THE THEORY OF
Price

THE MACMILLAN COMPANY
NEW YORK · BOSTON · CHICAGO · DALLAS
ATLANTA · SAN FRANCISCO

MACMILLAN AND CO., Limited
LONDON · BOMBAY · CALCUTTA · MADRAS
MELBOURNE

THE MACMILLAN COMPANY
OF CANADA, Limited
TORONTO

THE THEORY OF
Price

BY GEORGE J. STIGLER

PROFESSOR OF ECONOMICS, UNIVERSITY OF MINNESOTA

1946

THE MACMILLAN COMPANY · *New York*

PREFACE

The present volume is an augmented version of *The Theory of Competitive Price*, and now includes a survey of imperfect competition, multiple products, and interest theory. It thus covers the main topics of modern price theory, — that is, the mechanism of a stationary enterprise economy. The other two branches of economic analysis, the theory of fluctuations and the theory of development, are not discussed.

Parts I and II, which comprised the former volume, have been subjected to only trivial revision. This restraint is due chiefly to the desire to complete the volume according to original plan rather than embark on patch-work changes; it is not at all due to complacency. Yet dissatisfaction with the neoclassical theory of competition turns chiefly on questions of presentation; the theory of imperfect competition gives rise to deeper misgivings of which there is ample evidence in the text (Part III). One cannot present a wholly coherent and satisfying formal analysis nor can one concentrate on the (unknown) important phenomena of the real world. In its present state the theory of imperfect competition, despite its greater (or at least more explicit) empirical content, leans toward technical virtuosity. In short, economics is in an unsatisfactory state — it is hard to write a textbook!

I wish to express my indebtedness to J. N. Berrettoni and Thor Hultgren for valuable criticisms, and to The Macmillan Company, Harvard University Press, The University of Chicago Press, and *The New Yorker* for permission to use quotations which are identified in the text.

GEORGE J. STIGLER

MINNEAPOLIS, MINNESOTA

v

TABLE OF CONTENTS

PART I — INTRODUCTION

PART II — THE THEORY OF COMPETITION

PART III — THE THEORY OF IMPERFECT COMPETITION

PART IV — MULTIPLE PRODUCTS AND CAPITAL AND INTEREST

PART I

INTRODUCTION

CHAPTER 1

THE NATURE AND METHOD OF ECONOMICS

I. THE NATURE OF SCIENCE

Since economics is a science, it is appropriate to begin with an examination of the nature of science.* The fundamental characteristic of a science is the establishment of generalizations with respect to the relationship between various distinguishable phenomena. If one can say, if A, then B, one has a scientific law. This fundamental requirement is usually supplemented by a major and a minor requirement: the generalizations should be interrelated and, if possible, reducible to one comprehensive generalization; and the field of study should have fairly distinct boundaries. Some reasons for the former requirement are presented later. The latter requirement represents a necessary division of labor along lines which are always vague and usually shifting through time. The basic element, however, is the establishment of (scientific) laws.

The important purpose of a scientific law is to permit prediction, and prediction is in turn sought because it permits control over phenomena. That control requires prediction is self-evident, for unless one knows what "causes" a particular phenomenon, one cannot effect or prevent its occurrence. Prediction, however,

---

* It has come to be considered high praise of any field to call it a *science*, and conversely, few epithets are stronger than *unscientific*. Part of this prestige of science is of course due to the great achievements of the natural sciences, and a further explanation is provided by the typical looseness of popular usage of language: *unscientific* has become a synonym for *sloppy*. But without attempting to deprecate science in general, it is worth mentioning that the grounds for the prestige of science are nebulous. Surely usefulness is not the criterion, for cooking is more useful than astronomy; nor is æsthetics, for most men prefer music to chemistry. The difficulty of the subject matter of sciences is undoubtedly a factor, but here two things may be said. On the one hand, no subject is difficult to those with aptitudes and training in that direction — a modern Gauss could master higher mathematical analysis much more easily than an ordinary city dweller could learn to farm. And on the other hand, difficulty is a most ambiguous concept — there are many more men who can understand modern physics than can run 100 yards in 9.8 seconds. In sum, to say that economics is a science is a description, not an encomium.

requires a knowledge of *general* relationships. No matter how detailed our study of a particular phenomenon (say the price of wheat in March, 1874) may be, we would never be able to predict the movement of the price of wheat in similar circumstances, because the "similar" circumstance would differ in literally an unlimited number of respects. It is for this reason that general laws are sought between classes of phenomena, and the greater the scope of a law (given its content), the more useful it is in prediction.

The nature of a scientific law may be developed by way of an example.* The following is an economic law:

If: 1. An entrepreneur seeks maximum profits.
2. His marginal cost curve does not fall so fast as (or, rises more rapidly than) his marginal revenue curve.
3. These curves are continuous.

Then: He operates at the output where marginal revenue equals marginal cost.

There are two parts to this law: certain assumptions or hypotheses;† and a conclusion drawn from these hypotheses. A particular hypothesis may be true, i.e., in accordance with observation (assumption 2 is an example), or patently false (as with assumption 3), or partially true (assumption 1). The conclusion is the logical consequence of the assumptions; for those who are impressed by symbols it can always be derived mathematically.‡

The formal validity of a scientific law depends only on the logical rigor with which it follows from the assumptions. In the fore-

---

* *Law* might be replaced by *theory* at this and other points. It was once popular to call a *relationship* a *hypothesis* if it had not been tested, a *theory* if there were some evidence to support it, and a *law* if it were certain. This order contains a grain of truth, but it is essentially naïve and mistaken (witness the fact that no sensible hypothesis can be made about a subject matter of which one is completely ignorant, and no scientific "law" is ever certain). Historical accident plays a large part in such matters (Boyle's "law" of gases is only an approximation), and everyday usage has corrupted any possible distinction (why is relativity a theory and "supply and demand" a law?).

† Despite the widespread aversion of laymen toward hypothetical reasoning, it does not seem worth arguing at any length that all scientific laws require hypotheses. To paraphrase Newton by saying that objects fall with constant acceleration is obviously false; witness a quiescent book on a table. One may say this only *if* it is a freely falling body in a vacuum.

‡ In this case, let $C(x)$ be total cost, $R(x)$ total receipts, x output. Then profits are $R(x) - C(x)$, which attains a maximum (assumption 1) when $R'(x) = C'(x)$, the conclusion in the text. The sufficiency condition for maximum profits, $R''(x) < C''(x)$, is assumption 2. Differentiation of the functions requires assumption 3 (and strictly speaking, the curves or functions must also possess derivatives).

going example the conclusion does follow from the premises; so it is true even though one of the premises is always false and another only partially true. This test of logical derivation is the first test to apply to any scientific law, for two reasons.

First, if the assumptions are true but the conclusion does not follow logically, that conclusion is of course worthless. The following very popular economic theory is an example:

If: 1. In those industries where there are continuing economies of large-scale production, entrepreneurs will expand the size of their firms until they become monopolists or oligopolists.
2. It is desirable to produce a given output as cheaply as possible.

Then: The antitrust laws should not be enforced.

(Assumption 2 is an ethical postulate rather than an empirical observation, but this is not relevant to the present discussion.) In this case the conclusion is a *non sequitur* because monopoly and oligopoly arise for other reasons besides a reduction in production costs, and because there may be disadvantages to monopoly which outweigh gains in productive efficiency, to give only two reasons. Bad logic wastes good assumptions.

Second, even though the assumptions are not true, a logical conclusion may be very useful. The point will be examined in detail later; here an illustration may suffice. It was observed in the first example of an economic law that it appears to be completely unrealistic to assume that demand and cost curves are mathematically continuous. Yet if this assumption is not made, our previous conclusion need not be modified in any important respect. It need only be rephrased: Then the entrepreneur operates at the largest output for which marginal revenue is greater than or equal to marginal cost. This important theorem is thus virtually independent of the assumption of continuity.*

But if a science were to study only the logical implications of various propositions or assumptions, then logic (or mathematics) would be the only science. There is a second, and even more fundamental, test which a scientific theory must meet: it must explain the behavior of the phenomena in which we are interested;

* The reasons for making the assumption are discussed in Chapter 4.

the assumptions must correspond to the facts. It is necessary to emphasize that logic plays only a secondary role in this test: it is not possible to prove a priori that anything must be true of the real world. This view has not always been accepted: attempts have been made to deduce important economic laws from self-evident truths. John Stuart Mill's proof of the necessity for the law of diminishing returns provides an example:

> This general law of agricultural industry is the most important proposition in political economy. . . . If the land A yields a thousand quarters of wheat, to a given outlay in wages, manure, etc., and in order to raise another thousand recourse must be had to the land B, which is either less fertile or most distant from the market, the two thousand quarters will cost more than twice as much labour as the original thousand, and the produce of agriculture will be increased in a less ratio than the labour employed in procuring it.
>
> Instead of cultivating the land B, it would be possible, by higher cultivation, to make the land A produce more. . . . But, that it [the additional product] is obtained at a more than proportional increase of expense, is evident from the fact that inferior lands are cultivated. . . . If the additional demand could continue to be supplied from the superior lands, by applying additional labour and capital, at no greater proportional cost, than that at which they yield the quantity first demanded of them, the owners or farmers of those lands could undersell all others, and engross the whole market. *

This proof may be restated more schematically:

> *If:* 1. Land is cultivated in order to secure a maximum product, and only for this purpose.
> 2. No one would apply labor to land B unless he had reached the stage of diminishing returns on land A. †
> 3. Lands A and B are both cultivated.

Then: The law of diminishing returns must be true.

There are two comments to be made about this and similar proofs. First, observable facts are still indispensable: assumptions 1 and

---

* John Stuart Mill, *Principles of Political Economy*, Ashley ed., Longmans, Green, New York, 1929, pp. 177–178.

† This subsidiary argument is unfortunately very inconclusive. A person desiring a maximum product from a given amount of labor might be confronted by the following situation: The first 5 units of labor on acre A might each produce 12 units of product, all subsequent units of labor, 8 units of product. All units of labor on acre B might yield 10 units of product. Then if the individual possessed more than 5 units of labor, he would cultivate both acres. Yet on both acres the marginal product of labor is constant, and not diminishing.

3 are obviously empirical observations, and assumption 2 has subtle empirical content. These empirical elements might be held to be so pervasive and obvious that any dispute over their existence would be pedantic, but the history of science provides a long list of "obvious facts" which are now known to be untrue. Second, this "proof" is not a demonstration that the law of diminishing returns is the only possible explanation that is compatible with the observable facts (if they are facts) that land is cultivated only for a maximum product, that several acres of land are cultivated, etc. No amount of empirical evidence will ever make it certain that another theory might not better explain the facts, or explain a wider range of facts.

This last point, the impossibility of ever securing a conclusive proof of the empirical (in contrast with the logical) validity of a theory, deserves a few additional remarks. We may note first that although it can never be shown conclusively that a theory is empirically valid, it is possible to disprove an erroneous theory by showing important discrepancies between its assumptions or conclusions and observable facts. Most economists explain the fact that a given commodity has a uniform price in a market by pointing out that buyers and sellers can profit without risk, through arbitrage transactions, by eliminating any differences in price. Tarde, a French sociologist, explained the uniformity (as he explained almost everything else) by man's proclivity for imitation. The existence of price differentials based on transportation costs does not affect the principle of the economists' explanation. Tarde's theory as it stands cannot explain such disparities, and the necessary modifications in his theory (e.g., that imitation is inversely proportional to distance, that imitation is stronger over flat country and along water routes, etc.) are not empirically defensible.

A scientific law, moreover, will command greater confidence if it is consistent with other scientific laws which are compatible with observed facts. We could never be sure that the theoretical effects on prices of an excise tax are consistent with the observed effects of all excise taxes that ever have been or will be imposed, which is what a full proof would require. But we can show that if this theory of excise taxes is false, then the general theory of price is false, and that if the general theory is true, the special theory is true. Whatever empirical validity the general theory possesses is therefore conferred on, and reinforced by, that of the special theory. This is analogous to the fact that the law of the pendulum and the theory of tides are both accepted in part because they are parts of the general Newtonian system which has been shown to be empirically valid in many other fields.

But what if two alternative theories will explain all of the facts equally well? Thus the substitution or indifference theory of demand curves does not have any important advantage over the older marginal utility theory in explaining consumer behavior. The criterion for choosing between such theories is simplicity — which is not a simple notion.* The type of simplicity preferred might be called *analytical* simplicity, i.e., that explanation which requires fewer assumptions, and hence is more general in its applicability, is the simpler theory. Since the indifference theory of consumer behavior requires one less assumption than the marginal utility theory, the former is preferred. But this type of simplicity has nothing to do with familiarity or ease of comprehension, as will become evident to the student after reading Chapter 5.

ABSTRACTION

The question of realism has so far been discussed primarily in formal terms, and it is desirable to examine the material significance of the frequent charge that scientific and, in particular, economic theories are "unrealistic." Those who dislike theoretical analysis — perhaps only 95 per cent of the human race — will, if pressed, usually reformulate the indictment: although the logic of the particular theory seems to be correct, it is irrelevant because the hypotheses are false. This falsity can be of two kinds, which will be examined in turn.

First, a hypothesis may simply be contrary to everyday observation. (This charge is infrequent in the natural sciences, for everyday observation has long been known to be worthless, and now laymen delight in the "knowledge" that whipped cream and granite are nothing but small electrical charges flying about at enormous velocities.) For instance, Part II of this volume is based on the assumption of perfect competition, but anyone can see that competition is not perfect; many argue that it is dead; and some point

---

* See Morris R. Cohen and Ernest Nagel, *An Introduction to Logic and Scientific Method*, Harcourt, Brace, New York, 1934, pp. 213–215.

out that it never has existed. Why should anyone go to the trouble of learning theories which rest on such a faulty foundation? To this question we may give several answers.

First, empirical reality is too complex ever to be described fully. One could spend a lifetime describing the price of wheat in the North Central states on a certain day: a year describing the paper on which the prices are written, a year on the times and temperatures at which the sales were made, a decade describing (roughly) the physical characteristics of the various grains of wheat, etc., etc. In order to reduce any problem to manageable proportions, we must disregard almost all of what is termed *raw experience* and concentrate our investigation on *important* and *relevant* factors — and this is nothing more or less than abstraction. As a corollary, no scientific law will ever fully describe reality: no theory of rent will ever predict the 196th word in the lease or the disposition of the farmer's second cousin on rainy days. The examples were chosen to re-emphasize the point that no one is interested in complete reality.

Second, in order to predict one must be able to make true propositions about classes of phenomena, and not merely about individual phenomena. From the statement that Socrates was mortal one can conclude only that he was mortal. And thus we are led to justify a previous sentence: the greater the scope of a law (given its content), the greater its usefulness in prediction. But unfortunately the phrase in parentheses begs the fundamental difficulty: the greater the scope of a law the less will be its empirical content. A true proposition regarding the animal kingdom must contain fewer details than one about vertebrae, and one about vertebrae fewer details than one about mammals. Economic illustrations are perhaps more appropriate; let us consider three:

1. Since the chief markets for livestock in the United States are in the North Central and Atlantic states, and since transportation charges must be deducted from market prices to secure farm prices, the farm price of livestock is higher in Illinois than in Wyoming.
2. When two products are produced competitively in fixed proportions, a rise in the demand for one leads to a fall in the price of the other.

3. When a consumer has given tastes and income and seeks maximum satisfaction, he will buy such quantities of commodities Y and X that the marginal rate of substitution of Y for X equals the ratio of the marginal cost of X to that of Y.

As we go down the list, the theories lose content: the first tells us something definite about a specific object in specific places; the third does not (on its face) present any explanation of observable phenomena. But in parallel fashion the scope of the theories expands: the first does not contribute to the explanation of the price of wheat in Montana; the third applies to any products and under monopoly as well as competition. Abstraction, in the sense of reduced empirical content, is the inevitable price of generality of scope, and indeed *abstraction* and *generality* are virtually synonyms.

Third, perfect competition, to return to our example, contains elements of "real life," and these elements are so important that only theories which recognize these competitive elements can hope to be successful theories (i.e., yield predictions). This statement can be refuted, if it is untrue, only by someone who presents a better theory independent of these competitive elements. And when better economic theories are developed, it is certain that they will come from economists who have already mastered the existing theories.

Finally, pedagogically it is necessary to begin with simple cases. It is not yet completely established that economics and other social sciences cannot be mastered by reading one book or taking one course; the natural sciences have succeeded in instilling greater humility.

There is a second, and more sophisticated, version of the criticism based on abstraction: that the wrong, or at least the less important, phenomena have been studied. Thorstein Veblen and his followers provide an important example in their attack on economic theory.* They argue that only problems which are amenable to the orthodox technical apparatus are studied, that the broader factors (e.g., the roles of jurisprudence, technology, and religion) are taken as given when in fact they are the fundamental determinants of changes in our economy. Abstraction per se is not denounced, but the type of abstraction currently practiced is held to stultify real progress.

* See especially Thorstein Veblen, *The Place of Science in Modern Civilization*, Viking, New York, 1932.

It is not necessary to debate here the merits of this position.* Such criticism, and some of the replies usually made to it, are in considerable part intellectually imperialistic: some people do not like the topics that interest others. The most effective criticism of a theory is always to present a better theory: if price phenomena are better explained by Supreme Court decisions than by the elasticity of demand and marginal cost, the former field will not lack investigators.

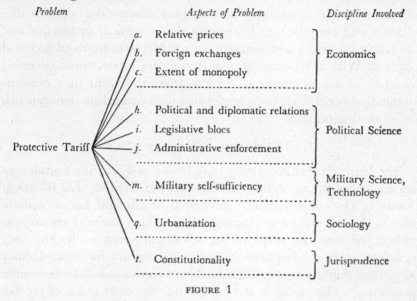

Problem	*Aspects of Problem*	*Discipline Involved*
	a. Relative prices	
	b. Foreign exchanges	Economics
	c. Extent of monopoly	
	h. Political and diplomatic relations	
	i. Legislative blocs	Political Science
Protective Tariff	*j.* Administrative enforcement	
	m. Military self-sufficiency	Military Science, Technology
	q. Urbanization	Sociology
	t. Constitutionality	Jurisprudence

FIGURE 1

There is, however, one point worth making. Division of labor also involves abstraction. It is not disputable that almost any important problem has many facets; this is illustrated by Figure 1, where some of the aspects of an economic problem are listed. Protective tariffs, the example chosen, have effects on relative prices, foreign exchanges, and the extent of monopoly, and such effects are studied by economists. A tariff also affects many variables which fall in other disciplines, and a few are noted in Figure 1. No one will argue that a complete analysis of tariffs is possible only in terms of economics.

Yet it is necessary to break the explanation down into parts. The type of mind which can use the intricate economic analysis

* In particular, the question of prediction of the future course of basic institutions of a society cannot be entered into here.

involved in this problem is not likely to be equally suited to deal with political and sociological phenomena, and in any case the necessary factual knowledge is beyond one man's powers of assimilation. Moreover, it is possible so to break down the problem: it does not turn out, for example, that the direct effects of the tariff on relative prices are offset by changes in people's tastes (a cultural phenomenon) or by transportation improvements (a technological phenomenon). This is an empirical observation, but it is a similar observation which underlies the working distinction between mechanics and chemistry — it appears that chemical properties are, for many purposes, unimportant in a study of motions of physical objects. Where the conventional division of labor would do great violence to a problem (e.g., an explanation of rent in a custom-dominated economy), the scientist tills the border line between two or more disciplines.

II. THE SCOPE OF ECONOMICS

The birth date of economics may be set in 1776; the founder, of course, a Scotsman, Adam Smith; and the treatise, *The Wealth of Nations*. The subjects which interested Smith and his immediate successors are, with few changes, those which interest economists today; the working scope of the science has not undergone any revolution. But it required more than a century for a satisfactory analytical definition to replace a table of contents as "the economic problem." This delay is not surprising, for most sciences receive satisfactory formal definitions only after a long period of development. Nor is the delay particularly alarming; no great harm was done so long as economists discussed the subjects which they were competent to discuss and did not say too much about the subjects of which they were ignorant. Oddly enough, one could make a good case for the thesis that they have usually erred more in the former respect than in the latter.

But let us pass to the formal definition of the economic problem. Economics is the study of the principles governing the allocation of scarce means among competing ends when the objective of the allocation is to maximize the attainment of the ends. There are thus three fundamental elements in the definition — given ends, scarce means, and the notion of a maximum — and each deserves a word of explanation.

The ends of economic activity are any objectives which motivate that activity. In building a house the economizing individual may seek warmth, or roominess, or prestige, or conformity to local architectural traditions, or a hedge against inflation (and then more ultimately, maintenance of his real income, which in turn may arise out of other ends). It is possible to view as the ends of economic activity either the immediate ends (e.g., a house, a phonograph) or those ends which, for lack of a better word, may be called *ultimate* (e.g., physical well-being, the respect of others), although economists usually deal only with the former. In order to be comparable, of course, the ends must necessarily be reducible to a common denominator, and this is called *satisfaction*.

The means (resources) consist of all things which are both scarce and versatile (i.e., capable of satisfying several ends) necessary to attain ends. Scarcity is relative to ends: although there are fewer bad eggs than good, Professor Robbins has observed, the latter are scarce, and the former are not. Scarcity is the most fundamental characteristic of an economic problem, for if the means are abundant, then all of the ends can be fully satisfied, and no problem of choice arises. The necessity for versatility in the means is equally evident, for if a given means can serve only one use, no choice can be exercised in its use, no matter how scarce the means may be.

The principle of the maximum is not strictly necessary, for an economic problem would arise if individuals sought to minimize the attainment of their ends, or if they sought 65 per cent of the maximum possible attainment of the ends, or any other specific objective. But it is enormously convenient and, on the present plane of generality,* very realistic to assume that a maximum fulfillment of ends is sought. Without some purpose to activity, in any case, no principles of correct behavior can be established.

A simple example may serve to illustrate the nature of economic decisions. Suppose that a small city has $10,000 left in its treasury after all regular expenses are met, and this surplus can be devoted to a partial fulfillment of any of three ends: education, public health, or the tourist trade. The funds are obviously insufficient to secure all

---

* Almost any activity can be viewed as oriented toward maximization of the attainment of ends. Carefully planned laziness can be looked upon as the maximization of not working; if it is not planned, it can be viewed as the simultaneous maximization of not working and not thinking.

of the students Ph.D.'s or to provide all of the inhabitants with the medical services they need or to attract all of the potential tourists. The fundamental steps in the rational solution of this problem may be sketched:

First, the city council must estimate the relative importance of various degrees of improvement of the educational system (in the light of other alternatives). The extension of a badly overcrowded school may be considered urgent; the increase of teachers' salaries will (it is to be feared) be a last resort. (As a matter of fact, this end is greatly simplified: a partial alleviation of overcrowding, repairs to the school furnace which cannot long be postponed, replacement of worn-out textbooks, then an additional extension of school space, may be the order of urgency.) Similar estimates must be made in the cases of public health and the tourist trade.

Second, these estimates of the importance of various degrees of educational reform must be compared with the importance of various degrees of attainment of other ends. Strictly speaking, this is already implicit in the estimates as first made. No specific end can be assigned an importance (i.e., a value) unless there are alternatives with which it can be compared. No need is always paramount, special pleaders to the contrary. Illiteracy must be stamped out — unless education involves starvation; and starvation is intolerable — unless the alternative is cannibalism!

Third, our council, which is by now no doubt inclined to refund the surplus tax receipts (still another alternative), requires another type of information. How efficient is a dollar in improving education, and in improving health? Obviously, if $100 will raise the intelligence quotients of 50 students from 100 to 190 (the level of Newton) and on the other hand cure only one mild case of sunburn, the sum will go to education; if it will raise the intelligence quotient of one "student" from 50 to 51 and on the other hand save several lives, it will go to public health. This is primarily a question of techniques.

Finally, the council allocates the $10,000 in such a way as to maximize the attainment of the original ends. This decision is the economic element in the problem, and the principles which govern it are among the most important parts of economic theory.

The precise roles of means and ends are further elucidated by considering technology and ethics.

I. *TECHNOLOGY*

Technology and economics are concerned with the same data, means and ends. But whereas the economist is concerned with the best allocation of scarce means among competing ends, the technologist studies the best means to attain a specific end. Economic factors will influence the selection of the best means, however. If land is free and labor expensive, it is a matter only of technique to decide how much land to use with a given amount of labor, i.e., the amount of land which will produce maximum output per worker. But if land also has a cost, then the technologist alone cannot determine the best means for producing the product, for this will obviously depend in part on prices. Thus 600 units of product may be procurable either by

25 acres and 500 man-hours of labor,
or by 26 acres and 300 man-hours of labor.

It might appear that the second combination should be used, because a 4 per cent increase in land permits a 40 per cent reduction in labor. But the reader can readily verify the fact that the first combination is preferable if the rent of an acre is $250 and the wage rate $1. What technology does study is the possibility of increasing the output of 25 acres and 500 man-hours from 600 units of product to some higher figure. In this examination economic considerations are virtually absent.*

II. *ETHICS*

Ethics is the study of values; so in the means-and-ends terminology ethics considers the relative desirabilities of the various ends. The philosopher, and not the economist, attempts to decide whether a consumer *should* prefer recitals of the modern dance to spiked beer. Strictly speaking, words like *ought* and *bad* cannot occur in an economic discussion — at most one may say that an action is not appropriate to the end in view.

The reason for assigning such an austere role to economics is this: it is the fundamental tenet of those who believe in free discussion that matters of fact and of logic can (eventually) be agreed upon by competent men of good will, that matters of taste cannot

* Actually, of course, it may be possible to discover by several lines of inquiry whether the output of 25 acres and 500 man-hours can be increased, and the technician will choose the most efficient method — which is in part an economic choice.

be reconciled by free discussion. Assuming this to be true,* it is apparent that if value judgments were mixed with logic and observation, a science would make but little progress. Disputes over undemonstrable value judgments would color disputes over demonstrable facts or relationships. A healthy skepticism, moreover, is very useful in examining conventional ethical judgments. But this austere economics has its disadvantages. An economist cannot, as a scientist, say that the legislation which requires the treasury to buy domestically mined silver is bad legislation. But it *is* bad legislation!

III. THE METHOD OF ECONOMICS

If economists do not utilize the best methods for discovering and verifying economic theories, it cannot be for lack of well-intentioned advice. Famous historians, psychologists, and biologists (to name only a few) have abandoned their own disciplines for embarrassingly short periods in order to master economics and point out an escape from the impasse in which they invariably find it. This chapter therefore concludes with a brief survey of the usual advices: experimentation and observation.

I. *EXPERIMENT*

Experiment has been a chief weapon in the natural sciences;† the natural sciences have made great progress; hence experimentation should be used by all sciences which wish to make great progress. This familiar, if rather sloppy, syllogism has a plausible ring. No one will deny the great advantage of a controlled experiment: it reduces to a minimum the dispute over facts. Nor, for that matter, will the natural scientist argue that experiments will be fruitful unless they are guided by hypotheses which are formulated by those who have disciplined imaginations and are familiar with the general subject. And a scientific imagination is disciplined by a knowledge of the known relationships in the field, that is, by a knowledge of the existing theories.

The great advantage of experiment, the verification of facts and hence of scientific laws, could be used with profit in economics. It is

---

* For a brief statement of the objections to this view, see George Stigler, "The New Welfare Economics," *American Economic Review*, XXXIII (1943), 355–359.

† But not, of course, the sole weapon. Many of the most important developments in physics (e.g., relativity) have at the time of their formulation possessed no empirical support.

disputed whether, in time of depression, a general cut in wage rates will increase employment: why not cut wage rates and see? The answer should appear on brief reflection: the experiment could not be controlled, so we would not be able to "see" what the net effect of wage rates on employment is.

This lack of control is due to two circumstances. Other factors besides wage rates affect employment, and it would be impossible to hold these other factors constant during the experiment. Even a dictator could not keep the average age of the population from rising, or prevent a business recession in an important foreign country, or prevent a crop failure. Moreover, even if all other factors could be isolated, we should not have attained a general scientific law from our results. For a particular result was secured in a particular constellation of circumstances, and a decade later a new experiment under different circumstances might reverse the quantitative results. Social relations are not invariant.

This is not to deny a modest role for experimentation in economics. For instance, a public utility might wish to discover the effect of its rates on the consumption of electricity. It can set different rates in a half-dozen towns which are similar in important respects,* and then record the differences in consumption. If the results are interpreted carefully,† it will be possible to say something about the effect of price on quantity purchased.

The limitations of this type of experimentation are evident. To be rigorous and conclusive, the various cases must be identical in all respects except the one which is being measured. In skillful hands such experiments are undoubtedly an important source of information. But even in the most skillful hands the experiments will usually yield information which is ambiguous: it is almost always possible that particular (and perhaps unknown) circumstances surrounding the experiment deprive the results of general significance. It may be said that experimental results will be more meaningful, (1) the more specific and carefully formulated the problems which are to be covered, (2) the more numerous the cases

* This list of important respects is really a portion of the hypothesis that rates affect consumption, unless their importance and comprehensiveness have already been "proved."

† Thus, the duration of the rate decrease or increase, technological changes in consumption during the experiment, changes in the general level of business activity, and similar disturbances must be "allowed for."

included in the experiment, and (3) the more fully developed the theory of the subject, i.e., the greater the experimenter's knowledge of probable relationships. But, to repeat, the possible field is very small; let us turn to a more promising alternative.

II. *STATISTICS*

The obvious difficulties involved in experimental determination of economic relationships have prevented any prominent economist from recommending wide use of this technique, but there are many who have argued that economic laws should be derived from, as well as based on, collections of empirical data. The German Historical School made this its fundamental tenet, and there are many modern, if less extreme, followers of this approach. Colin Clark, for instance, may be quoted:

> Not one in a hundred [of the academic economists] — least of all those who are most anxious to proclaim the scientific nature of Economics — seems to understand what constitutes the scientific approach, namely, the careful systematization of all observed facts, the framing of hypotheses from these facts, prediction of fresh conclusions on the basis of these hypotheses, and the testing of these conclusions against further observed facts. It would be laughable, were it not tragic, to watch the stream of books and articles, attempting to solve the exceptionally complex problems of present-day economics by theoretical arguments, often without even a single reference to the observed facts of the situation. Worse still is the practice of basing a book upon theoretical arguments and then selecting a limited number of facts to illustrate the conclusions already reached, thus effectively putting the theoretical cart before the factual horse. . . .
>
> Theory has a valuable, indeed an essential part to play in the development of economic science. But it must be theory which respects facts, not tries to supersede them. There is room for two or three economic theorists in each generation, not more. Only men of transcendental powers of reasoning can be candidates for these positions. Re-statements of economic theory, of which we are offered so many, are only occasionally needed, as factual knowledge advances and institutions change.*

The specific proposal may be left to the reader's mercies,† but what is the proper role of statistics in economics?

---

* Colin Clark, *The Conditions of Economic Progress*, Macmillan, London, 1940, pp. vii–viii.

† It is worth noticing, however, that such suggestions usually imply that most or many economists are economic theorists. This is surely wrong on any acceptable definition of an economic theorist (e.g., one who spends more than half of his professional

It should no longer be necessary to argue that it is impossible even to collect data without some preconceptions, which are more or less precisely formulated hypotheses. Nor should it be disputable that no economic generalization has ever "jumped out" of a collection of data; the elicitation of important generalizations from specific information calls for an extremely high order of scientifically disciplined imagination, a thorough knowledge of statistical reasoning, and vast patience. The real question is: what is the most fruitful role to assign to empirical research in the explanation of economic phenomena? The answer turns largely on the type of phenomena.

If the most general structure of a given type of economic system is in question, there is only a minor need for empirical information. The theory of competition is based fundamentally on about half a dozen assumptions. A more special theory, Ricardo's explanation of the determination of land rent, rested on three assumptions: that land is scarce (in the sense that its products cannot satisfy fully the desire for them); that its cultivation obeys the law of diminishing returns; and that competition rules between buyers and sellers. Historically, of course, no such general theory is from the first based on a complete, consistent, and clearly formulated set of assumptions; the logical refinement of a theory usually occurs only slowly. The real task at this level of analysis is not to discover and select the fundamental empirical data, for these are usually so prominent and matter-of-fact that almost any adult is familiar with them. Rather the task is analytical: to explore the implications of a set of assumptions.

But if the phenomena to be explained are of a specific nature, detailed information is necessary. No a priori argument from general premises (of the type just referred to) can tell us what the precise effects of a high excise tax on cigarettes will be, just as no degree of familiarity with mathematical physics will, of itself, indicate the necessary strength of the girders for a particular bridge. To analyze the effects of the tax, we must know the elasticity of demand, the possibilities of shifting to other products which are open to tobaccogrowers, and numerous similar facts.

time theorizing on economic problems) — at least 90 per cent of those who claim to be (or can be forced to admit that they are) economists spend over half of their time on "applied" or "empirical" subjects, and in fact only a small minority are even interested in "advanced" theoretical discussions.

This would suggest that empirical studies should provide quantitative measures of theoretical concepts, and indeed this is a basic — and difficult — task. But it is not enough. As a rule theoretical systems will fit a particular case fairly well; they would not be good systems if they failed to do so. But some of the relationships which the theory teaches us to look for may be unimportant, and certain observed facts will not fit into the theoretical scheme. As a result, it will be necessary to modify and extend the theory in the process of using it, and in this fundamental work the investigator must be an economist as well as a statistician or historian.

It is therefore a confession of weakness for a statistician to complain that an economic theory has not been formulated in such a way as to be capable of application to a specific problem, for actually this is a challenge to improve the theory. And it should not be considered too grave an indictment to say that the application of a theory requires facts or techniques which do not exist. It would be shortsighted to work only on problems which are easy to solve, and both facts and techniques grow and improve in response to the greater demands which are made of them. Complacency is at least as great a threat to scientific progress as despair.

RECOMMENDED READINGS

1. Cohen, Morris R., and Nagel, Ernest, *An Introduction to Logic and Scientific Method*, Harcourt, Brace, New York, 1934.
2. Robbins, Lionel, *The Nature and Significance of Economic Science*, 2nd ed., Macmillan, New York, 1935.
3. Knight, Frank H., "The Limitations of Scientific Method in Economics," in *The Trend of Economics*, Crofts, New York, 1924, and *The Ethics of Competition*, Harper, New York, 1935.
4. Parsons, Talcott, *The Structure of Social Action*, McGraw-Hill, New York, 1937.
5. Keynes, J. N., *The Scope and Method of Political Economy*, 4th ed., Macmillan, London, 1930.

CHAPTER 2

BASIC CONCEPTS: COMPETITION, STATICS AND DYNAMICS, AND EQUILIBRIUM

In the study of economic phenomena it is customary to use a framework or analysis which has become, through long experimentation, relatively standardized. In the same way there has developed a terminology which, although it contains few words which are not in every literate layman's vocabulary, have fairly precise (and sometimes peculiar) definitions formulated with a view to their convenience in theoretical analysis. The present chapter is intended to summarize this framework of analysis and certain important items in terminology. The framework is sketched in the first two sections on competition and statics and dynamics, and a fundamental methodological concept is presented in the section on equilibrium.

I. THE NATURE OF COMPETITION

It is necessary to define *competition*, and it is probably also desirable to explain the purpose of the concept. The nature of perfect competition is summarized in three conditions:

1. Each economic unit (household or firm) is so small relative to the market that it exerts no perceptible influence on the prices of the things it buys and sells.

2. All markets are free from special institutional restraints, or, more positively, prices and the mobility of resources are not restricted.

3. All economic units possess complete knowledge.

The first two conditions are those which would be dictated (in very different form) by common sense; the third is more technical in nature. All three will be examined in turn.

If an independent firm supplies so much of a commodity that when output increases the price falls perceptibly,* competition is

* The question of when a price influence becomes perceptible will be examined in Chapter 12; see also Chapter 6, problem 2.

21

not perfect. For the firm would then *regulate* the price by controlling output, and the power of controlling price is a distinguishing characteristic of what is popularly called *monopoly*. Competition requires that each economic unit * be so small as to consider market prices independent of its activities.†

Secondly, if special restrictions are placed on the prices or the mobility of resources in any field, it will generally be conceded that competition is impaired. The restriction may be governmental, as in the fixing of railroad rates, the examination of prospective physicians, or the prohibition of private liquor stores. Or a trade union may exclude laborers by high initiation fees or picket lines; an association of manufacturers may cut off supplies to dealers who engage in price-cutting. Custom may dictate that a son follow his father's occupation. All such restraints on prices and the use of resources are inconsistent with competition.

Nevertheless, there are tasks for society (operating chiefly through the state) even under competition. Contracts must be enforced; private property must be protected from seizure by individuals; and fraud and violence must be suppressed or at least punished. In any realistic discussion of competition, the state is also permitted to regulate weights and measures, to control banking and coinage of money, to assume social functions (education, health), and otherwise to control economic activity. But most of these latter functions are conceded only because of the lack of fulfillment of the third condition for competition: complete knowledge.

From what has just been said, it might be inferred that complete knowledge is assumed in order to reduce the activities of the state to those of a policeman or judge, but the requirement of knowledge is added for quite another reason. If consumers are ignorant of prices, they will buy at high prices when lower ones are available, and we will have several prices for one commodity in a market.

---

* These have already been itemized as households and firms. A combination of firms (cartel) would be the effective economic unit if the individual firms agreed on a common output and price policy, but such combinations, to the extent that they affect prices, are incompatible with competition.

† If we were appraising, rather than defining, competition, it would be necessary to investigate the conditions under which economic units will be small enough to fulfill this condition. In the case of consumer units, the realism of the assumption may be granted, with due respect to the cooperative movement. In the field of production, the question turns in part on economies of large-scale production (in the absence of state control over the size of unit), which are discussed at length in Chapter 11.

If laborers (or other owners of productive resources) are ignorant of wage rates, they will not always sell their services to the highest bidder. If entrepreneurs do not know costs and prices, they will frequently expand output and increase losses and other times contract output and reduce profits. The personnel of the economic system must be familiar with the system in order to make it work well.

But on reflection it will appear that complete knowledge implies much more. If consumers know the technical properties of all commodities, there will be no advertising, for all claims for a product would be true, and hence already known, or false, and then merely irritating. The entrepreneur foresees clearly future technical improvements (if any, see section 2), which usually raises the embarrassing question why he does not adopt them now. The capitalist makes his loans with full knowledge of the performance of the borrower throughout the life of the loan. We assume, so to speak, an economic republic in which everyone is a guardian.

Why bother with such an obviously unrealistic set of assumptions? This question has been raised by all of the intelligent and most of the other students of economics. The answer has already been sketched in Chapter 1, but it may be elaborated at this point:

1. Realism is a relative matter; competition is a better single assumption, even on the basis of realism, than monopoly. This will become clear once the theory of imperfect competition is presented (Part III), but the following remarks may serve as a temporary explanation. There are no monopolies which are sheltered from all rivalry — they must outbid other industries for labor, capital, and the consumer's dollar. These elements of rivalry are quantitatively weaker than in the case of competition, but they are probably more important than the elements of monopoly. On the other hand, there are so many types of monopoly (or better, of imperfect competition) that any one type is much less important than the more homogeneous group of near-competitive industries.

2. It is pedagogically necessary in all but the simplest problems to begin with piecemeal solutions. Complete economic reality is at least as complicated as complete physical reality. Yet the beginning student of physics does not demur at the absence of friction, or at Euclidean space, or, for that matter, at the frequent phrase, "It can be shown." Why then in economics?

3. But a first approximation is useful only if it is an approxima-tion. A frictionless physics would not be pedagogically sound if it had to be completely abandoned once friction was introduced. Competition also meets this test: it is invaluable as a steppingstone toward more realistic (and complicated) economic analyses. As a matter of fact, it is inconceivable that the modern theory of imper-fect competition could have reached its present state if a theory of competition had not already been well developed.

4. Competition was and is a policy as well as an analysis. This is in itself no excuse, or by analogy chemistry would still begin with a study of the element gold. But competition will continue to have policy implications because it offers a definition of an efficient economic system. The modern theory of socialism shares with the nineteenth-century theory of liberalism the view that the competitive system leads to the ideal allocation of productive services.

Because of the unfamiliarity of the economist's notion of com-petition, a few words may be added on the nature of such a system. Its essential feature is that all economic relationships are *impersonal*. The individual entrepreneur, for instance, is confronted by prices, not by rivals. He can buy all of the labor services he desires, at a fixed price. He can sell all of his product that he wishes, at a fixed price. He has no reason to wish ill of his neighbor who is in the same industry: how would the elimination of one rival help him, when there are thousands of others, and potentially any number necessary to eliminate his profits?

In everyday usage, unfortunately, *competition* is used in a very personalized sense. One football team competes with another; one brand of cigarettes attempts to gain the customers of another. Competition can be "cutthroat," — a contradiction in terms to the economist. Perhaps the best single warning to the student with regard to the use of *competition* is this: economic relationships are never perfectly competitive if they involve any personal relation-ships between economic units.

II. STATIONARY, DYNAMIC, AND HISTORICAL ANALYSES

Even where economic phenomena are completely understood, it is not desirable to analyze them in a single step: the explanation of complicated phenomena is usually also complicated, and there are pedagogical advantages in breaking the explanation down into several parts. This is one reason for the separation of stationary, dynamic, and historical economic analyses. There is, however, a second and more important reason for accepting this classification. Most economic phenomena cannot be completely explained in a scientific sense, i.e., they cannot be forecasted. In such cases, the economist may be able to provide a useful analysis of the phenomena by assuming that the fundamental data are stationary, even though he cannot explain dynamic and historical elements of the problem. The present section defines the three types of analyses.

A stationary (or static) economic theory is one which explains the equilibrium position (see section III) in the particular problem, on the assumption that the data of that problem do not change. To use a simple example, if the demand and supply curves of a given commodity are fixed, their intersection determines the equilibrium price and the quantity that will be purchased. A more elaborate example of stationary analysis is provided by a famous economic model, the stationary economy or state. This model will be used throughout most of the present volume, so its content deserves specification.

A stationary economy may be defined as one in which there are no changes in the three fundamental sets of data:

1. *Tastes.* The tastes or preferences of individuals for various commodities and services are fixed. This statement is to be interpreted broadly, e.g., the relative attractiveness of money income and leisure to laborers is assumed to be fixed. Under such conditions, no goods will ever become unstylish.

2. *Resources.* We may temporarily accept the classical summary of productive resources as land, labor, and capital. With respect to land, no soil will be washed away, nor new areas settled, no new ore deposits will be discovered, nor will existing deposits be depleted. The laboring population will not change in size, age or sex distribution, skill or education, etc. The capital equipment will neither increase nor decrease.

3. *Technology.* No new inventions will be developed, nor will changes be made in the existing organization of production by such developments as "scientific" management.

It deserves mention that a stationary economy need not be competitive, and indeed a competitive economy has never been (and probably could not be) stationary.

Dynamics is another concept borrowed from mechanics, but economists have been much less faithful to the original meaning in its use than in the case of *statics*.* The meaning of *dynamics* which will be employed here corresponds somewhat to its use in physics: dynamic economics is the study of the path by which a set of economic quantities (i.e., prices and quantities) reach equilibrium, within a static framework. An example of a dynamic problem is this: Assume that the demand and supply curves for a particular commodity are given, and that the condition for equilibrium is that 10,000 units be sold per unit of time at a price of $1. The price begins at $2. By what path does this price reach the equilibrium level? And does the path along which the price moves have any influence on the final equilibrium price? These are the fundamental questions in economic dynamics.

Finally, there are historical changes in the data, in wants, resources, and technology. A theory of historical economics would be a generalized explanation of the growth of population, of the discovery of new resources and new techniques, and of changes in wants. A theory of economic fluctuations would explain and predict the business cycle — to the eternal glory and temporary profit of economists. We do not enter on the problem of historical change in this volume.

III. THE NATURE AND CONDITIONS OF EQUILIBRIUM

Modern economics is frequently called *equilibrium* economics, for the study of the nature and conditions of equilibrium forms the core of price theory. In any specific investigation, the economist is interested in, e.g., the outputs of various commodities and their prices, in light of the data of the problem (the demand and supply conditions). These outputs and prices are in equilibrium if, given the governing data on demand and supply, there is no tendency for the outputs and prices to undergo additional changes. The conditions of equilibrium are the relationships which must be fulfilled

* In mechanics *statics* refers to the study of bodies in equilibrium, i.e., to problems in which the sum of the forces acting on a body is zero. The principle of the lever is a classical example. *Dynamics* refers to the laws of movements of bodies, or, more precisely, physical phenomena involving acceleration. The path of a projectile is a standard illustration. At present it is customary for physicists to treat statics as a special case of dynamics. In modern physics there is some use of the phrase *stationary state* (and of the corresponding *excited state*), but these phrases have very technical meanings which are totally unrelated to the (earlier) economic usage.

before outputs and prices are in equilibrium; these conditions summarize the important determinants of economic activity.

Equilibriums can be classified in several significant respects:

1. An equilibrium may be stable, neutral, or unstable. Pigou has summarized these forms:

> A system is in stable equilibrium if, when any small disturbance takes place, forces come into play to reestablish the initial position; it is in neutral equilibrium if, when such a disturbance takes place, no reestablishing forces, but also no further disturbing forces, are evoked, so that the system remains at rest in the position to which it has moved; it is in unstable equilibrium if the small disturbance calls out further disturbing forces which act in a cumulative manner to drive the system away from its initial position. A ship with a heavy keel is in stable equilibrium; an egg lying on its side in neutral equilibrium; an egg poised on one of its ends in unstable equilibrium.*

It is simple to concoct artificial economic situations in which neutral and unstable equilibriums exist, but in price theory concerned with real phenomena these cases are highly exceptional. A few cases of unstable equilibriums will be noted subsequently, but the conditions necessary to stable equilibrium (called the *stability* conditions) are usually fulfilled.

2. Equilibrium may be unique or multiple. A position of unique equilibrium arises if there is a single set of prices and quantities which fulfill the conditions of equilibrium. Multiple positions of equilibrium exist when several different sets of prices and quantities will meet the equilibrium conditions. The study of multiple equilibrium positions is essentially formal; no important empirical cases have yet been advanced to illustrate it. One or two possible situations of multiple equilibrium will be considered later, but in general a unique position of equilibrium will be treated as the typical case.

3. Equilibrium may be partial or general. A partial equilibrium is one which is based on only a restricted range of data: a standard example is the price of a single product, the prices of all other products being held fixed during the analysis. General equilibrium is ostensibly based on all of the data relevant to the problem which is being studied: the corresponding example would be the prices and outputs of all industries. The method of partial equilibrium

* A. C. Pigou, *Economics of Welfare*, 4th ed., Macmillan, London, 1932, pp. 794–795.

analysis is associated with Marshall and the Cambridge School; that of general equilibrium with Walras and the Lausanne School.

But *general* equilibrium is a misnomer: no economic analysis has ever been general in the sense that it considered *all* relevant data. The Walrasian system, for instance, does not include the business cycle, the excise-tax system, or technological improvements, nor does it, on the other hand, treat of detailed characteristics and peculiarities of specific industries. The most that can be said is that general equilibrium studies are *more* inclusive than partial equilibrium studies, never that they are complete. Moreover, the more general the analysis, the less specific its content must necessarily be — this is almost a corollary of the fact that the human mind can handle only a relatively few problems at one time. From the viewpoint of formal analysis the wide scope and small content of the general equilibrium studies offer no objections. But in a specific problem, such as the explanation of the price of milk in one city, the complexity of the problem requires that the investigator's limited powers of analysis be concentrated on only the most relevant data. It is not useful, even though it is correct, to say that the price of milk in one city depends upon, among other things, all the other prices in America.

Nevertheless, the study of general equilibrium serves important purposes in addition to providing a fascinating problem for analysis. First, it provides a demonstration that equilibrium in any particular sector of the economy is not incompatible with equilibrium in other sectors, and this conclusion is scarcely self-evident.

Second, it provides an outline of the general structure and workings of our economy. Pedagogically this is important, and the next chapter is devoted to this end. Third, it is of great assistance in discovering which data are relevant to any specific problem and teaches us the implications and limitations of considering only one industry at a time and treating all others as in some sense constant. This last role, in particular, will receive numerous illustrations in the subsequent discussion.

4. An equilibrium may be "long" or "short" run. An equilibrium position may be dependent on time, in the sense that with the passage of time the data of the problem change. This could be considered to be a particular instance of the application of the

distinction between partial and general equilibriums, in which short-run analysis is partial and long-run analysis general.

The standard illustration of changes in the data of a problem with the passage of time is found in the theory of production. It is assumed by Marshall, for instance, that a producer can alter the rate of production in an existing plant more rapidly than he can alter the plant itself. Then the price based on variation in the rate of production from a fixed plant is called the *short-run* normal (equilibrium) price, and if both the size and number of plants are permitted to vary, there results the *long-run* equilibrium price.

5. An equilibrium may be dependent on, or independent of, the path by which it is reached. In general, one would expect the final position of equilibrium to depend on the path by which it is reached. Suppose, for example, that the equilibrium price of cotton is 10 cents per pound this year, in the sense that if this price were established immediately, there would be no tendency for it to change. If in fact the price begins below the equilibrium point and rises as the excess of the quantity demanded over the quantity supplied becomes apparent, it may continue to rise to perhaps 12 cents, merely because, on the basis of experience, sellers withhold a portion of the supply in anticipation of further price increases. On the other hand, the initial low price may never rise to the original equilibrium level because consumers have stocked up at low prices and divert a portion of their incomes to other clothing materials.

There is no general theory of the effect of the path of movement of economic phenomena on their ultimate equilibrium, and the phenomena are so complicated that it is not likely that such a theory will be developed. The importance of influences of the path of movement on the final equilibrium position cannot be estimated a priori, of course; these influences are dependent on peculiarities of each market situation. It does appear reasonable to believe that the less the fluctuations in prices and outputs, the less the final equilibrium position will be affected, and if this be so, there are many cases in which it is safe to take the final position as fixed.

The problem can be eliminated by postulating that the final equilibrium is attained immediately, and this is a general practice among economists. The method by which influences of the path of movement are eliminated is provided by Edgeworth's principle of recontract. According to this scheme, all the individual buyers and sellers in a market enter into contracts which are provisional with respect to prices and quantities. No exchanges take place on the basis of these preliminary contracts; each buyer (or seller) is privileged to recontract with any seller or buyer with whom he can secure better terms. When the recontracting has continued long enough, no buyer or seller can improve his position by any change in price that would be agreeable to anyone else. This is, of course, the position of equilibrium in that market, and exchange then takes place after this position is reached.

The conditions of equilibrium are the relationships which must be fulfilled if the economic system in question is to be in equilibrium. Given the data of a problem, the conditions of equilibrium contain a complete summary of all the forces that are influential in the final outcome of the economic process. A problem in economic theory is therefore solved once its conditions of equilibrium are known.

The outstanding characteristic of the conditions of equilibrium is that they are equal in number to the unknown quantities and prices which are to be determined. The conditions are, in mathematical terminology, the equations of the economic system, and prices and quantities are the unknowns. This important characteristic of equality in number of conditions of equilibrium and unknown prices and outputs may be illustrated by two examples:

1. In the simple case of a fixed supply of a commodity, we have two data: the quantity available and demand curve of the commodity. In addition, we have one condition of equilibrium: that the quantity demanded at the equilibrium price equal the quantity available. With this relation between the data, we can determine the unknown price.

2. The second case is the long-run equilibrium in a competitive industry. In this case the conditions of equilibrium (which are studied in Chapter 9) are: (a) Every firm is operating at the output which will maximize its net profits; (b) the price is such that the quantity supplied equals the quantity demanded; and (c) the price is such that each firm is earning only the competitive rate of return on investment. From these conditions (plus the data of the problem) we can determine (a) the number of firms in the industry, (b) the output of each firm, and (c) the price of the product.

In addition to these necessary conditions of equilibrium, there are certain other so-called *sufficiency* or stability conditions, which are sufficient to ensure that the equilibrium is stable. These stability conditions can be illustrated by recourse to the explanation of market price. The familiar supply and demand curves for a commodity are given in Figures 2A and 2B. In both cases, the necessary conditions (one price, and quantity supplied equals quantity demanded) are fulfilled at a quantity of OA and a price of OB. In Figure 2A the situation is stable, for a small disturbance of price above OB will lead to an excess of the quantity supplied over the quantity demanded and force the price down again to OB, and vice versa in case the price is below OB. But in Figure 2B the stability conditions are not fulfilled, for if the price were slightly lower than OB, the quantity supplied would exceed the quantity demanded and the price would cumulatively fall, and if the price were slightly above OB, the quantity demanded would exceed the quantity supplied, and the price would cumulatively rise. The stability condition in this case is that the demand curve cut the supply curve from above.

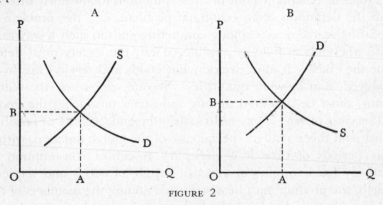

FIGURE 2

RECOMMENDED READINGS

1. Knight, Frank H., *Risk, Uncertainty and Profit*, London School Reprints of Scarce Works, No. 16 (1933), Chs. 1, 5, 6.
2. Robbins, Lionel, "On a Certain Ambiguity in the Conception of Stationary Equilibrium," *Economic Journal*, XL (1930), 194–214.
3. Knight, Frank H., "Statics and Dynamics," reprinted in *The Ethics of Competition*, Harper, New York, 1935.
4. Kaldor, N., "A Classificatory Note on the Determinateness of Equilibrium," *Review of Economic Studies*, I (1934), 122–136.

CHAPTER 3

THE FUNCTIONS OF AN ECONOMIC SYSTEM: THE ENTERPRISE SYSTEM

The present chapter is in a sense the synopsis of the theory of economics. The major economic problems which confront any society are summarized, and then the general method by which an enterprise system solves these problems is sketched. Most of the remainder of this volume is devoted to filling in some of the more important details of this general picture.

I. THE FUNCTIONS OF AN ECONOMIC SYSTEM

Five functions of any economic system have been distinguished by Professor Knight.* Four of these functions follow fairly directly from the definition of an economic problem, i.e., the problem of allocating scarce means among competing ends in such a way as to satisfy the ends as fully as possible. First, the society must determine the ends — it must decide what goods and services are to be produced, and in what quantities. Second, resources (the scarce means) must be allocated among industries producing the goods and services in such a way as to satisfy the ends as fully as possible. Third, and this is really a special case of the fourth function, within short periods of time it is necessary to adjust consumption to relatively fixed supplies or rates of supply of goods and services. Fourth, the product must be distributed among the members of the society — it must be decided whose wants are to be satisfied, and to what extent. Finally — and this function transcends the economic problems of a stationary state — provision must be made for the maintenance and expansion of the economic system. Although these functions obviously overlap, it is useful to discuss them individually.

* This section is based directly on Frank H. Knight, "Social Economic Organization," in *Syllabus for the Second-Year Course in the Social Sciences*, 2nd ed., University of Chicago, Chicago, 1933, pp. 130–137.

The determination of the quantities of the various goods and services that are to be produced can be considered from three viewpoints. From the individual's viewpoint, those goods and services are demanded which will most satisfactorily meet his personal wants (however these latter may be determined). This is an economic problem, the solution of which is contained in the theory of demand (see Chapter 5). From society's viewpoint there are two additional problems. There is the question of how a given quantum of goods is to be distributed, in what proportion the goods are to be divided among the members of the society. This problem of distribution is treated separately as the third function. But in addition, society influences the personal wants of individuals. In part this influence is conscious and deliberate, as in the prohibition on the use of certain commodities like drugs. A far greater influence is exerted unconsciously and indirectly, for the wants of individuals are dominated by the kind of society in which they live. Economic theory has little to contribute to the understanding of this last phenomenon, the culture of a society.

In this connection it is worth repeating Professor Knight's point that the determination of what is desirable to produce (that is, the set of values to attach to goods) is indispensable to the notion of efficiency. Students frequently define *efficiency* as the ratio of output to input when in fact the first law of thermodynamics assures us that this ratio is always unity. Efficiency in the economic sense is the ratio of useful output to useful input — we are not directly influenced in our judgment of the efficiency of a candle by the heat it generates or by the oxygen it consumes.

The second function, the organization of production, is in considerable part a technological problem, but it also involves important economic decisions. The organization of production entails three tasks: (1) the allocation of the productive services among industries which produce the goods we desire; (2) within each industry, the allocation of productive services to various production units (plants and firms); and (3) within each production unit, the efficient combination of the various productive services. The first task is obviously economic in nature, but it might appear that the second is exclusively technological. This is not true: there may be, for example, a choice between producing in one plant and saving machinery or producing in several plants and saving transportation, and machinery and transportation can be compared only in value terms. The third task is exclusively technological once the productive services are allocated to a production unit, but the technical way in which various services combine will react on the allocation among industries. If productive service A is a good technical substitute for B in producing commodity X, and B is both scarce and indispensable in producing Y, then clearly it is (economically) wise to allocate most or all of B to Y.

The third function, the adjustment of consumption to relatively fixed rates of supply, is a short-run problem. Given sufficient time to build plants and train laborers, it is possible to increase greatly the production of goods of which we desire more — this is in fact the second function of the economic system. But in cases where the rate of supply is fixed temporarily (and sometimes permanently, as with early Shakespeare folios) society must somehow ration the goods directly among the individual consumers, and if in addition the goods are perishable in consumers' hands, the rationing system must also distribute them over the period which lasts until the rate of production is increased.

The fourth function is to distribute the product among the members of the economy. It has already been suggested that the distribution of income plays a large part in determining what products shall be produced. In a slave economy the products will be cheap foods and clothing for the slaves and luxuries for their owners. In the not-very-different totalitarian society, the products will be essentials for the population and munitions for the dictator. The distribution of income need not be closely correlated with the performance of economic services, as indeed these examples show.

Finally, society must provide for the maintenance and expansion of the economic system. On the side of resources this implies growth in the size of population and improvement of its skills, discovery of additional natural resources, and the accumulation of capital equipment. With respect to technology it implies the development of new production techniques and new forms of business organization. Finally, the wants of the citizens will undergo change. These changes will be influenced in some part by technological developments and by deliberate economic activities (e.g., advertising), but again the fundamental explanation must embrace all elements of the culture.

Economic decisions play a part in the determination of the optimum rate of progress (which here means a rise in national income, and not necessarily a better civilization) because progress is costly. This is most apparent in the case of a resource which is fixed in supply (e.g., petroleum), for the more that is allocated to the future, the less we may consume now. But the same choice exists with permanent resources; we can accumulate a larger amount of capital equipment only by consuming less at present. Hence the society must decide the rate and direction of expansion, the organization of resources to secure this end, and the distribution of costs of the expansion.

II. THE STRUCTURE OF AN ENTERPRISE SYSTEM

An enterprise system may be characterized as follows: the owners of productive resources (laborers, capitalists, and landowners) sell the services of their resources to entrepreneurs (usually organized on a corporate basis) for money, and then spend the money to buy the products of the entrepreneurs. This form of organization should be contrasted with a handicraft system, where the owner of the productive resources produces and sells the complete product. In this latter economy there is no problem of distribution, the total product belongs to the person who makes it. The handicraft system is still present in the professions and in agriculture, but our subsequent discussion will be restricted to the more complex enterprise system, which of course includes the handicraft system as a special case.

It will simplify our discussion without affecting any important principles to assume that all businesses are vertically integrated, so that each firm engages in all stages of production from the extraction of raw materials to retail merchandising. We shall further ignore the important economic activities of the state. By thus eliminating interfirm and governmental transactions, we are left with only two kinds of markets, those for consumers' goods and those for productive services.

In the first type, consumers'-goods markets, the entrepreneur sells goods and services to consumers in exchange for money. Examples of such markets are those for foodstuffs, permanent waves, and symphony concerts. In the second type, the resources markets, the entrepreneur exchanges money (secured from consumers) for the use of productive resources (including labor, land, and capital) which he requires to produce consumers' goods. If the commodity in question is produced and sold continuously throughout the year, as is frequently the case, the entrepreneur is in both markets simultaneously and continuously.

One additional point is necessary to complete this broad picture: consumers secure their incomes as owners of productive resources. In an enterprise economy there is no other source of income than the sale of productive services; charity and gifts (other than the nicely balanced exchanges at Christmas) are strictly speaking non-economic (but not necessarily uneconomic). Hence there is a

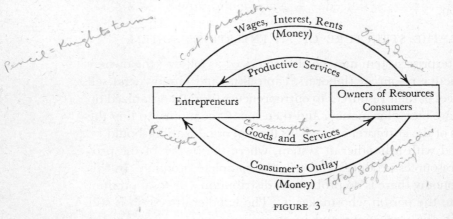

FIGURE 3

complete circulation of purchasing power — from consumers to entrepreneurs to owners of resources, and so *ad infinitum*. This gives rise to the well-known "wheel of wealth" portrayed in Figure 3, although it might better be called the "itinerary of income" if the alliteration must be preserved.

If the economy is stationary, as previously defined, these flows will be constant through time in both magnitude and composition. In that case the flow of income manifests itself in four different forms. From the viewpoint of consumers, it is paid out as the cost of living, and as a corollary it represents the receipts of business. On the other side, the receipt of the flow by consumers is personal income, and its payment by entrepreneurs is the cost of production.

Should the economy be progressive, minor modifications must be made in this picture. The disbursements of consumers now consist of the cost of living plus savings, and these latter are placed at the disposal of entrepreneurs (directly or through financial institutions) in exchange for the payment of interest or dividends. On the other side, the entrepreneurs invest the savings in research, exploration for new resources, and construction of new capital equipment. The annual returns from these investments accrue slowly through time and serve to pay the interest or dividends necessary to secure the savings. Again the economy is in general equilibrium, although now the national income (which equals any of the four flows) will rise each year.

In an enterprise system the five economic functions are solved through the price system. An enterprise system need not be perfectly competitive, as indeed our own economy amply testifies, but it will simplify the exposition of the workings of the price system if all deviations from perfect competition are ignored.

1. THE FIXING OF VALUES

Within the limits set by law and custom, consumers may spend their incomes as they wish. Naturally they will offer high prices for the things they desire greatly and low prices for the things which yield less want satisfaction. Since entrepreneurs are motivated by the desire for profits, and in any case must cover costs to remain solvent, they will devote their productive facilities to those commodities whose prices are high (relative to the outlay necessary to produce them) — i.e., to those commodities which are most urgently desired. It is for this reason that an enterprise system is frequently characterized as subject to "consumer sovereignty."

It is important to note that an individual consumer's control over production is limited by the size of his income. Every dollar of income (or expenditure) is a vote for the types of goods and services the possessor of the dollar desires to have produced. It follows, therefore, that the constituents of the flow of annual income of an economy are determined in large part by the distribution of ownership of resources. In an economy in which economic equality prevailed, there would be fewer domestic servants and more butter. Yet in the field of consumption goods and services this influence is not as great as many people suppose; Adam Smith observed that "the desire of food is limited in every man by the narrow capacity of the human stomach." Income distribution is a major element in determining the amount of new savings, but this is a topic which will be investigated much later.

II. *THE ORGANIZATION OF PRODUCTION*

It has been suggested that entrepreneurs must sell the products which consumers desire in order to cover the costs of production. But what are the costs of production? Costs are merely the amounts the productive services would secure if they were transferred to some other use or uses. The cost of day labor to building contractors is the value of the product the day labor could produce in railroad construction. The cost to a farmer of land for corn is the amount the land would earn if devoted to wheat or oats. Therefore, if an entrepreneur is not covering costs, this means that the resources could be used elsewhere to satisfy wants for which the consumers are willing to pay higher prices.

Although this statement contains the fundamental argument, it may be well to elaborate it in terms of the three tasks in production organization (see page 33). High prices for products enable entrepreneurs to pay high prices for productive services and hence to draw resources away from industries whose products are less urgently desired — thus price allocates resources among industries. The allocation among firms is similarly on a price basis, for those firms which are more efficient can sell the product at a lower price or pay a higher price for the productive services. Finally, within the firm the desire for profits will lead to the substitution of services with low prices for those with high prices.

The organization of production by prices is the chief defense for the enterprise system. If resources are used where they secure the highest rates of remuneration, if they are used efficiently in these industries, and if they are used to produce the products which consumers most desire, then it may be concluded that output is as large as possible. This argument is important and valid, but the fundamental assumptions on which it is based must not be forgotten: the economy is competitive, and the distribution of income is accepted.

III. *SHORT-RUN RATIONING*

The allocation of fixed supplies is a direct product of the price system. If there is little wheat, the quantity demanded can be curtailed by progressive increases in its price, and there is always a price sufficiently high to restrict the quantity demanded to the amount available. Similarly, most of the wheat will not be consumed the first six months of the crop year. If it were, the price thereafter would become very great. In the early part of the period speculators buy in anticipation of a future price rise, and their operations serve to equalize the rate of consumption (and to moderate the price fluctuations) by raising the price in the early part of the year and lowering it in the latter part of the year.

iv. DISTRIBUTION OF THE PRODUCT

Since incomes are secured by the sale of productive services, the money income of any consumer depends upon the types and amounts of productive resources he owns and the prices their services command, and his real income depends in addition upon the prices of consumers' goods. The ownership of resources is of course affected by economic factors, but a much more prominent part must be assigned to the institution of private property. The prices paid for productive services have already been considered as costs of production, and it was pointed out in this connection that the price system directs resources to the industries where they are most needed. The analysis can be carried a step farther: the price system also affects the type of resources. If an occupation is relatively well paid, men will seek the education and training necessary to enter it.

v. ECONOMIC PROGRESS

The maintenance and expansion of the economic system cannot be explained exclusively, or perhaps even primarily, in terms of the price system. Technological improvements, for instance, are only partially due to economic incentives; Pasteur did not develop his method of sterilizing milk in order to become wealthy. Again, the explanation of population size no longer runs in the simple biological and economic terms of Malthus' theory. A full explanation of economic progress involves a study of the society's entire culture.

Yet there is one important price, the interest rate, which does exert great control over economic expansion. The importance of the interest rate as an inducement to save has been much debated. But it unquestionably serves to ration the demand for new capital. Even in the absence of important technological improvements there is a great number of possible investments which would yield some return. We could build toll highways, or air-condition all homes, or eliminate all grade crossings. Those which yield low returns must be excluded, or the economy will fail to attain the maximum possible expansion of income. The selection of investments which should secure funds is the basic service of the interest rate.

This simplified picture should not obscure the fact that in its detailed structure and workings the price system is almost fantastically complex. No sprinkling of statistics can remedy this deficiency, but some idea of the intricacy of the price structure is suggested by a study of the textile industries.* Over 200 markets are distinguished, and this is of course a great understatement, for on the one hand, many of these markets (e.g., hats) must be subdivided for detailed analysis, and on the other hand, many closely related markets (textile labor and machinery, dyes) are not included. It is probably very conservative to estimate the total number of individual textile products at two or three hundred thousand; there are several thousand kinds of sewing thread alone.

The multiplicity of products and prices is less important than the fact that they form an interdependent system. Prices are related by substitution possibilities: cotton goods compete with wool and with other cotton goods; wool competes with reworked wool; and cotton competes with paper in bagging. Moreover, there are intricate cost relations among fibers, yarns, gray goods, finished goods, and fabricated goods. And finally, if the complete explanation of the structure of the textile industries were desired, one would have to investigate also other agricultural industries, transportation, competing demands for labor, and eventually by these and other channels, the entire economy.

RECOMMENDED READINGS

1. Knight, Frank H., "Social Economic Organization" and other chapters, in *Syllabus and Selected Readings for the Second-Year Course in the Social Sciences*, 2nd ed., University of Chicago, Chicago, 1933.
2. Cassel, G., *The Theory of Social Economy*, rev. ed., Harcourt, Brace, New York, 1931, Bk. I.
3. Schumpeter, J., "The Nature and Necessity of a Price System," in *Economic Reconstruction*, Columbia University, New York, 1934.
4. Lange, O., "On the Economic Theory of Socialism," *Review of Economic Studies*, IV (1936), 53–71.

* See *Textile Markets*, National Bureau of Economic Research, New York, 1939, pp. 3–142, and also the market chart at the end of the volume.

CHAPTER 4

FUNDAMENTAL QUANTITATIVE RELATIONSHIPS

The study of quantitative economic phenomena requires certain tools of analysis. For some purposes arithmetic is adequate, but there are several objections to complete reliance on numerical illustrations. Tables of numerical data are relatively awkward and laborious to handle. Moreover, arithmetical examples may lead to generalizations which are correct only in special cases. As an example, John Stuart Mill argued, on the basis of a numerical illustration, that a certain type of agricultural improvement (one that raised the marginal productivity curve of capital by a fixed percentage) always led to a fall of land rents. This was wrong: it is easy to set up a numerical example where an improvement of this type will increase land rents.* Finally, particular numerical examples may raise theoretical difficulties which are essentially irrelevant or unimportant, and thus unnecessarily complicate the theory. Here Böhm-Bawerk provides an example: he established the clumsy and misleading theory of "marginal pairs" of buyers and sellers to circumvent difficulties arising out of his choice of indivisible commodities (horses) to illustrate the theory of value.†

As a result of these weighty objections, the arithmetical method has yielded much ground to graphical analysis, and even symbolic mathematical analysis (the infinitesimal calculus in particular) has increased in popularity — or perhaps one should say that it has decreased in unpopularity. The preference for geometrical analysis

---

* See John Stuart Mill, *Principles of Political Economy*, Ashley ed., Longmans, Green, New York, 1929, pp. 717–718. The error is discussed by A. Marshall, *Principles of Economics*, 8th ed., Macmillan, London, 1920, pp. 836–837.

† See Eugen von Böhm-Bawerk, *Positive Theory of Capital*, Stechert, New York, 1930, Bk. IV, Ch. 3. The theory is appraised by F. Y. Edgeworth, *Papers Relating to Political Economy*, Macmillan, London, 1925, Vol. I, 37–39. He characteristically observes that Böhm-Bawerk is "riding a one-horse illustration to death." Mill also supplies an example of this point; see J. Viner, *Studies in the Theory of International Trade*, Harper, New York, 1937, p. 541.

is largely justified: graphs are relatively easy to handle, and yet they are adequate to derive very general theorems.

The relationships between economic quantities are usually considered to be continuous. Thus, if the price of butter falls from 35 to 34.99 cents per pound, it is assumed that the quantity of butter a consumer will purchase increases from (say) 30 to 30.01 pounds per year. Quite obviously this is untrue; butter is not sold in such small units. Nevertheless, economists usually assume that economic magnitudes can vary by arbitrarily small amounts, for several important reasons. It is extremely convenient to treat of continuous rather than discrete variation. The geometry (and the more advanced mathematical analysis) of continuous relationships is much simpler than that of discontinuous relationships. Moreover, for most purposes the error introduced by treating discontinuous relationships as continuous is very small; there will be no serious consequences for the analysis of demand, for instance, if we do assume that the consumer will increase his consumption of butter by one hundredth of a pound. Where discontinuous relationships do give significantly different answers, they will be used.

Most of the necessary apparatus will be developed in the present chapter; the nature of indifference curves and of envelopes will be taken up at appropriate points in later chapters. The important relations between total, average, and marginal quantities will be taken up twice, first with discrete numerical illustrations and then with continuous curves. The same propositions are true in both cases, but they are more difficult to prove in the latter case. Thereafter the relations between these quantities and the concept of elasticity will be developed.

I. TOTAL, AVERAGE, AND MARGINAL QUANTITIES: THE DISCRETE CASE

The present discussion will center about the important relationships between a total quantity, an average quantity, and a marginal quantity. This exposition will be presented in terms of specific problems, e.g., the product secured by cultivating land with increasing intensiveness, but every conclusion here established will be equally applicable to any other quantitative problem which involves these types of quantities.

Table 1 is the basis for the immediate discussion: it presents the product (in bushels) secured by cultivating a hypothetical farm with a variable amount of composite units of capital-and-labor. The definitions now to be given are illustrated from this table:

TABLE 1

Units of Capital-and-Labor	Total Product (bushels)	Average Product (bushels)	Marginal Product (bushels)
0	0	0	0
1	5	5	5
2	13	$6\frac{1}{2}$	8
3	23	$7\frac{2}{3}$	10
4	38	$9\frac{1}{2}$	15
5	50	10	12
6	60	10	10
7	68	$9\frac{5}{7}$	8
8	75	$9\frac{3}{8}$	7
9	81	9	6
10	86	$8\frac{3}{5}$	5
11	90	$8\frac{2}{11}$	4

1. Total Product. The total product of a given number of units of capital-and-labor, when applied to this hypothetical farm, is obviously the number of bushels of product secured by the assistance of that quantity of capital-and-labor. The second column of Table 1 gives the various total products.

2. Average Product. The average product of *n* units of capital-and-labor is the total product of *n* units divided by *n*. The third column of Table 1 gives the average products.

3. Marginal Product. The basic definition of *marginal product* is

$$\frac{\text{increase in total product}}{\text{corresponding increase in quantity of capital-and-labor}}.$$

As a special case of this definition, we may define the marginal product of *n* units of capital-and-labor as the increase in total product which results from increasing the quantity of capital-and-labor from (*n* − 1) units to *n* units. Restating this second definition: marginal product is the amount added to total product by the addition of one more unit of capital-and-labor.* The last column of Table 1 gives the marginal products.

> *Proposition 1:* The sum of the first n marginal products is equal to the total product of n units of capital-and-labor.

This proposition follows directly from the definition of the marginal product of capital-and-labor, for

marginal product of 1 unit = amount added by first unit

marginal product of 2 units = amount added by second unit

marginal product of 3 units = amount added by third unit

. . . .

marginal product of n units = amount added by nth unit.

If these marginal products (the left sides of these equations) are added, they equal the total product of n units of capital-and-labor (the right sides of the equations). Table 1 illustrates the proposition: the sum of the marginal products of the first six units of capital-and-labor is $5 + 8 + 10 + 15 + 12 + 10 = 60$.

> *Proposition 2:* When the average product is increasing, marginal product is greater than average product.†

This proposition is illustrated in Table 1, where average product is increasing up to the fifth unit of capital-and-labor, and the marginal product is greater than the average product for the first five units of capital-and-labor. (The equality of average and marginal product when one unit of capital-and-labor is employed is due to the discrete nature of the data.) An algebraic proof of the relationship is given in a footnote.‡

* A common definition of *marginal product* is that it is the amount added to total product by the *last* unit of capital-and-labor. Two implications of such a statement are undesirable:
1. It is the task of economics to discover which is the last unit; this is not known until the end of the analysis.
2. This definition may suggest that the "last" unit of capital-and-labor differs from the preceding units either in its nature or its duties. But all units of capital-and-labor are assumed to be homogeneous (see page 112): all are equally efficient, and all do equally important things. It is for that reason that the text speaks of the marginal product of n units, not the marginal product of the nth unit.

† Note that it is not said that the marginal product increases when the average product increases, for this is not necessarily true.

‡ Let N units of capital-and-labor yield a product of P, so the average product is P/N. By adding n more units of capital-and-labor, total product is increased by p, and the new average product is

Proposition 3: When average product is decreasing, marginal product is less than average product.

This proposition is also illustrated in Table 1, where average product declines after the sixth unit of capital-and-labor is applied, and marginal product is less than average product.*

Proposition 4: When average product is at a maximum, marginal product equals average product.

This is a corollary of propositions 2 and 3, for if average product is at a maximum, at that point it is neither increasing nor decreasing, and therefore marginal product is neither greater than nor less than average product. This point is illustrated in Table 1 at six units of capital-and-labor. (In the table, average product appears to have two maximums of 10; this again is due to the discrete nature of the data.)

Proposition 5: The addition (or subtraction) of a fixed sum from all of the total products will have no effect on the marginal products.

In order to verify this proposition, the reader can add (say) 10 bushels to each of the total products in the second column of

$$\frac{P+p}{N+n}.$$

Since the new average product is larger than the former,

$$\frac{P+p}{N+n} - \frac{P}{N} > 0.$$

Bringing these terms over a common denominator,

$$\frac{NP + Np - PN - Pn}{N(N+n)} > 0,$$

or $\quad\quad\quad\quad\quad\quad Np - Pn > 0,$

or $\quad\quad\quad\quad\quad\quad \dfrac{p}{n} > \dfrac{P}{N}.$

Find a k (greater than unity) such that

$$\frac{p}{n} = \frac{kP}{N},$$

then $\quad\quad\quad\quad\quad \dfrac{p}{n} = \dfrac{kP+p}{N+n} > \dfrac{P+p}{N+n}.$

In this last equation p/n is the marginal product (for it is the increase in total product divided by the increase in the quantity of capital-and-labor), and $(P+p)/(N+n)$ is average product, so it follows that when average product is increasing, marginal product is greater than average product.

* The preceding algebraic proof holds for this case, if "less than" is substituted throughout for "greater than."

Table 1. It is obvious that the difference between any two total products (i.e., the marginal product) will not be affected.

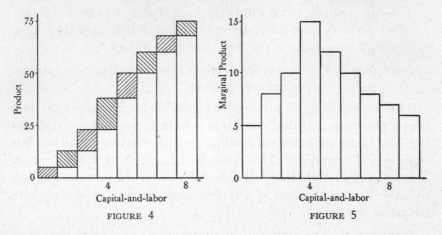

FIGURE 4   FIGURE 5

II. TOTAL, AVERAGE, AND MARGINAL QUANTITIES:
THE CONTINUOUS CASE

If the variable quantity of capital-and-labor is measured along the horizontal axis (or axis of abscissas) and the total product is

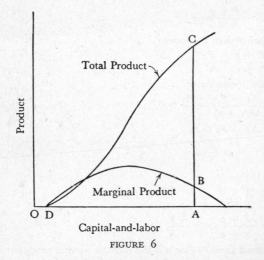

FIGURE 6

measured along the vertical axis (or axis of ordinates), it is possible to represent the data in Table 1 by rectangles such as those in Figure 4. The area of each rectangle corresponding to the excess product over the preceding total product is crosshatched in Figure 4; these shaded areas are by definition the marginal products. They are plotted separately in Figure 5 (note change in vertical scale).

Proposition 1: The area under the marginal product curve up to any point is equal to the height of the total product curve at that point.

The area enclosed by n rectangles in Figure 5 is equal to the area of the nth rectangle in Figure 4 — this is true by construction. If these rectangles are suffi-ciently narrow (i.e., if the units of capital-and-labor are made small enough), con-tinuous curves are approxi-mated. Such curves are shown in Figure 6, where at any quantity (A) of capital-and-labor, the area under the marginal product curve (OBA) is equal to the height of the total product curve (AC). Figures 4 and 5 sug-gest that this is true; it cannot be proved by ele-mentary methods.*

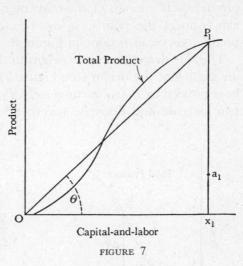

FIGURE 7

In order to prove the next four propositions, it is necessary to explain the derivation of the average and marginal product curves from the total product curve. The average product is derived in Figure 7. For any quantity of capital-and-labor (x_1), there is a corresponding total product (P_1). Average product is the latter divided by the former, or P_1/x_1. This ratio can be computed by measuring P_1 and x_1; it is found to be x_1a_1.

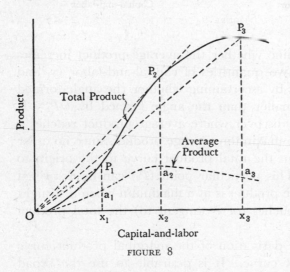

FIGURE 8

* The proof is as follows: Let x be capital-and-labor, $f(x)$ the total product, and hence $f'(x)$ marginal product. Since $f(0) = 0$,

$$\int_0^x f'(x)\,dx = f(x).$$

Average product is computed for three different quantities of capital-and-labor in Figure 8; x_1a_1, x_2a_2, and x_3a_3 are these average products. If enough of these average products are computed, we can connect the points, a_1, a_2, a_3, etc., by a continuous average product curve, as is done in Figure 8.

The line drawn from the origin to the total product curve forms an angle θ at the origin (see Figure 7). The size of this angle can be measured by P_1/x_1, or conversely, P_1/x_1 can be measured by θ: the two increase and decrease together.* This relationship is useful;

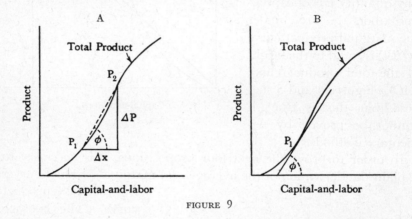

FIGURE 9

it is possible to determine whether the average product increases or decreases between two quantities of capital-and-labor (x_1 and x_2, for instance) merely by ascertaining whether the angle formed by OP_1 is larger or smaller than the angle formed by OP_2. It is now also possible to discover where average product reaches a maximum: x_2 yields the maximum average product, since no other line can be drawn from the total product curve to the origin to form a larger angle. This particular point (P_2) can be described more generally: average product is at a maximum when a straight line from the origin touches (or is tangent to) the total product curve.

The final task is the derivation of the marginal product curve from the total product curve. It is desirable to use the broad definition of the marginal product: marginal product is the change (increase) in total product divided by the change (increase) in the

* This amounts only to the trigonometrical definition, $\tan \theta = P_1/x_1$.

quantity of capital-and-labor which brought it about.* In Figure 9A the increase of capital-and-labor is labeled Δx (where Δx means a small amount of x), and the resulting increase of product is labeled ΔP (where ΔP is the corresponding small increase of P). The marginal product is then $\Delta P / \Delta x$.

As the increase of capital-and-labor is made smaller and smaller, P_2 approaches P_1 (see Figure 9A), and the line joining them becomes the tangent of the total product curve at P_1 (see Figure 9B). It was observed in connection with the discussion of the average

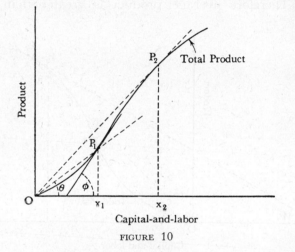

FIGURE 10

product curve that θ is a measure of P_1/x_1; similarly ϕ is a measure of $\Delta P / \Delta x$. We have reached the conclusion: marginal product is equal to the slope of the total product curve, and the marginal product will increase (or decrease) with the increase (or decrease) of the angle which the tangent to the total product curve forms with the horizontal axis.

Proposition 2: When the average product is increasing, marginal product is greater than average product.

This proposition is demonstrable for continuous curves by means of Figure 10. Up to x_2 of capital-and-labor, the average product of capital-and-labor is increasing. At any point x_1 in this region erect a perpendicular line to P_1. Then the average product is

* Marginal product is properly defined in terms of change rather than increase, since the total product may decrease when the quantity of capital-and-labor increases, in which case the marginal product is negative.

measured by θ, where θ is the angle formed by OP_1. The marginal product is measured by ϕ, where ϕ is the angle formed by the line tangent to the total product curve at P_1. Since ϕ is greater than θ up to x_2, marginal product is greater than average product up to x_2.

> *Proposition 3:* When average product is decreasing, marginal product is less than average product.

Figure 11 serves to prove this proposition. Beyond P_2 the average product is decreasing, and it is evident that in this region θ is larger than ϕ. Therefore average product is greater than marginal product.*

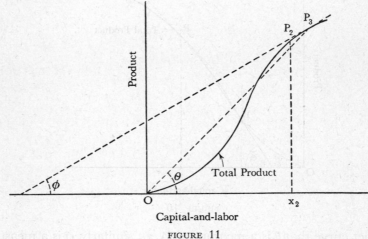

FIGURE 11

> *Proposition 4:* When average product is at a maximum, marginal product equals average product.

At the point where average product reaches a maximum, θ and ϕ coincide (see Figure 8, for instance), and therefore average and marginal products are equal.

> *Proposition 5:* The addition (or subtraction) of a fixed quantity from a total curve will not affect its marginal curve.

For the demonstration of this proposition it is convenient to shift to another example: total cost. In Figure 12, TVC is total variable cost, and TC is total cost; they differ by the constant amount of

---

* If the total product is decreasing, marginal product becomes negative, and the proposition is still true.

total fixed cost. At any output x_1, the two curves are therefore equidistant, so their slopes are equal ($\phi_1 = \phi_2$). Hence marginal cost is the same for both curves.

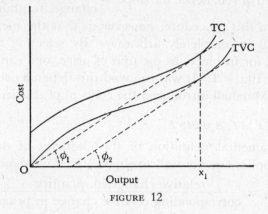

FIGURE 12

III. THE CONCEPT OF ELASTICITY

The use of the concept of elasticity to describe demand (and less frequently supply) curves has become almost universal. It is therefore indispensable to understand fully what an elasticity is, if the current literature of economics is to be read, quite aside from the positive advantages to be derived from its use.

TABLE 2

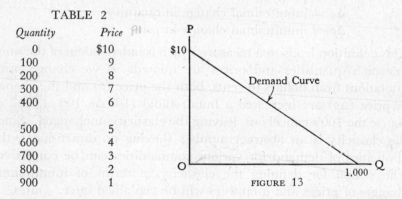

Quantity	Price
0	$10
100	9
200	8
300	7
400	6
500	5
600	4
700	3
800	2
900	1

FIGURE 13

The purpose and advantages of the elasticity measure can best be understood by examining a specific demand schedule and curve. The demand curve corresponding to the schedule in Table 2 is plotted in Figure 13. The simplest type of demand curve, a straight line, has been chosen. It would be possible to measure the responsiveness of sales to price changes by the slope of the demand curve: in this example a fall in price of \$1 leads to an increase in quantity purchased of 100, hence the slope $= \dfrac{\text{change in price}}{\text{change in quantity}} = \dfrac{1}{100}$. The defect in this procedure, however, is that the measure of the slope (1/100) is completely arbitrary. By selecting cents rather than dollars, for instance, as the unit of price, one can change the slope to $100/100 = 1$. It was to avoid this dependence on the size of unit that Marshall introduced the concept of elasticity.*

I. *ELASTICITY AT A POINT*

The fundamental definition of the elasticity of demand (the definition applies equally well to supply) is, if we denote elasticity by η,

$$\eta = \frac{\text{relative change in quantity}}{\text{corresponding relative change in price}}$$

when both of these changes are infinitesimally small. In symbols,

$$\eta = \frac{\dfrac{\Delta q}{q}}{\dfrac{\Delta p}{p}} = \frac{\Delta q}{\Delta p} \cdot \frac{p}{q}$$

where
q = quantity
p = price
Δq = infinitesimal change in quantity
Δp = infinitesimal change in price

This definition leads to a measure which is independent of the units in which quantities and prices are quoted. If we change price quotations from dollars to cents, both the price (p) and the change in price (Δp) are increased a hundredfold ($100\,\Delta p/100\,p$), and of course the 100's cancel out, leaving the elasticity unchanged. Since the elasticity is an abstract number (having no dimensions), the elasticities of demand for various commodities can be compared. The reason for defining the elasticity in terms of infinitesimal changes of prices and quantities will be explained later.

II. *MEASUREMENT OF ELASTICITY AT A POINT*

If a demand curve is known, the elasticity may be computed either symbolically or geometrically; the latter method will be

* A. Marshall, *op. cit.*, pp. 102–103 note, pp. 839–840.

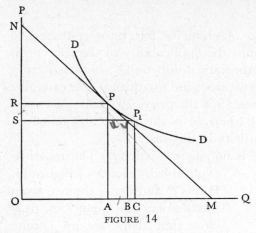

FIGURE 14

used in the text.* The problem is to measure the elasticity of the demand curve, *DD*, in Figure 14, at point *P*. First draw a line *NM* which touches (is tangent to) *DD* at *P*. If the price falls from *OR* to *OS*, the quantity increases from *OA* to *OC*. But if the price change is very small (that is, if P_1 is very close to *P*), *OB* will be approximately equal to *OC*. Turning now to our formula,

$$\eta = \frac{\dfrac{\Delta q}{q}}{\dfrac{\Delta p}{p}} = \frac{\dfrac{AB}{OA}}{\dfrac{RS}{OR}} = \frac{AB}{RS} \cdot \frac{OR}{OA}.$$

But by a well-known theorem on similar right triangles, $AB/RS = AM/RO$, so $\eta = \dfrac{AM}{RO}\dfrac{OR}{OA} = \dfrac{AM}{AO}$, whence, finally, since $AM/AO = PM/PN$,

$$\eta = \frac{PM}{PN}.$$

This is the measure of the elasticity of a demand curve at point *P*.

In the case of a demand curve, quantity increases when price decreases, and vice versa; so the changes are of opposite sign. The elasticity of demand is therefore negative. If the elasticity is − 1, it is called *unitary* elasticity. If the elasticity is numerically greater than − 1, for instance − 2, the demand is called *elastic*. If the elasticity is numerically less than − 1, for instance − ½, the demand is *inelastic*.

* The symbolic procedure is as follows: let $q = f(p)$ be the demand curve. The elasticity of demand is defined as
$$\eta = \frac{dq}{dp}\frac{p}{q}.$$
For a linear demand curve, $q = ap + b$, $\dfrac{dq}{dp} = a$, and $\eta = ap/(ap + b)$. If the demand curve is $q = kp^n$, where k and n are constants, $\dfrac{dq}{dp} = nkp^{n-1}$, and $\eta = nkp^{n-1}p/kp^n = n$.
Hence if the demand curve is of the form $q = kp^n$, it has the same elasticity at all points, and this elasticity equals n. (If the demand curve is to have a negative slope, of course $n < 0$.)

III. *ARC ELASTICITY*

Until now the discussion of elasticity has been restricted to elasticity at a point; this limits the applicability of the concept to continuous curves and mathematical functions. But frequently data are secured for only a few prices and quantities. For example, it may be observed that when $5 is the price, 200 units of a commodity are purchased, and when $4 is the price, 300 units are purchased. What is the elasticity in this case?

The answer is that there is no single elasticity. The reason is explicable by means of Figure 15. Points P_1 and P_2 are the two given sets of prices and quantities. It is clear that there are an infinite number of different curves on which these two points may lie, and every one of these curves has a different elasticity at P_1 and P_2.

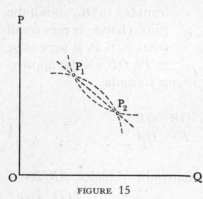

FIGURE 15

Nevertheless, an approximation to the true point elasticity can be secured even in this case. The following tests are open: (1) Trace the behavior of total receipts (see next section); (2) draw a freehand curve through the points or fit a curve by various statistical methods, and then use the geometrical method; or finally, (3) define an arc elasticity to meet the problem.* The arc elasticity is an average elasticity; it may be represented as follows:

$$\eta = \frac{q_0 - q_1}{q_0 + q_1} \bigg/ \frac{p_0 - p_1}{p_0 + p_1} = \frac{q_0 - q_1}{q_0 + q_1} \cdot \frac{p_0 + p_1}{p_0 - p_1},$$

where q_0, p_0 is one set of prices and quantities, and

q_1, p_1 is the other set of prices and quantities.

This measure is more accurate, the closer q_0 is to q_1 and the closer p_0 is to p_1. Applying it to our example:

$$\frac{\dfrac{200 - 300}{200 + 300}}{\dfrac{5 - 4}{5 + 4}} = \frac{-\dfrac{1}{5}}{\dfrac{1}{9}} = -\frac{9}{5} = -1.8.$$

* Only one such definition is given here; for a comprehensive treatment see R. G. D. Allen, "The Concept of Arc Elasticity of Demand," *Review of Economic Studies*, I (1934), pp. 226–229.

IV. RELATIONS BETWEEN ELASTICITY AND TOTAL AND MARGINAL QUANTITIES

If the demand curve has an elasticity of unity at all points, the proportional changes in quantity and price are equal and opposite in sign, and exactly offset one another. Total receipts (quantity times price) therefore remain unchanged when price changes; this case is illustrated in Figure 16A. The reader can readily verify for himself (by using the geometrical test) that the demand curve has an elasticity of unity at all points. At price OB, quantity OA is taken, and total receipts are $OB \times OA$. At price OC, quantity is OF, and total receipts are $OC \times OF$ ($= OB \times OA$).

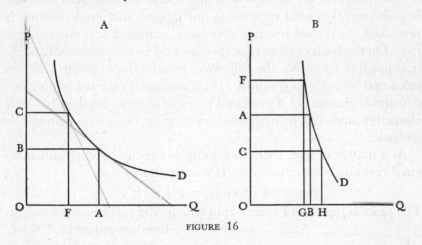

FIGURE 16

If the demand curve is inelastic (i.e., elasticity is numerically less than unity), the relative change in quantity will be less than the relative change in price from which the quantity change results. This holds true of the demand curve in Figure 16B, as can be verified by the geometrical test. In this case, if price falls from OA to OC, total receipts fall from $OA \times OB$ to $OC \times OH$. If price rises from OA to OF, total receipts rise from $OA \times OB$ to $OF \times OG$. If the demand curve is elastic, these conclusions are reversed. The relations are summarized in Table 3.

Marginal revenue may be defined as the change in total revenue divided by the corresponding change in output. If output increases by only one unit, then the resulting change of total revenue is marginal revenue. The relations between total and marginal revenue

TABLE 3

	Inelastic Demand	Unitary Elasticity	Elastic Demand
Price Rise . . .	Receipts rise	Receipts unchanged	Receipts fall
Price Fall . . .	Receipts fall	Receipts unchanged	Receipts rise

are identical with those between total and marginal product. It follows immediately from this definition that, given an increase in the quantity, (1) if total revenue increases, marginal revenue is positive; (2) if total revenue is unchanged, marginal revenue is zero; and (3) if total revenue decreases, marginal revenue is negative. On the basis of these relationships and by reference to Table 3, it is possible to derive the following relationships, given a fall in price and increase in quantity: (1) if marginal revenue is positive, demand is elastic; (2) if marginal revenue is zero, demand has unit elasticity; and (3) if marginal revenue is negative, demand is inelastic.

As a matter of fact, the relationship between elasticity and marginal revenue is more precise. It can be shown that

$$\text{marginal revenue} = p(1 + 1/\eta).$$

The proof is based on Figure 17, in which NM represents a straight-line demand curve.* Select

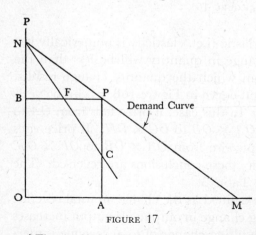

FIGURE 17

a point P on NM. Then designate the marginal revenue corresponding to output OA by AC (which is still to be determined). The proof of the formula follows in two steps:

1. AC is determined by the fact that $BF = FP$. For total revenue = output times price, or $BPAO$, and total revenue also =

* The proof holds also for nonlinear demand curves; see J. Robinson, *The Economics of Imperfect Competition*, Macmillan, London, 1933, pp. 32–34.

the sum of the marginal receipts, or $NCAO$ (by proposition 1). But if $BPAO = NCAO$, then right triangles NFB and FPC are of equal area. Since angle $NFB =$ angle PFC, therefore $BF = FP$.

2. Marginal revenue $= p(1 + 1/\eta)$, or $AC = AP(1 + 1/\eta)$. For $AC = AP - CP$, and since $BN/BP = AP/AM$ and $CP = BN$, therefore $CP = (AP/AM)BP$. Substituting,

$$AC = AP - CP = AP - AP(BP/AM)$$
$$= AP(1 - BP/AM).$$

But $BP/AM = OA/AM = NP/PM = -PN/PM = -1/\eta$,*
so $AC = AP(1 + 1/\eta)$
or,   marginal revenue $=$ price $(1 + 1/\eta)$.

RECOMMENDED READINGS

1. Robinson, J., *The Economics of Imperfect Competition*, Macmillan, London, 1933, Ch. 2.
2. Allen, R. G. D., *Mathematical Analysis for Economists*, Macmillan, New York, 1938. Even the antimathematical reader will profit from Chapters 1, 2, and 5.

PROBLEMS

1. In the following numerical example,
   a. Compute average cost, average variable cost, and marginal cost.
   b. Verify the five propositions stated in this chapter.

Output	Total Cost	Total Variable Cost
1	$ 40	$ 10
2	49	19
3	57	27
4	66	36
5	76	46
6	87	57
7	99	69
8	112	82
9	126	96
10	141	111
11	157	127
12	174	144

* Observe that PN is negative and opposite in sign to NP. It is by this convention as to sign that the elasticity of demand, PM/PN, is negative.

2. In Figure 18, there are drawn the total variable cost and the total cost curves of a firm. Prove geometrically that
   a. Average variable cost attains a minimum at P_1.
   b. Average cost (total cost divided by output) attains a minimum at P_2.
   c. P_2 must lie to the right of P_1.
   d. Marginal cost equals average variable cost at P_1.
   e. Marginal cost equals average cost at P_2.

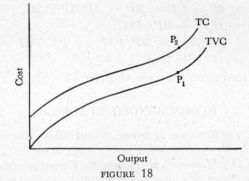

Output

FIGURE 18

3. In Figure 19, prove that the elasticity of SS at P_1 is equal to AB/OB.
4. Compute the elasticities of demand by the arc-elasticity formula:

   a. p 10   10   b. p 10   5
      q 20   40 q 20   20

   c. Compute the elasticities between all adjacent prices and quantities in Table 2.
   (Hint on a: To find the value of say 6/0, let the denominator approach zero. Thus, find the values of 6/1, 6/.1, 6/.01, etc.)

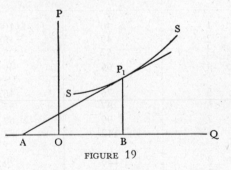

FIGURE 19

5. Prove that all straight-line supply curves passing through the origin have an elasticity of $+ 1$.
6. Create a numerical example of a demand schedule in which price (average revenue) always decreases as quantity sold increases, but in which marginal revenue increases as quantity sold increases, over a

region of quantity sold. (Hint: From marginal revenue $= p(1 + 1/\eta)$, if marginal revenue is to increase when p decreases, η must become large.)

7. In Figure 20, there are two parallel demand curves.
   a. Which is more elastic at quantity OA?
   b. Which is more elastic at price OB?

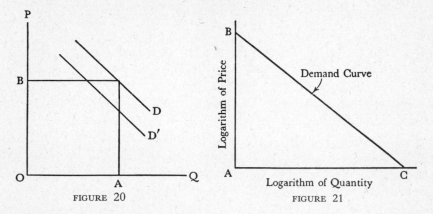

FIGURE 20   FIGURE 21

8. It was proved (page 53, note) that all demand curves with uniform elasticity (i.e., the same elasticity at every point) can be written $qp^n = k$, where q is quantity, p is price, n is a positive number numerically equal to the elasticity of demand $(n = -\eta)$, and k is a positive constant. If this equation is rewritten in terms of logarithms,

$$\log q + n \log p = \log k$$
$$\text{or} \quad \log q = \log k - n \log p$$

Hence, if the logarithms of p and q are plotted (or, what is the same thing, if p and q are plotted on double logarithmic paper), they will fall on a straight line (if the elasticity of demand is the same at all points), and the line will have a slope (with respect to the log p axis) equal to the elasticity of demand. Thus, in Figure 21, the elasticity of demand is AC/BA.

   a. Make up figures for a demand curve with an elasticity of -1, and plot these figures on double logarithmic paper, and verify the elasticity.
   b. Do the same for elasticities of $-\frac{1}{2}$ and -2.
   (Hint: If $\eta = -\frac{1}{2}$, then $qp^{\frac{1}{2}} = \$100$ (say). Then assign values to p, and read off the corresponding values of q. Thus if $p = \$4$, then $q\,4^{\frac{1}{2}} = \$100$, or $q = 50$; if $p = \$9$, then $q\,9^{\frac{1}{2}} = \$100$, or $q = 33\frac{1}{3}$.)

PART II

THE THEORY OF COMPETITION

CHAPTER 5

THE THEORY OF DEMAND

The purpose of demand theory is to explain the behavior of consumers. Each consumer has, in a given time period, a fairly definite money income which he allocates among various commodities and services. If his income, or the other factors governing the allocation, should change, there will be a corresponding change in the consumption pattern. The theory of demand isolates these factors which control the consumption pattern, and this alone would be illuminating. Moreover, the theory develops the precise functional relationships between these factors and the consumption pattern, so that changes in the pattern may be predicted from changes in the factors.

I. BASIC CONSIDERATIONS

There are three fundamental assumptions necessary to derive the theory of demand:

First, it is assumed that individuals (or, more properly, the heads of family units) have specific and complete information concerning the things which they desire. By *things* we mean general ends of activity, such as the satisfaction of hunger and the attainment of prestige. It is worth remarking that human beings seem to possess no desires for specific commodities. We need food, but the vegetarian and the cannibal satisfy the need differently; we desire personal adornment, but our culture dictates whether we wear togas or tuxedos.

Second, it is assumed that consumers know the technical means by which these general ends may be attained. More specifically, we are to know of the effects of pork chops on hunger and physical efficiency, and of a new car on our neighborhood position.

Third, it is assumed that consumers utilize their information in such a way as to maximize the attainment of the ends they desire. This assumption is known, somewhat notoriously, as the concept of an "economic man." No thoroughgoing defense of the assumption is possible here, but two things may be said in its behalf. The concept of a "maximizing individual" is indispensable if economic phenomena are to be treated scientifically, that is, if economic generalizations are to be secured. The second point is that the concept of an "economic man" does not imply (as almost all of its critics state) that the individual seeks to maximize money or wealth, that the human soul is a complex cash register. It does not affect the formal theory of demand in the least whether the individual maximizes wealth, religious piety, the annihilation of crooners, or his waistline.

On the basis of these assumptions, it is possible to indicate certain quantitative relationships for each individual:

1. Variations in the quantity of each commodity purchased when its price varies
2. Variations in the quantity of each commodity purchased when the individual's income varies
3. Demand relationships between two or more commodities

If the ends of the consumer (assumption 1) or the means to their satisfaction (assumption 2) change in a known way through time, these three quantitative relationships will change in a predictable fashion. The technical derivation of these relationships is presented in the second part of this chapter.

CERTAIN OBJECTIONS CONSIDERED

Some of the more important objections that can be raised against these assumptions are worth considering. A discussion of the objections will clarify the meaning of and the realistic limitations on the assumptions.

We may begin with a spurious objection: it is alleged that individuals desire commodities they do not purchase, and on the other hand they purchase commodities they do not desire, even when they possess the relevant information. For instance, a college instructor goes to his president's reception, even though he would rather see a wrestling match. But this objection is essentially terminological. The instructor's behavior shows that he places agreeable relations with his president (or his wife) above seeing a wrestling match — he is attaining the end he thinks is more important.

Turning to a more substantial objection, it is frequently held that individuals do not have known or definite ends. The one type of activity which seems to illustrate this objection is termed *explorative* activity, the importance of which is emphasized by Professor Knight:

> The individual who is acting deliberately is not merely and perhaps not mainly trying to satisfy given desires; there is always really present and operative, though in the background of consciousness, the idea of and *desire for a new want* to be striven for when the present objective is out of the way. Wants and the activity which they motivate constantly look forward to new and "higher," more evolved and enlightened wants and these function as ends and motives of action beyond the objective to which desire is momentarily directed. The "object" in the narrow sense of the present want is provisional; it is as much a means to a new want as end to the old one, and all intelligently conscious activity is directed forward, onward, upward, indefinitely. Life is not fundamentally a striving for ends, for satisfactions, but rather for bases for further striving; desire is more fundamental to conduct than is achievement, or perhaps better, the true achievement is the refinement and elevation of the plane of desire, the cultivation of taste.*

The explorative element is clearly important, and perhaps it plays a dominant part in consumers' demand for nonrecurrent commodities — it is proverbial that few people are long satisfied with the homes they build. But in the case of commodities which are frequently purchased — and such commodities secure most of the consumer's dollar, of course — the explorative element seems to exert only a minor influence. It is to these commodities that our theory of demand will be most relevant. Human activity which is value-realizing is beyond analytical treatment, for then it is aimless and purposeless from any but the ethical viewpoint. It is possible that statistical studies of large numbers of individuals will be of assistance, as they have already been in such literally explorative activities as migration.

Another substantial objection turns on the second assumption: it is held by some that people rarely know the means by which their ends can be attained. There is a plethora of examples of consumers who behave very stupidly (in the light of the facts) because they are ignorant of the technical properties of commodities. But on the other hand, every consumer is something of an expert in buying

* Frank H. Knight, *The Ethics of Competition*, Harper, New York, 1935, pp. 22–23.

some commodities. Our technical ignorance is not spread like a thick veil over all goods. If a thing is simple and frequently purchased (lettuce), we are good at buying; if it is complex and infrequently purchased (an appendectomy), we are bad at buying. And it must be added that ignorance per se does not upset the theory of demand. If a consumer thinks that an apple a day really keeps the doctor away and acts economically on this belief, it is possible to analyze his behavior. What is disastrous for the theory is vacillation.

Finally, apropos of the third assumption, it is said that an individual may have the facts concerning his desires and their means of satisfaction, and yet irrationally fail to act in such a way as to maximize his satisfactions. There are two types of illustrations. First, an individual may fail to attain a maximum position because the effort involved in reaching a nice mathematical balance is more than that nice balance is worth — Professor J. M. Clark has spoken of the "irrational passion for dispassionate rationality." These cases must be frequent, but they are individually unimportant, and even collectively they are probably not important enough to worry about. They can always be handled in the formal theory by introducing a minimal discrimination. The only effect of this change is to make our theoretical conclusions fuzzy; it does not vitiate them or alter their qualitative content. The second type of illustration usually arises in sporadic and, let us hope, widely separated cases (chronologically ordered), when the individual goes on a "spree." Alternatively, however, a spree can be viewed as a rationally planned vacation from close planning!

Habit is worth a few words in this connection. Habit is a device for economizing on attention and decision-making, and its existence is not a priori evidence of a failure to maximize. And habit will effectually prevent the individual from overcoming small deviations from a maximum position, but it becomes progressively less powerful, the farther the deviation from the maximum position. A person may be attached to X beer, but the attachment will not survive a price premium of five cents a glass.

To summarize, our theory of demand should be reasonably accurate in describing those commodities and services which are purchased regularly. When the purchases are infrequent and of a complex technical nature, the theory will be less informative.

II. INDIFFERENCE CURVES AND THEIR ANALYSIS

Once the tastes or preferences of the consumer are given, there remains the technical problem of determining the quantities of various commodities he will purchase at various prices and incomes. In this section we shall derive the demand curve and the expenditures curve of a consumer for any specific commodity.

It is of basic importance to the theory of demand that the consumer can substitute one commodity for another. It is obvious that this power is possessed in the case of similar commodities: one can substitute Chevrolets for Plymouths, tea for coffee, and airplane for railroad transportation. But on reflection it will appear that relatively dissimilar commodities are also substitutes for one another: houses for automobiles, travel for clothes, and books for opera. Nor need the substitution be direct: an automobile may be an indirect substitute (by way of an electric refrigerator) for ice. In some cases the competition of two commodities is apparently so remote, however, as to consist primarily of competition for the consumer's limited income, or for his limited time and energy.

There is one large class of exceptions to this general relationship of substitution between commodities. Some pairs of commodities are complementary, so that the consumer uses more of one, the more he uses of the other. Obvious examples are gasoline and tires, chairs and tables, cups and saucers, silk hats and white ties, and travel and luggage. Complementary commodities will be studied after the more common relationship of substitution has been analyzed.

If the consumer can substitute one commodity for another, he can find several combinations of the two commodities, X and Y, which are equivalent.* Thus the consumer may be confronted by the choice between the following combinations:

$$(1.3) \quad 13 \text{ units of } X + \; 8 \text{ units of } Y$$
$$(1.0) \quad 12 \text{ units of } X + 10 \text{ units of } Y.$$

It may be that he prefers combination (1.3) to (1.0) — in other words, he thinks that two additional units of Y are not sufficiently useful to him to offset the loss of one unit of X. In that case more of Y can be added to combination (1.0) until, for this individual, it

* The argument is applicable to any number of commodities; it is restricted to two in order to simplify the exposition.

becomes as attractive as (1.3). Suppose this additional amount of Y to be one unit; then we say that the following combinations

(1.3)   13 units of X +   8 units of Y
(1.4)   12 units of X + 11 units of Y

are equivalent, or that the consumer is indifferent between them. It is possible to make up many combinations which are equivalent; a few are listed in section (1) of Table 4.

TABLE 4

(1)				(2)			
Combination	X	Y	S_{yz}	Combination	X	Y	S_{yx}
(1.1)	15	5	—	(2.1)	15	6	—
(1.2)	14	6	1	(2.2)	14	9	3
(1.3)	13	8	2	(2.3)	13	13	4
(1.4)	12	11	3	(2.4)	12	18	5
(1.5)	11	15	4	(2.5)	11	24	6

The combinations of Table 4 are represented by small circles in Figure 22, where units of X and Y are measured along the two axes. If these commodities are highly divisible, we may draw a continuous curve (I_0) through all such points. The curve I_0 is called an *indifference curve* because the consumer is indifferent as to which of the combinations of X and Y on curve I_0 he possesses.

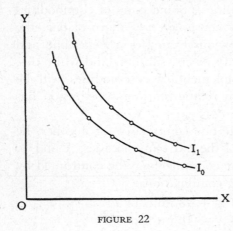

FIGURE 22

It is also possible to find a new combination which is preferable to any given combination of X and Y. Of the two combinations

(2.3)   13 units of X + 13 units of Y
(1.3)   13 units of X +   8 units of Y

the consumer surely prefers the former, since it contains as much of X and 5 more units of Y. And, by an extension of the previous argument, it follows that it is possible to find combinations which are equivalent to (2.3); examples are given in section (2) of Table 4. It is to be observed that since combination (2.5) is by definition equivalent to (2.3); and since combination (2.3) is preferable to (1.3), therefore (2.5) is preferable to (1.3). Every combination in column (2) is preferable to every combination in column (1). This new and preferable set of equivalent combinations is represented by the curve I_1 in Figure 22. The curve I_1 lies above I_0 because it contains more of each commodity (in terms of consumer preferences). Since the commodities are assumed to be divisible, an indifference curve can be drawn between I_0 and I_1, and in general another in- difference curve between

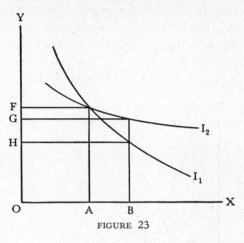

FIGURE 23

any two indifference curves.   Hence the number of possible indifference curves is unlimited.

1. *PROPERTIES OF INDIFFERENCE CURVES*

1. Indifference curves cannot intersect. This can be proved by assuming the contrary, that two indifference curves do intersect (as in Figure 23) and showing that an absurd conclusion emerges from this assumption. Since all combinations of X and Y on one indifference curve are equivalent, therefore,

$$OA \text{ of } X + OF \text{ of } Y = OB \text{ of } X + OG \text{ of } Y \text{ (on } I_2)$$
$$OA \text{ of } X + OF \text{ of } Y = OB \text{ of } X + OH \text{ of } Y \text{ (on } I_1)$$

It follows that

$$OB \text{ of } X + OG \text{ of } Y = OB \text{ of } X + OH \text{ of } Y$$

or OG of $Y = OH$ of Y

But this conclusion is absurd, for OG of Y is clearly preferable to OH of Y. Hence indifference curves cannot intersect.

2. The slope of an indifference curve is negative; as the quantity of X increases, that of Y must decrease. This is a universal prop- erty, for it is impossible that two combinations of desirable goods

be equivalent if one combination contains more X and as much Y as another combination.

At this point we must introduce a <u>definition: the marginal rate of substitution of Y for X is the amount of Y necessary to offset the loss of one (small) unit of X.</u> The marginal rate of substitution is thus in effect a comparison of two adjacent and equivalent combinations. Moving from combination (2.1) to (2.2) the consumer requires three additional units of Y to compensate for the loss of one unit of X; hence the marginal rate of substitution (written S_{yx}) equals 3 Y for 1 X. It may be noted that $S_{yx} = 1/S_{xy}$.

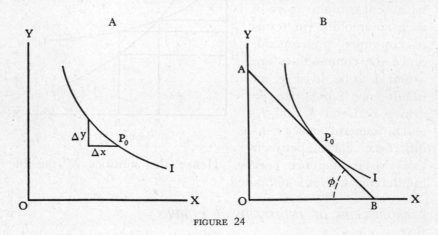

FIGURE 24

The concept of the marginal rate of substitution of Y for X is illustrated geometrically in Figure 24. The individual starts at position P_0. He gives up a small quantity (Δx) of X, and requires a certain increase (Δy) of Y in order to maintain the same level of satisfaction. We define $\dfrac{\Delta y}{\Delta x}$ to be the marginal rate of substitution of Y for X. By a familiar argument (page 49), it follows that if the units are made small enough,

$$S_{yx} = \text{slope of the line } AB = OA/BO = \tan \phi.^*$$

---

* It should be observed that by this definition, $\dfrac{\Delta y}{\Delta x}$ is negative, for Δy is positive (the increase of Y) and Δx is negative (the decrease of X). To avoid the complication of sign, the marginal rate of substitution is defined as $-\dfrac{\Delta y}{\Delta x}$; so it is always positive. It is with this understanding that the term is used here.

3. The marginal rate of substitution of Y for X increases as the quantity of Y increases relative to that of X. This hypothesis seems to possess very general validity. The more of Y and the less of X that the consumer possesses, the less attractive an additional unit of Y will appear relative to the loss of an additional unit of X. Suppose that X is leisure, and Y is money income from work. Then as the individual moves from (1.1) to (1.2), he demands \$1 more of income to compensate for one less hour of leisure. But if he moves from (1.2) to (1.3), he requires \$2 of income to compensate for another hour's reduction of leisure for two reasons: (i) he has less

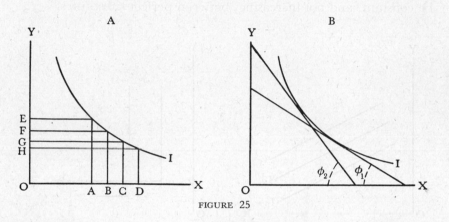

FIGURE 25

leisure left, so its relative desirableness increases, and (ii) he has more money income, so the relative desirableness of additional dollars decreases.*

The principle of increasing marginal rate of substitution is illustrated in Figure 25. Let AB, BC, and CD be equal quantities of commodity X; then the consumer requires increasing quantities of Y ($GH < FG < EF$) to offset the loss of each of these additional amounts of X. If the units of X and Y are taken to be infinitesimal, the slope of the indifference curve (which equals S_{yx}) increases as the consumer moves upward along the curve; hence, $\tan \phi_2 >$ $\tan \phi_1$ (and $\phi_2 > \phi_1$). The principle may be restated: the indifference curves are convex to the origin.

* The principle of an increasing S_{yx} corresponds to the older theory of diminishing marginal utility of a commodity as its quantity increases. More precisely: if S_{yx} is increasing, then the marginal utilities of Y and X must be decreasing; if the marginal utilities of Y and X are decreasing, then S_{yx} is probably, but not necessarily, increasing.

a. The flatter the indifference curves between two commodities, the better substitutes they are for one another. An illustration is provided by nickels and dimes, for nickels are almost perfect substitutes for dimes in the ratio two for one. This example is shown in Figure 26A. It may be observed that if two commodities are perfect substitutes for one another, they are for all practical purposes the same commodity, and there is no point in distinguishing between them. If consumers were completely indifferent whether they possessed green or red ash trays, then there would really be only one type of ash tray. The marginal rate of substitution would be constant, and not increasing, between perfect substitutes.

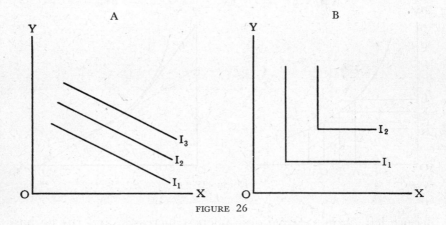

FIGURE 26

b. The other extreme exists when two commodities cannot be substituted at all for one another; they must be used in fixed proportions. Left and right shoes are an example; the normal consumer simply will not buy them in other than a one-to-one ratio. This case is illustrated by Figure 26B.

II. *THE INDIVIDUAL'S DEMAND CURVE*

With the assistance of the foregoing apparatus it is possible to determine the quantities of each commodity that a consumer will buy at various prices. The following data are assumed to be known to the individual consumer:

1. His indifference curve system for the two commodities
2. His income, which is assumed to be constant (Variations in income are treated in the next section.)

3. The prices of the commodities, which are not affected by the
  quantities of the commodities that he buys *

Let p_x and p_y be the known prices of X and Y, and let R be the individual's income.

The indifference curves for X and Y are drawn in Figure 27.
It is assumed that the
individual allocates his
entire income between
X and Y, so

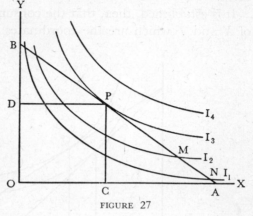

FIGURE 27

$$xp_x + yp_y = R,$$

where x and y are the
quantities of X and Y
that the individual con-
sumes. If the individual
spends his entire income
on X, he can purchase
R/p_x units of X — this is
marked off as OA in Fig-
ure 27. Similarly, if he spends his entire income on Y, he can
buy R/p_y ($= OB$) units of Y. If A and B are connected by a
straight line (which is called the *price* line), this line represents all
possible combinations of X and Y that the individual can purchase
with an income of R, given p_x and p_y. The equation of this line is
of course $R = xp_x + yp_y$.†

The individual will by hypothesis spend his entire income (and
no more); so he must buy a combination of X and Y falling on line
AB. He will seek the most preferable combination, i.e., the combination on the highest possible indifference curve. This highest
possible indifference curve is I_3, and the individual will buy OC of

---

* I.e., he buys such a small portion of the total supply of each commodity that he
exerts no perceptible influence on its price.

† This is evident if it is recalled that A and B are two points on $R = xp_x + yp_y$ (for
the cases where y and x, respectively, equal zero), and two points determine a line.
More precisely, the equation of a straight line that cuts OX at A and OY at B is

$$\frac{x}{A} + \frac{y}{B} = 1,$$

and since $A = R/p_x$ and $B = R/p_y$,

$$\frac{x}{\frac{R}{px}} + \frac{y}{\frac{R}{py}} = 1,$$

or

$$xp_x + yp_y = R.$$

X and OD of Y. The price line intersects lower indifference curves (I_1 and I_2); so the individual could stop at points M and N; but point P is preferable since I_3 represents more desirable combinations. On the other hand, the combinations on I_4 are even more preferable, but the individual's income is insufficient to purchase them.

It is established, then, that the consumer will buy the quantities of X and Y which are the coordinates of the point at which the

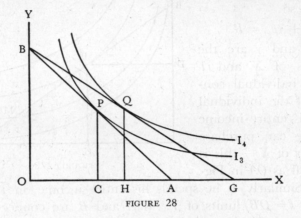

FIGURE 28

price line touches the highest possible indifference curve.* But the slope of the price line is

$$\frac{OB}{OA} = \frac{R/p_y}{R/p_x} = \frac{p_x}{p_y},$$

and the slope of I_3 at P is equal to the marginal rate of substitution of Y for X. Since these slopes are equal at P (for I_3 and AB are tangent there), we secure the fundamental rule: For the individual to be at a maximum position, it is necessary that the marginal rate of substitution of Y for X equal p_x/p_y.

The rationale of this rule will appear evident from a study of its terms. The term S_{yx} is the measure of the consumer's subjective rate of conversion of X into Y, and it is independent of the prices of X and Y. The price ratio, p_x/p_y, on the other hand, is the rate at which one commodity can be exchanged for another in the market; if $p_x = \$1.00$, $p_y = \$.25$, then $p_x/p_y = 4\ Y$ for $1\ X$. If $S_{yx} > p_x/p_y$,

---

* Since indifference curves slope down to the right, it is possible for the price line to touch one of them. Since they are convex to the origin (S_{yx} increases) and do not intersect, the price line can touch only one of them.

then the individual values a unit of Y less relative to X than does the market — he will exchange Y for X and reduce S_{yx}. If $S_{yx} < p_x/p_y$, the individual values Y more relative to X than does the market — he will exchange X for Y and increase S_{yx}.*

To derive the demand curve for X, it will simplify the exposition if Y is taken to be the money income of the consumer. Then $p_y = 1$, for the price of \$1 is always 1, in terms of dollars; the slope of the price line AB becomes $p_x/1 = p_x$. The original position (P) is reproduced in Figure 28. Now let the price of X fall a certain amount, so that (1) a larger amount of $X (= OG)$ can be purchased with the given income, and (2) the new price line BG (whose slope equals p_x) becomes flatter. The individual will move to point Q on a higher indifference curve (I_4) where he consumes OH of X. We then possess two points on a demand curve:

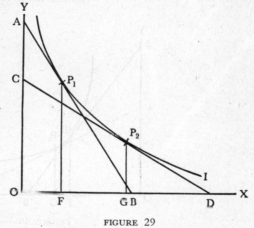

Price of X	Quantity of X
OB/OA	OC
OB/OG	OH

FIGURE 29

If the price line is allowed to take on all possible positions, all of the points of the demand curve for X will be secured.

Returning to the original hypothesis that both X and Y are commodities, it is easy to show the reason why the demand curve for a commodity is elastic or inelastic. The commodities X and Y are very good substitutes for one another, in the case illustrated in Figure 29, so the indifference curve is very flat. The two price lines represent different relative prices of X and Y. Since the slope of a price line $= p_x/p_y$, and CD is flatter (has less slope) than AB, therefore CD represents a lower price for X relative to that of Y. Corresponding to this reduction in the relative price of X, there is a large increase (FG) in the quantity of X purchased. Hence the demand

* Using these prices, and an income of \$16.25, the reader can verify that the consumer will choose combination (2.3) of Table 4. This is as preferable a combination as he can afford, and $S_{yx} = p_x/p_y = 4\ Y$ for $1\ X$.

for *X* (and for *Y*) is elastic. In general, the better the substitutes for a commodity, the more elastic its demand.

The case of very poor substitutes is illustrated in Figure 30. In this case a very considerable reduction in the relative price of *X* leads to a very small increase (*FG*) in the quantity of *X* purchased. This suggests the generalization: the demand for a commodity will be inelastic if there are no good substitutes for it.

It may be well to collect at this point the various assumptions which have been used in deriving the demand schedule:

1. The consumer is able to decide whether two combinations of goods are equivalent or whether he prefers one to the other. But

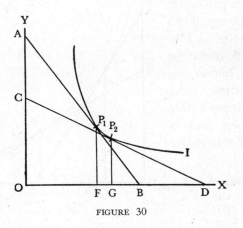

FIGURE 30

it is not assumed that he can tell by how much he prefers one combination to the other; this is the fundamental difference between the present and the older (marginal utility) theory of demand.

2. Prices of the commodities are fixed for the individual. This amounts to the statement that he buys so small a fraction of the supply that he has no influence on its price. This assumption is not necessary, but it describes the typical consumer market.

3. The consumer's money income is fixed. (It follows as a corollary that general movements of price levels [changes in the value of money] are ruled out.)

4. If a continuous demand curve and continuous indifference curves are drawn, it is implied that the commodity is divisible. This assumption will be examined later.

III. *THE EXPENDITURES CURVE*

The demand curve represents the quantities of a commodity which will be purchased at various prices, given the income of the consumer. The expenditures curve represents the quantities of a commodity which will be purchased at various incomes, given the prices of the commodities. This latter curve is easily derived by an extension of the technique used to secure the demand curve.

The development is based on Figure 31. The consumer's original position was P, for at this point the price line touched the highest possible indifference curve, $- S_{yx}$ was equal to p_x/p_y. Now let the consumer's income increase by (say) 20 per cent. He will then be

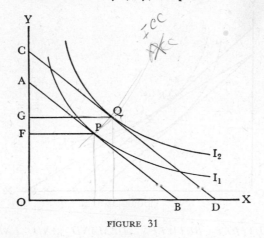

FIGURE 31

able to buy 20 per cent more of X or Y or any combination of the two. Hence there will be a new price line, CD, where AC is 20 per cent of OA and BD is 20 per cent of OB. (CD is parallel to AB since p_x/p_y has not changed.) The individual will move to a new equilibrium position, Q, where he will consume OG of Y. If income takes on all possible positions, all of the points on the expenditures curve are described. The two points determined in Figure 31 may be tabulated:

Consumer's Income	Quantity of Y
OA	OF
OC	OG

In drawing the expenditures curve, it is customary to let OX represent the consumer's money income and OY the quantity of commodity Y purchased.* If the expenditures curve rises to the right, so the individual purchases more of the commodity as his income increases, the commodity is termed *normal*. If the expenditure curve falls to the right, so that the individual buys less of Y as his income increases — as with margarine — it is an *inferior* commodity. Two comments may be made on this classification: (1) If a large bundle of commodities, such as "food," is studied, it will always be "normal," while if specific commodities such as spareribs are considered, they will frequently be "inferior." (2) It is possible for a commodity to be "normal" at some income levels and "inferior" at others.

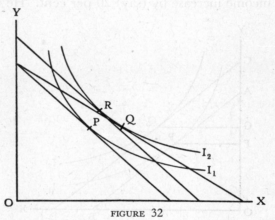

FIGURE 32

IV. *THE RELATION BETWEEN DEMAND AND EXPENDITURES CURVES*

The relationship between demand and expenditure curves can be developed with the assistance of Figure 32. Point P is the consumer's original position; a fall in the price of X leads him to move to point Q on a higher indifference curve. This move from P to Q can be thought of as involving two steps:

1. A movement from P to R due to what is in effect an increase in income (i.e., the fall of p_x is equivalent to an increase of money income). This is the "income effect."
2. A movement from R to Q due to a fall in p_x relative to p_y. This is the "substitution effect."

* Strictly speaking, OY usually represents the amount of money spent on Y ($= yp_y$), rather than the physical quantity ($= y$). But y is, of course, proportional to yp_y (since p_y is held constant); so the elasticity of the expenditures curve is not affected.

The "income effect" may be positive or negative, i.e., a consumer may increase or decrease the quantity of X he purchases when his income increases, depending on whether the commodity is "normal" or "inferior." The "substitution" effect is always in favor of X; a fall in the relative price of X always leads to the substitution of X for Y. In general the substitution effect will be dominant (the quantity of X purchased will increase) even if the commodity is "inferior," but exceptions (leading to rising demand and falling supply curves) have been noted.*

III. APPLICATIONS OF INDIFFERENCE CURVES

1. BARTER BETWEEN TWO INDIVIDUALS

The first application of the indifference-curve apparatus by its discoverer, Edgeworth,† was to prove that if two individuals engage in barter, the exchange rate between the two (or more) commodities bartered is indeterminate. That is to say, given only the preferences of the individuals and the supplies of the commodities, it is not possible to ascertain the precise rate at which the two commodities will exchange. The most that can be done is to indicate the limits within which the exchange ratio must lie; its actual position within these limits is determined by the relative abilities of the two individuals to bluff, to coerce, to harangue, and the like.

In Figure 33, the indifference curves of individual A are represented by solid curves. The indifference curves of individual B are represented by broken curves, and these indifference curves are drawn up side down (i.e., rotated 180 degrees), with reference to axes $O'X'$ and $O'Y'$. The location of $O'X'$ and $O'Y'$ is determined by the fact that OA is the total amount of commodity X, and OB the

---

* See A. Marshall, *Principles of Economics*, 8th ed., Macmillan, London, 1920, p. 132; J. R. Hicks, *Value and Capital*, Oxford University, London, 1939, pp. 31 ff. The quantitative relationship may be written:

elasticity of demand for $X = - k_x$ (income elasticity of X)
$+ (1 - k_x)$ (substitution elasticity),

where k_x is the proportion of total income spent on X. Only if the income elasticity (the "income effect") of X is negative (so X is an "inferior" good) is it possible, but not necessary, for the demand curve of X to rise. The "substitution effect" increases with the flatness of the indifference curves; it is equal to

$$\frac{\text{relative change in } (y/x)}{\text{relative change in } S_{yx}}.$$

† Edgeworth, F. Y., *Mathematical Psychics* (1881), London School Reprints of Scarce Works, No. 10, pp. 20 ff.

total amount of commodity Y that the two individuals together possess.

Assume that A possesses OC units of Y and CD units of X, before exchange begins. Then A will not make any exchanges which would put him on an indifference curve lower than I_a. Also B possesses $O'F$ units of Y and FD units of X at the outset of the bargaining, and he will not engage in any exchange which would put him on a lower indifference curve than I_b.

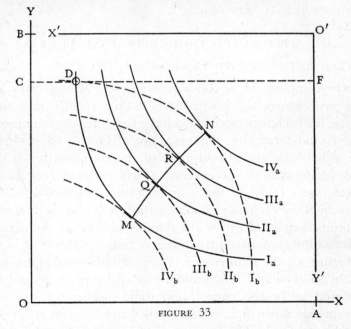

FIGURE 33

It will be recalled that A will exchange Y (of which he has relatively much) for X until the marginal rate of substitution of Y for X (i.e., the slope of his indifference curve) equals p_x/p_y. Similarly, B will exchange X (of which he has relatively much) for Y until his marginal rate of substitution of Y for X equals p_x/p_y. Since the exchange ratio between Y and X (that is, p_x/p_y) must obviously be the same for both individuals, it follows that the marginal rates of substitution of Y for X must be the same for both individuals. This condition is satisfied wherever the indifference curves of A and B touch one another.

But the two sets of indifference curves touch at infinitely many points, only a few of which (M, Q, R, and N) are shown in Figure 33.

If these points are connected by a curve MN, that curve represents all possible positions of equilibrium (where the marginal rates of substitution of the two individuals are equal). Hence MN is called the *contract curve* — every point on the curve represents a position of final contract between the two individuals. Ultimate equilibrium will be near M if B is the more resourceful bargainer, and near N if A is the more resourceful.

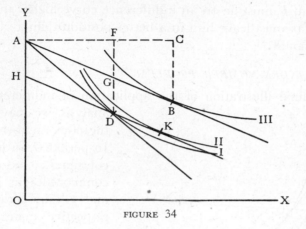

FIGURE 34

It can be demonstrated that the length of the contract curve decreases as the number of bargainers increases, and that with very many buyers or sellers or both, it reduces to a single point.

II. *A PROPOSITION IN TAXATION*

A second application of the indifference-curve apparatus lies in the field of taxation. The theorem in question is: the individual taxpayer will be on a higher indifference curve if a certain sum of money is taken from him by a personal income tax than if it is raised by means of a commodity (excise) tax.

The theorem will be demonstrated by means of Figure 34. In this figure, OX represents the commodity taxed and OY the individual's money income, and I, II, and III are indifference curves. The taxpayer's money income is equal to OA. Draw the price line AB, whose slope is equal to p_x/p_y; since p_y is unity (the price of \$1 is 1), the slope of AB equals p_x. The individual, if not taxed, will buy AC of the commodity taxed (say, cigarettes) at a total expenditure of CB dollars.

If a tax is imposed on cigarettes, their price will rise to AD, and the individual will buy AF of cigarettes at a total cost of FD, of which DG will be taxes.* If an equal sum is raised by an income tax, the individual's income is reduced to OH (where $HA = DG$), but the price line, HK, retains its former slope since the price of cigarettes is unaffected. The consumer will move to point K on indifference curve II. Since the indifference curves are convex to the origin, K must lie on an indifference curve higher than I; the income tax must leave him in a better position than a sales tax of equal amount.†

III. *THE INDEX-NUMBER PROBLEM*

As a final illustration of the application of indifference-curve analysis, we may consider the index-number problem. In period O an individual consumes q_0 and q_0' of two commodities at prices p_0 and p_0'; in period I, the respective quantities and prices are q_1, q_1', p_1, and p_1'. (The results are not affected if more than two commodities are involved.) The index-number problem is this: has the individual's standard of living risen or fallen in I compared with O?

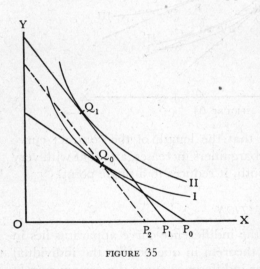

FIGURE 35

In order to make any progress, it is necessary to assume that the individual's preferences have not altered between the two periods. For if in O a person likes and consumes many bananas, and in I he acquires a dislike for bananas and comes to like and consume many apples, there is no basis for comparison of his standard of living in the two periods. This fundamental necessity for constant tastes

* It is assumed that the price of cigarettes will rise exactly the amount of the tax. This assumption merely simplifies the problem.

† For the more elaborate geometrical and algebraic analysis from which this presentation was taken, see M. F. W. Joseph, "The Excess Burden of Indirect Taxation," *Review of Economic Studies*, VI (1939), 226–231.

implies that cost-of-living comparisons between distant points (temporal or spatial) are virtually meaningless.

Granted constant tastes, we may employ one set of indifference curves in both periods. The price line P_0 and the equilibrium position Q_0 represent the consumer's income and position in O; P_1 and Q_1 represent his position in I (see Figure 35). If we knew the indifference curves, we should see at once that the individual had a higher standard of living in I, for Q_1 is on a higher indifference curve. In the (customary) absence of knowledge of indifference curves, what can be said?

Even without knowledge of the indifference curves we can proceed as follows:

1. All combinations to the left of P_0 are obviously less preferable than Q_0, for they fall on lower indifference curves.

2. All combinations preferable to Q_0 must lie to the right of P_0, since all higher indifference curves lie to the right of P_0.* Similar things can be said of Q_1 and P_1. Since Q_0 lies to the left of P_1, Q_0 must be less preferable than Q_1 (by rule 1); the individual's standard of living has risen in I.

This can be restated algebraically. The total expenditure in I was $p_1q_1 + p_1'q_1'$. If the combination Q_0 (rather than Q_1) had been purchased in I, it would have cost $p_1q_0 + p_1'q_0'$. If Q_1 is preferable to Q_0, then the cost of Q_0 at the prices ruling in I must be less than the cost of Q_1, i.e.,

$$p_1q_1 + p_1'q_1' > p_1q_0 + p_1'q_0'$$

or writing sums,

$$\Sigma p_1q_1 > \Sigma p_1q_0.$$

(In geometrical terms, at the relative prices ruling in I [i.e., given a price line with slope equal to that of P_1], the combination Q_0 falls on a price line P_2 which lies to the left of the price line (P_1) which actually existed in I.) Similarly, if the individual was better off in O, then

$$\Sigma p_0q_0 > \Sigma p_0q_1.$$

Let us now define three index numbers. The first measures the change in the consumer's income:

$$E = \frac{\Sigma p_1q_1}{\Sigma p_0q_0}.$$

* It is not true, however, that all combinations to the right of P_0 are preferable to Q_0. Indifference curves lower than that on which Q_0 lies continue beyond P_0.

The second is an index number based on O quantities (called the *Laspeyre index*):

$$L = \frac{\Sigma p_1 q_0}{\Sigma p_0 q_0}.$$

The third is an index number based on I quantities (called the *Paasche index*):

$$P = \frac{\Sigma p_1 q_1}{\Sigma p_0 q_1}.$$

If the individual is better off in I, $\Sigma p_1 q_1 > \Sigma p_1 q_0$, and dividing both sides of this inequality by $\Sigma p_0 q_0$, $E > L$. Conversely, if the individual was better off in O, $\Sigma p_0 q_0 > \Sigma p_0 q_1$, and dividing by $\Sigma p_1 q_1$, $1/E > 1/P$, or $E < P$. Four cases are possible in any statistical study:

1. E is greater than either P or L. Then the individual's standard of living has risen, for $E > L$. ($E > P$ can be disregarded.)
2. E is less than either P or L. Then the individual's standard of living has fallen, for $E < P$. ($E < L$ can be disregarded.)
3. $L > E > P$. Then neither test works, and no conclusion can be drawn.
4. $P > E > L$. This set of inequalities proves that the individual's standard of living has both risen and fallen! Such a contradiction is usually explicable in terms of a change of tastes (new indifference curves) in I.

Some further progress can be made in narrowing the range of indeterminacy (case 3) by making more detailed hypotheses concerning the indifference curves.*

RECOMMENDED READINGS

1. Knight, Frank H., *Risk, Uncertainty and Profit*, London School Reprints of Scarce Works, No. 16 (1933), Ch. 3.
2. Wicksteed, P. H., *The Commonsense of Political Economy*, Routledge, London, 1933, Vol. I, Bk. 1, Chs. 1–3.
3. Allen, R. G. D., and Bowley, A. L., *Family Expenditure*, King, London, 1935, Ch. 3, Appendix.

* This summary is based on J. R. Hicks, "The Valuation of Social Income," *Economica*, N. S. VII (1940), 105–124. For references to the literature, see R. Frisch, "The Problem of Index Numbers," *Econometrica*, IV (1936), 1–38.

4. Hicks, J. R., and Allen, R. G. D., "A Reconsideration of the Theory of Value," *Economica*, N. S. I (1934), 52–76, 196–219.
5. Hicks, J. R., *Value and Capital*, Oxford University, London, 1939, Part I.
6. Knight, Frank H., "Economic Psychology and the Value Problem," *Quarterly Journal of Economics*, XXXIX (1925), 372–409, reprinted in *The Ethics of Competition*, Harper, New York, 1935.

PROBLEMS

1. Explain what would happen to a consumer's allocation of income between commodities X and Y if the indifference curves were:
   a. Concave to the origin
   b. Straight lines
2. Draw the indifference curves for an individual who likes X very much relative to Y.
3. Draw the indifference curves that will yield a demand schedule which contains a range of indeterminacy, e.g.,

Price of X	Quantity of X Purchased
$1.00	9 to 10
1.50	7 to 8
2.00	5 to 6

4. Construct a set of indifference curves such that beyond a certain point the quantity of X demanded decreases as the price of X falls. Then show that the quantity of Y demanded decreases as income increases.
5. Pareto believed that if a line is drawn parallel to the OX axis through a set of indifference curves, the curves become flatter along this line as one moves to the right. Illustrate graphically and explain.
6. Show that if there are two A's and two B's, each set of individuals with identical indifference curves and initial stocks of X and Y, the contract curve will be shorter than with only one A and one B. (See Edgeworth, *Mathematical Psychics*, p. 32.)

CHAPTER 6

TOPICS IN DEMAND THEORY

The derivation of demand and expenditure curves of individual consumers has been developed in a very general and formal way in the preceding chapter. These findings will now be summarized in less technical fashion, and the analysis will be extended to include (1) the relation of individual to market demand curves, and (2) certain complications in demand theory when new factors such as time are introduced.

I. THE DETERMINANTS OF INDIVIDUAL DEMAND

From the formal theory of demand it appears that four fundamental factors determine the quantity of each commodity that will be purchased by any consumer.

The first and most obvious determinant is the price of the commodity which is being purchased. No one who has ever observed a free market (one in which rationing is not practiced) has failed to note that in general larger quantities of a commodity will be purchased at lower prices. And almost everyone has also observed that a 10 per cent reduction of price will lead to very different percentage increases of purchases of various commodities; the elasticities of demand (see Chapter 4) for various products are most diverse. The customary explanation of sophomores and laymen is that the demand for necessaries (salt) is inelastic, the demand for luxuries (Scotch whisky) elastic. But if pressed to classify all commodities into these two groups, the nonprofessional economist will find that some "luxuries"* have inelastic demands (for example, cigarettes) and some "necessaries" have elastic demands (for example, probably margarine) — or else he will classify commodities in accordance with their elasticities to make sure that he is right. Our analysis has suggested the real basis of elasticity: commodities for which there are good substitutes will have high demand elasticities; commodities for which there are only poor substitutes will have low elasticities.

* The most satisfactory definition of a *luxury* is perhaps that supplied by a friend: a luxury is something that some people think that others should do without.

86

The second determinant of the quantity demanded by a consumer is his income. There is no universal relationship between income and quantity of a commodity purchased. A rich southerner buys more automobiles, but less sowbelly, than a sharecropper. There will be some correlation between income and demand elasticities, however. If a person will not buy much more of a commodity when its price falls, he will usually increase his purchases only moderately when his income rises.*

A few complications which arise in more detailed analyses of income variations may be commented upon. The permanence of a change in income is important in determining how expenditures are affected. Temporary windfalls (realization of capital gains from investments, bonuses, and inheritances, for instance) cannot be made the basis of a permanent expansion of the recipient's standard of living (except to the extent of interest that can be secured by investing the windfalls). They will therefore be allocated to more permanent objects, the leading alternatives being durable consumers' goods (houses, automobiles), repayment of debts, and new investment.† The immediate and ultimate effects of a sudden but permanent change in income are also likely to differ considerably. The immediate impact will be similar to that in the preceding case: the income change will show up chiefly in investment categories. Only gradually does an individual change his consumption pattern. In part the lag is due to habit. But in part it is also due to technological restrictions — the old house must be sold; the cheaper suits of men's clothing worn out; and a trip must be planned.‡

* For the precise relationship, see above, page 79, note.

† An attempt was made to discover by questionnaire how veterans were going to spend the payments on their adjusted compensation certificates in 1936. The statistics are wretched but relevant: important percentages were repayment of debt, 31; building and repairing homes, 13; buying homes and farms, 11; investment in own business, 7; cars and trucks, 6; furniture, 6 (*Business Week*, January 18, 1936, p. 30). Similar results were secured in an earlier study, which also included, for employed veterans, a mysterious and intriguing 9.3 per cent for "expenditures resulting in no practical benefit" — taxes? (*Hearings of the Ways and Means Committee of the House of Representatives*, 72nd Session, 1st Congress, April 26, 1932, p. 589.)

‡ This lag was ingeniously exploited by one faculty wife:

Mrs. Kranich, wife of the professor of Anglo-Saxon, was an equally prominent subject for gossip. . . . It was said that every year Mrs. Kranich went through the list of instructors promoted to the rank of assistant professor to select a husband for her daughter Gretchen. She had a theory that the time when a young man was most amenable to suggestions of marriage was in the interval between his promotion and the drawing of his first decent salary check. After he once tasted the joy of possessing enough for one person to live on, he began to dream about a summer in Europe, and was hopeless.

(W. F. Neff, *Lone Voyagers*, Houghton Mifflin, Boston, 1929, p. 29.)

The third determinant of demand is the set of prices of substitutes, and this calls for more detailed discussion. The relationship between two commodities is generally one of two types: the commodities are competing or complementary. If beef falls in price, this will usually lead to a fall in the demand curve for pork (i.e., less will be purchased at any price), and in general, the demand curve of any commodity will move in the same direction as the changes in the prices of its substitutes. On the other hand, if the price of typewriters falls, there will be an increase in the demand for typewriter ribbons, and in general, the demand curve for any commodity will move in the opposite direction from the changes in the prices of complementary commodities.

CROSS-ELASTICITY OF DEMAND

Demand and income elasticities summarize our information concerning the first two determinants of demand; similarly the cross-elasticity of demand affords a useful measure of the relationship between the demands for two or more commodities. The elasticity of demand for X in terms of the price of Y is defined as

$$\eta_{xpy} = \frac{\text{relative change in quantity of X}}{\text{relative change in price of Y}},$$

the price of X being held constant. An arc cross-elasticity is given by a simple modification of the previous arc elasticity formula (page 54), i.e.,

$$\eta_{xpy} = \frac{x_0 - x_1}{x_0 + x_1} \bigg/ \frac{p_0 - p_1}{p_0 + p_1},$$

where the x's are quantities of X and the p's prices of Y. Except in certain cases,* the cross-elasticities offer a satisfactory basis for classifying pairs of commodities into the two classes of competing and completing goods. From the discussion in the previous paragraph, it is seen that η_{xpy} is positive if the commodities are substitutes (i.e., a rise in the price of Y leads to an increased sale of X), negative if they are complements.

A numerical illustration may serve to illustrate the use of the cross-elasticity. Assume that if the retail price of beef is 50 cents a

* The possible (not necessary) exceptions are commodities whose income elasticities are large. See H. Schultz, *The Theory and Measurement of Demand*, University of Chicago, Chicago, 1938, pp. 622 ff., and the references in the next footnote.

pound, a consumer will annually purchase the following quantities
of beef:

Price of Substitute	Quantity of Beef Purchased
1. Pork (Mutton 50 cents)	
40 cents	60 pounds
50 cents	65 pounds
2. Mutton (Pork 50 cents)	
45 cents	60 pounds
55 cents	66 pounds

The cross-elasticity of demand for beef in terms of the price of
pork is:

$$\frac{65 - 60}{65 + 60} \Big/ \frac{50 - 40}{50 + 40} = \frac{5}{125} \Big/ \frac{10}{90} = .36.$$

By a similar computation the cross-elasticity of demand for beef in
terms of the price of mutton proves to be .48. This latter elasticity
is larger, so if these hypothetical data were true, beef would be a
better substitute for mutton than for pork. The cross-elasticities
provide a convenient index of the readiness with which consumers
substitute one commodity for another.

It must not be inferred that, because in computing η_{xp_y} we hold
p_x constant, the price of X will really remain unchanged when the
price of Y changes. (In fact, p_x is held fixed only so that the effects
of the change in p_y may be isolated.) If the price of pork rose from
40 to 50 cents per pound, it would be impossible for beef to remain
at 50 cents per pound: the increased price of pork would cause
consumers to shift to beef and hence raise the latter commodity's
price.*

The final determinant of demand is the consumer's tastes or
preferences. It has already been observed that men are not en-
dowed by nature with specific wants. Consider physiological needs.
Dieticians estimate that an adult male daily requires approximately
3,000 calories, 70 grams of protein, .7 gram of calcium, 1.3 grams
of phosphorus, 15 milligrams of iron, and certain quantities of the
various vitamins. (At no time in history has a majority of the
human race attained such a level!) But these are not specific wants;

* As samples of the extensive and technical literature on complementarity, see
J. R. Hicks, *Value and Capital*, Oxford University, London, 1939, Ch. 3.
   H. Schultz, *The Theory and Measurement of Demand*, University of Chicago, Chicago,
1938, Chs. 18, 19.
   O. Lange, "Complementarity and Interrelations of Shifts in Demand," *Review of
Economic Studies*, VIII (1940), 58–63.

calories, for instance, can be secured from sugar, dairy products, grain products, meats, fish, or potatoes within our present social system. Elsewhere in the world they are secured from rice, blubber, and earthworms. It is quite clear that physiological needs are not specific, and this is even more true of clothing, shelter, and recreation.

It is impossible to understand the wants of the individual without knowing the society within which he lives, for all of his specific wants are determined by that society. One wears a necktie because that is done in his society. Even the iconoclast has his images chosen

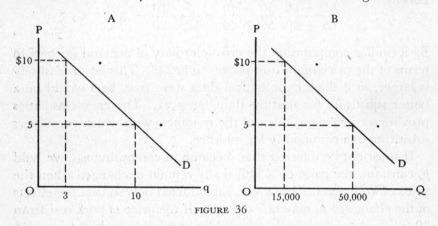

FIGURE 36

for him. Thus a comprehensive theory of consumer preferences must rest on the laws of formation and structure of social cultures. The discovery of these laws is the enviable task of social anthropology, and the economist qua economist can render only modest assistance in this important work.

II. INDIVIDUAL AND MARKET DEMAND CURVES

So far we have been concerned only with the individual consumer's demand curve, but most economic analysis is devoted to the behavior of markets and here market demand (and supply) curves are necessary. On the other hand, in the analysis of the output of the individual firm, it will be necessary to have that firm's (partial) demand curve, i.e., the curve representing the quantities which the firm can sell at various prices if all other firms sell at a given price. The formal derivation of market and partial demand curves will first be presented; and then the nature of a "market area" will be examined.

A *market demand curve* may be defined as representing the total quantities which will be taken by all consumers in the market at all possible prices. The process of building up a market demand curve is very simple, once the number of individuals in the market is known. Let the demand curve of an individual be represented by Figure 36A, and let there be 5,000 individuals with identical demand curves in the market. By multiplying the quantity demanded at each price by 5,000 we secure the quantity demanded by the

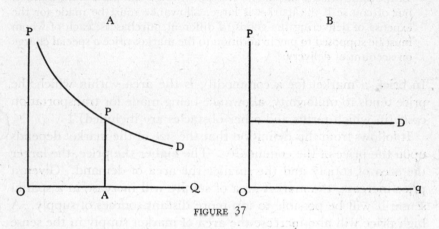

FIGURE 37

market at that price. The market demand curve (Figure 36B) is a graphic representation of the points thus secured. If each individual has a different demand curve, these curves are summed horizontally rather than multiplied.

The construction of a partial demand curve involves the opposite procedure: the market demand curve is viewed from the viewpoint of one of a large number of competitive sellers. Assume that there are 10,000 independent sellers of approximately equal size, and that they are selling quantity OA at price AP (Figure 37A). If one producer increases his sales by 100 per cent, the total quantity sold in the market will increase by 1/100 of 1 per cent. This is an increase which is relatively so small that it cannot be shown in Figure 37A, and the resultant fall of price will be economically, as well as graphically, imperceptible. The individual seller will therefore take his (partial) demand curve to be a horizontal line. This partial demand curve is exhibited in Figure 37B; it should be noted that Oq is only 1/10,000 of OQ.*

THE CONCEPT OF A MARKET AREA

In order to know the proper number of individuals to include within the market for a commodity, the market area for the product must be established. Marshall's definition of a *market* is generally accepted:

> Thus the more nearly perfect a market is, the stronger is the tendency for the same price to be paid for the same thing at all parts of the market: but of course if the market is large, allowance must be made for the expense of delivering the goods to different purchasers; each of whom must be supposed to pay in addition to the market price a special charge on account of delivery.†

In brief, a market for a commodity is the area within which the price tends to uniformity, allowance being made for transportation costs (in which tariffs and other obstacles are included).‡

It follows from this definition that the size of the market depends upon the price of the commodity. The higher the price, the larger the area of supply and the smaller the area of demand. Given a price increase, the market area of supply will increase in a spatial sense; it will be possible to tap more distant sources of supply. A high price will also increase the area of market supply in the sense of diversion of the commodity from other uses,§ but this factor is already incorporated in the individual demand or supply curves. In similar fashion, a low price will lead to a contraction of the market area of supply by cutting off distant supply sources.

We shall generally be concerned with highly organized markets, so it may be well to examine briefly their characteristics. The fundamental requirement of a well-organized market pertains to knowledge. Buyers and sellers must, at a minimum, be familiar with

---

* Partial demand curves for each of a few producers (who cannot sensibly neglect the influence of their output on price) will be taken up in the theory of duopoly.

† A. Marshall, *Principles of Economics*, 8th ed., Macmillan, London, 1920, p. 325.

‡ The preceding addition of individual demand curves to secure the market demand curve is modified by the presence of transportation costs. If some particular point (e.g., Detroit for automobiles) is the market center, the demand curves at a distance from this point should have the transportation costs per unit subtracted (vertically) before being summed.

§ For example, if the price of fluid milk is relatively high, milk will be diverted from the production of cheese and ice cream.

prices asked and offered throughout the market; if this is not true, it may happen that several prices will be quoted simultaneously. Since a price quotation is meaningful only if it refers to a specific commodity, the commodity must be homogeneous or at least capable of specification. If the commodity is unique (e.g., a plot of land), moreover, short sales will be impossible; one cannot sell a commodity he does not possess (with the hope of covering the sale later by purchase at a lower price) unless he can secure the commodity on competitive terms.

In a perfect market it is always possible to buy or sell any desired quantity at the ruling price. This implies, of course, that the market is competitive. A market may be perfect on only one side — one can buy as many packages of Lucky Strikes at a fixed price as one wishes, but the American Tobacco Company can sell only a definite quantity at that price.

III. THE INFLUENCE OF TIME

The passage of time has at least two implications for the individual and market demand curves for a commodity. First, for reasons about to be explored, the individual and market demand curves of a commodity increase in elasticity when the time period is lengthened. Second, if prices fluctuate through time, consumers will be influenced by the prices anticipated to rule in the future as well as by currently quoted prices. These two problems will be considered in turn.

1. *DEMAND ELASTICITY THROUGH TIME*

It is generally accepted that the elasticity of demand for a commodity increases with time, e.g., a 1 per cent decrease in price may lead to only a half of 1 per cent increase in the quantity purchased immediately after the price cut, but later the quantity may increase by 2 or 5 per cent. It is assumed that consumers' tastes do not change; if the rule of increasing elasticity through time were based on changes of tastes, it would be merely a dubious historical generalization.

Three possible reasons may explain this phenomenon. The first is technological. The consumer does not have the ability to make immediate and complete readjustments of his consumption pattern to price changes. The commodity whose price has fallen may require complementary commodities whose purchase is expensive and may require advance planning. Thus a fall in the price of electricity will have its full effect on sales only after new appliances are purchased. This example also suggests a second technological restriction on the consumer: durable goods (e.g., gas stoves) may have to be worn out before a shift is made to the product whose price has fallen.

Of course, durability may also lead to the contrary phenomenon: the short-run elasticity of demand may possibly be greater than the long-run elasticity. Thus, suppose purchases of a certain commodity at a certain price are exclusively for replacement. A fall in price will lead to the acquisition of new customers, but after a period of time the replacements of these new customers come to be spread evenly through time, so that the sales are less in later years than in the first year after the price cut. This is a special case of what is known as the *acceleration principle* in business-cycle theory.

A second factor leading to demand elasticity increasing with time is imperfect knowledge. A price fall may not be known immediately, and naturally its full effects will not be realized until every potential customer is informed of the price cut. This is presumably a factor of small importance in the case of frequently purchased staples, but some unstandardized commodities which are purchased infrequently (houses, furs) may be considerably affected by it.

Habit, the third factor, is of general applicability and importance. A price cut requires some time to make its full impact on consumers. Budgets must be rearranged, and the relative merits of other commodities must be reappraised.* The inertia which prevents instantaneous readjustment of consumer behavior contains some rational elements. The consumer, for example, may deem the effort to readjust his purchases excessive in the light of the probable reward, and the readjustment may come only after a considerable number of price changes make it worth while to reappraise his consumption pattern. (This factor is better calculated, however, to explain the fact that a large price cut may achieve more than, say, twice the response of two price cuts each of which

---

* There may also be some delay to discover whether the price will fall further (see next subsection).

is half as large.) But the fundamental explanation of consumer inertia is the task of psychology, and it is not necessary for present purposes to enter this terrain.*

ii. ANTICIPATED PRICES

If prices fluctuate through time, as of course a vast majority of prices do, the consumer bases his purchases in part on his anticipations of future prices. Except in the case of perishable commodities, he will attempt to store up supplies of commodities when their prices are low, and postpone purchases when prices seem high.

There are striking examples of this evident fact. In the last days before New York City imposed a tax of two cents on every package of cigarettes, the customers of Macy's purchased on the average of five cartons of cigarettes a person. In the week after the war began (September 2 to 8, 1939), American consumers (remembering the sugar shortages during the World War, and wholesale prices as high as 26.5 cents per pound in June, 1920) purchased virtually all of the immediately available sugar, and the average retail price rose 23 per cent. Cases of postponement of purchases are not so easily found, for a variety of reasons.† Some cases could be culled from tariff history, for occasionally tariff reductions have gone into effect long after the acts were passed.

The example of sugar is sufficient to prove that generally held anticipations of future prices are important even when the basis of the anticipations (in this case, a shortage of sugar) proves to be completely erroneous. The important task is not to explain what will happen if consumers anticipate a certain price change, for they will obviously buy at what they believe are low prices, and postpone purchases when prices seem high.‡ The question is rather: how are the anticipations formed?

All rational men base their anticipations of the future on their experience in the past; there is no other basis for prophecy. But past experience is highly complex, and it is often impossible to be

---

* See, however, J. M. Clark, "Economics and Modern Psychology," *Journal of Political Economy*, XXVI (1918), 1–30, 136–166, reprinted in *Preface to Social Economics*, Farrar and Rinehart, New York, 1936.

† The chief of which is that definite ideas concerning future price cuts are uncommon among consumers. Price cuts are seldom announced in advance, simply because sales would temporarily stop.

‡ The precise analysis must allow for the interest factor. See Chapter 9.

certain which portion of experience provides the correct basis for forecasting future events. Most American consumers thought, in early September of 1939, that their experience with the first World War with high sugar prices and rationing was the proper basis for forecasting. But actually the correct basis was the fact that world sugar production had increased over 60 per cent since 1917, and that 1939 stocks in America were at an all-time high.

The more knowledge (i.e., experience) an individual possesses, the closer are the historical analogies that he can find for a given situation, and the better his prophecies will be. But knowledge is not enough. It is truistical that history never repeats itself; every new situation contains elements or combinations of elements which have never occurred before. The signs are rarely all in one direction; frequently experience will provide a dozen reasons why a price should go down and as many more why it should rise or remain unchanged. The ability to recognize, to evaluate, and to combine these conflicting indications is in part the product of logical analysis, but it is much more the product of judgment. The prophet is an artist, not a scientist. And because his technique is an art, it cannot be formulated into generalizations which will permit others to forecast mechanically with precision.*

These comments would suggest the impossibility of any analysis of anticipations of the future, but this is too strong an inference. It is possible to analyze in detail how people will behave if they entertain particular anticipations, and it is also possible to isolate, in certain cases, the factors which usually determine these anticipations. Some attention will be devoted to these points subsequently, but in the case of consumer demand no extended analysis seems worth while.

For future prices do not seem to play an important role in most consumer markets — or perhaps one should say that consumers usually behave as if they did not expect current prices to change in the future. The demand for a large sector of consumer goods (many foods and style goods, for example) is not postponable, nor are supplies storable, so that there is limited scope for variations in rate of purchase. Another very considerable group of commodities (branded goods, public utility services) does have stable prices.

---

* Although an interesting history could be written of "systems" that have been developed to "beat" stock markets, horse races, and gambling games.

There are also certain general grounds for questioning the importance of anticipations of price changes. The typical consumer, whatever else his characteristics, is usually not well enough informed to make even a definite (to say nothing of sensible) forecast of the future behavior of the prices of the hundreds or thousands of commodities he buys. And even if he possesses this knowledge, the inconvenience of buying commodities before he wishes to use them seems to be something of a deterrent.

It is not our purpose to retract the original statement that consumers base their purchases in part on estimates of future prices. But it is fair to conclude that perhaps generally these future prices are treated as if they were going to be equal to current prices. In those cases (such as the imposition of a new tax, or annual clearance sales) where definite knowledge is possessed of future price movements, it is possible to allow for this factor, in both theoretical analyses and, with less ease, the administration of economic policy.

IV. INDIVISIBLE COMMODITIES

The smooth, continuous demand curves which are customarily drawn are, of course, applicable only in the case of finely divisible commodities, such as sugar and gasoline. When one treats of the demand for houses or men's suits, it is less realistic to hypothesize small variations in the quantity purchased when there are small variations in the price. It may be remarked that discontinuous demand curves (in which the quantity demanded does not vary continuously with price) are due to the nature of the commodity, rather than to its expensiveness. The typical consumer's demand curve for telephone service is probably no more continuous than that for automobiles.

In the case of market demand curves, the problem is not acute. A small reduction in the price of automobiles may well leave some potential customer unaffected, but there will usually be others for whom that small reduction is decisive. This is a particular application of the familiar "law of large numbers": phenomena which in individual cases may seem irregular and discrete take on a regular and continuous appearance when many cases are combined.

There is no analytical difficulty in analyzing the discontinuous demand curve of an individual consumer for a particular commodity. If only a certain quantity of the commodity is purchased, regardless of the price (within certain limits), the demand curve takes on the appearance suggested in Figure 38. In this example, the consumer buys one unit at any price over $5, two units at any price between $3 and $5, and three units at any price below $3.

But in general a consumer's demand does not behave in the manner portrayed in Figure 38. With surprisingly few exceptions, a consumer does buy *more* of a commodity when its price falls. A fall in rents leads to an increased purchase of housing, if in housing we include space, airiness, attractiveness of decoration, location, and similar factors which make up a "house." A fall in the price of automobiles leads to the purchase of more car, e.g., a larger car or the more frequent purchase of a new car.

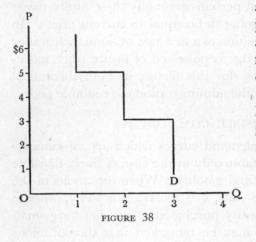

FIGURE 38

It is tempting to label the horizontal axis of a demand graph as, e.g., *automobile* and not as *1942 Chevrolets*. If this practice were followed, there is no doubt but that the individual's demand curve for most "indivisible" commodities would become much more continuous. The defects in this procedure, however, are two: the demand curves for specific commodities (e.g., 1942 Chevrolets) are indispensable in explaining market prices, for it is specific commodities, and not a composite commodity, that are sold in the market. This objection is not serious, since both specific and composite demand curves can be retained, the former to explain the market prices and quantities of specific commodities, and the latter to describe the individual's reaction to price changes.

The second objection to the composite demand curve is that it is difficult to combine heterogeneous factors such as, in the case of a house, size of rooms, number of rooms, layout, exposure, decorations, location, and behavior of neighbors. There can be no doubt but that the consumer does combine these factors (most of which could of course be broken down into further constituent parts); to do so is necessary before coming to a decision whether to rent or buy any particular house. The basis on which the factors are combined will vary from one consumer to another — some consumers wish large rooms, others many; some wish to be near a church, others near a saloon. The real objection, however, is that the basis for combining these factors in any particular case cannot, at least at present, be determined empirically.* A specific purchase can be rationalized, but it cannot be predicted.

Since indivisible commodities are in a sense a limitation on the consumer's ability fully to satisfy his desires, it is frequently profitable to transform them into divisible commodities. The first, and most obvious, method of achieving divisibility is simply to produce commodities of different sizes and qualities. One may generalize that typically a new commodity is produced in increasingly diverse forms with the passage of time. One can find exceptions (witness the era of model-T Fords), but usually standardization gives way to the variety of consumer preferences. Second, divisibility is attained by the system of hire — the taxicab and the for-hire car are examples in the automobile field. And finally, joint ownership may be used to secure divisibility. In one very important form this involves socialization, as in the provision for highways on which to drive, but there are narrower forms, such as the private school, the group library, and the neighbor's lawn mower. The restraint on consumer choice offered by indivisible commodities is constantly weakened by these and related devices.

RECOMMENDED READINGS

(See references on pages 84, 89, note.)

1. Marshall, A., *Principles of Economics*, 8th ed., Macmillan, London, 1920.
2. Pigou, A. C., *The Economics of Stationary States*, Macmillan, London, 1935, Ch. 15.
3. Smith, H., "A Note on Time Elasticity of Demand," *Economica*, N. S. IV (1937), 309 322.

PROBLEMS

1. Compute all of the sensible demand, income, and cross-elasticities for fluid milk in the following series. Remember that a demand elasticity computation, for example, is meaningless if the individual's income changes simultaneously with the price of fluid milk. Why? When tastes change, do not compare years before and after the change of

---

* It deserves mention that if the consumer's scale of preferences as between size, location, etc., is known, the formal theory can easily predict his behavior.

tastes, and always compare years as close together as possible. Explain why the remainder of the elasticities are meaningless. (There are 198 possible computations.)

Year	Price of Fluid Milk (cents)	Quantity Purchased (quarts)	Family Income	Price of Canned Milk (cents)
1	10	200	$ 1000	7
2	11	190	1000	7
3	11	200	1100	8
4	11	210	1100	9
5	10	200	1100	7
6	10	210	1100	8
7	10	200	1000	8
8	12	210	1100	8
9	12	190	1100	7
10	13	180	1100	7
11	13	200	1300	8
12	13	210	1400	8

2. There are 1,000 similar firms in an industry whose demand curve is given by $pq = \$300,000$ where p is price and q is quantity. The price is $30, the output of each firm 10 units. Compute the demand schedule (by unit steps up to 10) for a new firm on the assumption that the 1,000 old firms will sell at any price necessary to maintain outputs of 10 units. Compute the arc elasticity of demand for the new firm.

3. Each of the five cities in a market has a demand curve described by $p = 100 - q$.
   a. Compute the total market demand schedule on the assumption that transportation costs are zero.
   b. Compare the elasticity of demand (at any price) of one city with that for the market. Explain the result.
   c. Compute the total market demand schedule on the assumption that one city is at the center of the market area, and the other four cities must pay transportation costs of $5, $10, $15, and $20 per unit respectively.

4. Appraise: "Since elasticity measures variations in quantity (demanded or offered) divided by variations in price, the elasticity of demand for anything will be seven times as large for seven similar demanders as it is for one."

5. Appraise: "Recent studies of domestic consumption in low-cost municipalities demonstrate that the demand for electric current is highly

elastic, expanding rapidly as the cost declines. The national average consumption of the United States was 604 kilowatt-hours in 1933. The average charge to consumers on October 1, 1934, for the whole country is reported as 5.4 cents per kilowatt-hour. In Seattle where the average cost is 2.58 cents the average consumption is 1,098 kilowatt-hours. In Tacoma, the charge is 1.726 cents and the consumption 1,550. In 26 cities of Ontario, the average charge is 1.45 cents and the consumption 1,780. Finally, in Winnipeg, where the average net charge is only 8 mills per kilowatt-hour the average per capita consumption exceeds 4,000 kilowatt-hours." (*Report of the National Resources Board*, December 1, 1934, Government Printing Office, Washington, 1934, p. 39.)

CHAPTER 7

THE NATURE OF COSTS AND THE PRODUCTION FUNCTION

I. THE NATURE OF COSTS

Since most of the modern theory of price turns on costs of production, it is necessary to examine the nature of costs in some detail. It may be well to emphasize at the outset that money expenses of business men are not all costs, nor are they the only costs, as the economist uses the word. Certain of these outlays exert no influence on prices, and their actual computation is frequently subject to arbitrary accounting conventions. The costs which concern the economist are those which influence the relative prices of commodities and the allocation of productive services among firms and industries.

The generally accepted explanation of costs is contained in the alternative (or opportunity) cost theory. The cost of any productive service X in the production of any commodity A is the maximum amount that X would produce of any other product (B, C, ···). If capital funds can earn four per cent elsewhere, that is their cost to the automobile industry. If an acre of land can earn $6 a year in oats, that is its cost in producing wheat.

In the simple case where there are only two commodities which a given productive service can be used to produce, it is a matter of indifference whether the cost (i.e., the alternative product) is stated in physical terms (bushels of oats) or in money terms — under competition the two will always be proportional for any firm. But when more than two alternative products are available, so that one must consider the maximum amount that the productive service could yield elsewhere, it is necessary to reduce these alternative products to comparable (money) terms.

Of course, if the productive service is actually used simultaneously in two or more fields, as is usually the case, the values of the products of a unit of the service in each field must be equal. For if the product of a unit of the service in producing A is worth $5 and that in B, $3, there is an obvious gain of $2 for the owner of the service by shifting a unit from B to A. As this transfer continues, the value of units of B will rise and those of A fall (for reasons to be explained shortly), until equality is established. The allocation of productive services is in equilibrium when no owner of a service can increase his return by shifting the service from one use to another.

One noteworthy feature of this definition of costs is that costs depend on demand prices. It is impossible to know the money cost of growing wheat until one knows the price of oats. The more valuable the alternative products (B, C, ⋯) of a given productive service, the greater will be its cost in producing A.

It may be objected that oats are expensive because the use of land is expensive, so that it is circular reasoning to argue that the use of land is expensive because oats command a high price. Because of the desirability of an illustration of the nature and determination of cost, and only incidentally to refute the charge of circularity, a detailed numerical example will be presented. For simplicity, it will be assumed that only land is used to produce oats and wheat; no other productive services are necessary. The demand schedules for these products are given by consumers' preferences and incomes, in a manner already analyzed.

Assume that there are 1,000 ten-acre farms of homogeneous land, and that each acre will supply 30 bushels of oats or 40 bushels of wheat. Let the demand schedules for oats and wheat be those given in Table 5. If 500 farms were devoted each to oats and wheat, there

TABLE 5

Wheat		Oats	
Price (cents)	Quantity	Price (cents)	Quantity
80	200,000	80	80,000
70	220,000	66⅔	105,000
60	240,000	50	120,000
50	260,000	30	150,000
40	280,000	20	180,000

would be produced 200,000 bushels of wheat and 150,000 bushels of oats. According to the demand schedules, wheat would sell at 80 cents and oats at 30 cents. But then if a farmer shifted one acre of land from oats to wheat, he would give up 30 bushels of oats, worth $9, to secure 40 bushels of wheat, worth $32. This profitable move would be made, and the shift of land to wheat would continue until the rent of wheat land equaled that of oat land. By inspection, this would occur when 650 farms were raising wheat and 350 raising oats. An acre of land in either wheat or oats would then yield a rent of $20. It is not circular to say that the cost of producing oats is $20 per acre even though the rent of land would be less if no oats were produced (since the entire 1,000 farms would be turned to wheat, and its price would fall).

The argument may be restated in terms of equilibrium analysis. The following data are given: the demand conditions for wheat and oats, the supply of land, and the productivity of land in growing wheat and oats. The conditions of equilibrium are three: (1) that no farmer can gain by shifting an acre from one product to the other; (2) that the price of wheat be such that the quantity demanded equal the quantity supplied; and (3) that the price of oats be such that the quantity demanded equal the quantity supplied. These three conditions uniquely determine the three unknowns: the price of wheat, the price of oats, and the rent of land. There is no circularity; rather we say that these three magnitudes are simultaneously (or mutually) determined.

A second feature of the theory of cost is that the analysis is not vitiated by the fact that usually two or more productive services cooperate to make any commodity. It is possible, as will be shown in the next chapter, to isolate the contribution which one of several cooperating services makes to the total product; this separate product is known as the *marginal product* of the service. Once this marginal product is isolated, we may restate the definition of costs: the cost of productive service X in the production of A is equal to the value of the marginal product of X in its other uses (B, C, ⋯).*

This definition of costs would suggest that if a productive service can be used in producing only one product, then, since there are no foregone alternatives, it has no cost. From the viewpoint of the

---

* One must replace *value of the marginal product* by *marginal value product* if the analysis is applied to imperfect competition; see Chapter 13.

industry (the group of firms making a product) this is undoubtedly correct. If a mid-ocean island can be used only for refueling planes, for instance, then to the air transportation industry there is no cost in using the island; the industry, if it acted as a unit, could hire the island for $1 a year. But if many competing airlines each sought such a base (of which there were relatively few), then the cost of the use of an island to the firm which secured it would be the amount the use of the island was worth to the other airlines. Similarly, the rental of land covering an oil pool is not a cost to the petroleum industry, if the land has no other use, but it is a cost to any particular company which must bid the land away from rivals.

Productive services which can be used only by one industry are sometimes called *specific*. Payments for their use are not costs of production from the viewpoint of the industry and may therefore be termed *noncost outlays*.* It may be that a productive service, for example, the acting of a movie star, is worth $100,000 a year to the movie industry and only $2,000 elsewhere (perhaps driving a milk truck). In this case $98,000 would be noncost outlay, and $2,000 the cost to the movie industry. To any one of many competing movie producers, to repeat, the entire $100,000 would be a cost.

It follows from the determination of costs, that in competitive equilibrium the allocation of productive services is ideal, in the sense that no other allocation would increase the product (measured in terms of what consumers are willing to pay). No unit of a productive service could produce more if transferred to another firm (in the case of specific factors) or to another industry (in the case of nonspecific factors).

This famous generalization is subject to two possible exceptions, one illusory and the second real. It is worth considering first the illusory exception, since it has appeared in the writings of even outstanding economists.

This exception turns on the difference between the cost of a productive service to a competitive firm and to the industry of which it is a member. Suppose that the industry employs 50,000 units of a particular productive service, and that a new firm enters the industry and hires an additional 1,000 units of the service.

---

* *Noncost outlay* is used in preference to the more customary word, *rent*, simply because the everyday use of this latter word is hopelessly different from the special meaning sometimes accorded to it in economics.

Assume, further, that the price of the service was $1.00 per unit when 50,000 units were hired, and rises to $1.01 when 51,000 units are hired.* The total cost to the industry in the two cases is as follows:

$$50,000 \text{ times } \$1.00 = \$50,000$$
$$51,000 \text{ times } \$1.01 = \$51,510$$

The additional cost of the 1,000 units to the industry is therefore $1,510.† The cost to the new firm, however, is only 1,000 times $1.01, or $1,010, because the increase in the price of the productive service to the other firms plays no part in its costs.

It has been argued that this situation leads to overinvestment in such an (increasing cost) industry. The firm will enter the industry if the 1,000 units of the productive service yield a product worth $1,010, whereas the (marginal) cost to the industry (and to society) is really $1,510.‡ The new firm should be discouraged from entering the industry by a tax or some similar restraint.

Here is an apparent disharmony between private and social interests, but a closer examination of the example reveals its illusory nature. The cost of a productive service to society is, as in the case of the individual firm, the value of the foregone alternative product. It is tempting to call the $1,510 cost to the industry this social cost. But what is the value of the foregone product of a unit of the productive service? It must be $1.01, and not $1.51, or the industry would not be able to secure 51,000 units at this price. The increase of $.01 in the price of the 50,000 units previously employed is necessary to equalize the price for all units of a homogeneous supply. This extra sum of $500 (50,000 times $.01) is a noncost outlay from society's viewpoint; it represents no foregone alternative, and is merely a transfer from entrepreneurs (and ultimately the consumers of the product) to the owners of this productive service.

The second discrepancy between private and social cost is valid

---

* It should be noted in passing that the price rises to $1.01 for each of the 51,000 units, which are assumed to be homogeneous. Under competition it would be impossible to pay different prices for various units of a homogeneous supply.

† The marginal cost of the service to the industry is (see page 43):

$$\frac{\text{increase in total cost}}{\text{increase in quantity of the service}} = \frac{\$1510}{1000} = \$1.51.$$

‡ It is similarly argued that there will be too little investment in decreasing-cost industries, but this case involves special difficulties; it will be considered later.

and, indeed, important. It arises when nontransfer costs are smaller (or greater) for the firm than for society.* For example, the cost of a product may be $10 from the producer's viewpoint; it may be $20 if cognizance is taken of the damage done by the smoke which pours from his factory's chimneys. An example where cost to the individual exceeds cost to society is provided by the drainage of a swamp on one farm if this involves drainage of adjacent farms.

An impressive list of such disharmonies between individual and social cost can easily be assembled.† No single principle underlies them, and they are eliminated largely by *ad hoc* policies. Such policies include not only private activity (for example, cooperation) but also state interference by the use of the police power (zoning), taxes (automobiles, liquor), subsidies (conservation), dissemination of information (foods, drugs, securities), and numerous other devices.

CERTAIN COMPLICATIONS IN THE THEORY OF COSTS ‡

The foregoing statement of the theory of cost is complete only under relatively simple conditions. Certain complications in the theory appear when productive services are used under a system of "division of labor" (i.e., when each unit of productive service is employed in only one occupation). These complications will be discussed with reference to labor, but they are also applicable to other productive resources.

The first complication is that hours of work of a given type of labor will differ between occupations and localities. Thus, for a given daily wage carpenters will usually work for fewer hours in strongly unionized cities than they will in adjacent suburbs. (The reasons for this difference are fairly evident, and in any case they are not relevant to the present problem.) This phenomenon does not impair our concept of costs: the cost of labor to a suburban builder will be equal to the wage that a carpenter would receive in the city. The suburban builder will receive more product per dollar

* *Nontransfer* is meant to exclude only the type of transfer item just discussed.

† See A. C. Pigou, *The Economics of Welfare*, 4th ed., Macmillan, London, 1932, Part II, Ch. 9.

‡ This section is based primarily on the following writings of Professor Frank H. Knight, " 'The Common Sense of Political Economy' (Wicksteed Reprinted)," *Journal of Political Economy*, XLII (1934), 660–673; and "Bemerkungen über Nutzen und Kosten," *Zeitschrift für Nationalökonomie*, VI (1935), 28–52, 315–336.

of expenditure on wages, and suburban houses will cost less to build. But productive services are still distributed so as to equalize their money returns in various uses.

The second complication is more serious. Assume that independent mechanics (operating their own garages) receive $1,200 a year in wages and hired mechanics receive $1,500, and assume further that this is an equilibrium situation because the privilege of working for oneself is valued at $300 per year. The cost of a hired mechanic's service to a garage is now $1,200 (the amount he could secure if working for himself), although $1,500 is actually paid in wages. How is the discrepancy to be explained? It appears necessary to include in the cost of the hired mechanic's services not only the $1,200 in cash, but also the foregone pleasure of working for oneself. The definition of costs must be reformulated: the cost of productive service X in making A is equal to the amount of B that X could produce plus (or minus) the nonpecuniary returns (or costs) attached to producing B. The notion of objective cost must then be abandoned. In addition, the theorem on maximum product is no longer true; it is now possible for productive services to be transferred from one occupation or locality to another in such a way as to increase the *money* product of the services.

It would appear possible to evade this difficulty by converting nonpecuniary into pecuniary returns. Thus in our example the independent mechanics show, by their unwillingness to work for others unless paid $300 more per year, that independence is worth $300. By this device it is possible to reduce the returns of a given type of labor in various uses to a common monetary denominator and restore objectivity to the cost concept. This expedient is available, however, only under simplified conditions. At least two difficulties in the comparison may be noted. First, it is very difficult to ascertain what the money costs (and hence the net money income) of an occupation are — should the doorman's uniform be considered a cost if he has always nurtured the desire to appear an admiral? Second, the pecuniary and nonpecuniary returns of two dissimilar occupations are difficult to compare. Work in different occupations or localities involves different modes of life and, as a result, different systems of preferences (indifference curves). Equal money incomes will yield different (and in fact, incomparable) satisfactions, and the comparison of the nonpecuniary returns of different occupations will also be subject to the same difficulty.

Finally, we may note that a group of laborers is rarely homogeneous in attitudes toward different occupations. To return again to our example, some mechanics will appraise the right to work for themselves at $600, others at $300, and still others at − $100. Those mechanics who value independence highly will work for themselves; those who place little value on it will work for others. Therefore a hired mechanic may have an alternative cost of $1,500 ($1,200 cash plus $300 of nonpecuniary returns), but he may also have an alternative cost of $1,100 ($1,200 cash minus $100 of nonpecuniary costs). All hired mechanics will receive equal money incomes because they produce equal products (by assumption), but a considerable share of the returns will be noncost outlays. This is an additional reason for saying that the money return of a given type of productive service may not be maximized, and indeed it is even improper to treat as one type laborers who have dissimilar attitudes toward different occupations.

These vexatious (and in part, insuperable) difficulties in the alternative cost theory are more important as a barrier to a neat formulation of cost theory than because of their empirical significance. As Professor Knight remarks,

> It is very doubtful that laborers or owners of other productive agents sacrifice money return for other considerations to any large extent on the whole. The classical theory of non-competing groups rested on the observation of Mill as well as Cairnes, and indeed of every thoughtful person, that in general it is the people with high money incomes who get the other pleasant perquisites of productive life, that the more disagreeable work pays the lower wages. From another point of view, all observation concurs in the judgment that observed wage differences are mainly traceable to other facts than the relative subjective advantages or disadvantages of the work.*

II. THE PRODUCTION FUNCTION

A production function may be defined as the relationship between inputs of productive services per unit of time and outputs of products per unit of time. Production functions are descriptive of techniques or systems of organization of productive services, and they are therefore taken from disciplines such as engineering and

* Knight, F. H., "Bemerkungen über Nutzen und Kosten," *loc. cit.*, p. 332.

industrial chemistry: to the economic theorist they are data of analysis.*

It is clear that from a given quantity of various productive services it is usually possible to secure numerous different amounts of the same product,† depending on the technique (i.e., the production function) that is employed. It is customary to rule out this situation by assuming that the best (or, as with Marshall, the average) technique is employed; that is, the technique is employed which maximizes the product from the given combination of the productive services. Given "the state of the industrial arts," this assumption serves to define a unique production function, which involves prices only in the determination of what should be classed as economic product. Should, however, two or more products be secured from the given combination of productive services, it becomes necessary to introduce the precise prices of the various products in order to determine the maximum total product. Suppose that a farmer could, with given resources, produce 5 more pounds of cotton by giving up 25 pounds of cottonseed; there is no possibility of determining whether this should be done unless the relevant prices are known.

Instead of speaking of the maximum product of given productive services, however, it is preferable to consider the minimum cost of securing a given product, for it is in this form that the problem of production usually presents itself to the entrepreneur. The solution requires two related types of information: (1) the types of productive services to use in production, and (2) the quantities of each that should be employed. In our terminology, the problem of production consists in selecting the most appropriate production function and then determining the inputs which will minimize costs. The decision on these two questions must be simultaneous, for the quantities of the services cannot be known until the services

* The production function is usually written, $P = \phi(A, B, C, ...)$, where P is product and $A, B, C, ...$ are productive services, all per unit of time. Leon Walras was apparently the first economist to give a general symbolic statement of the production function (see *Eléments d'économie politique pure*, 1st ed., F. Rouge, Lausanne, 1874, § 307), although J. H. von Thünen had already deduced empirical production functions for his famous estate (*Der isolierte Staat*, 3rd ed., Fischer, Jena, 1930, Part I, passim), and the law of diminishing returns is only one example of the importance of the notion even in the Ricardian economics.

† Where *product* must be defined (at least qualitatively) in economic terms, or this statement becomes a senseless denial of the law of conservation of energy.

themselves have been selected, and the services cannot be selected until the quantities that will be required under various techniques are known. The principles by which the decision is governed will be presented in Chapter 8.

Production functions can be divided into three classes, on the basis of the nature of their coefficients of production. A production coefficient of a given productive service, following Walras, is the quantity of that service necessary to produce one unit of product. In illustration, if an acre of land will annually produce 40 bushels of wheat (with the help of appropriate amounts of cooperating services), then 1/40 is the production coefficient of this type of land in producing wheat. Symbolically, if A produces a product of P, then $A/P = a_p$ is the coefficient of production of A in the production of P.

The first possibility is that all of the production coefficients are fixed, so that there is only one possible ratio between the productive services which will yield any product. The baking of bread would provide an example if (contrary to fact) 1,000 loaves of bread could be made only with the following ingredients, in pounds: flour, 690; water, 386; salt, 10.3; sugar, 18.4; milk, 13.8; etc. (As a matter of fact, another popular baker's recipe calls for flour, 686; water, 417; salt, 12.3; sugar, 4.9; milk, 27; etc.) There is no dispute among economists that this form of production function is very unrealistic. One must resort to fields like (theoretical) chemistry to find cases where all of the "ingredients" must be combined in fixed proportions. This case will therefore be passed over without further comment.*

The second possibility is that all of the production coefficients are variable (or compensatory), and this is the most popular hypothesis concerning their nature. In this case, the same amount of product can be secured by varying amounts of any one productive service, if the amounts of the other productive services are varied in a compensatory manner. Twelve bushels of winter wheat per acre, for instance, can be grown either by 2.2 man-hours (and much machinery) as is done in Kansas and Texas, or by 22.8 man-hours (and very crude equipment) as is done in Georgia.† The

* For a history of the use of this and the following two hypotheses concerning the nature of the production coefficients, see George J. Stigler, *Production and Distribution Theories*, Macmillan, New York, 1941, especially Ch. 12.

† See *Changes in Technology and Labor Requirements in Crop Production: Wheat and Oats*, Works Progress Administration, Philadelphia, 1939, pp. 37, 52, 108.

writer accepts the view of a majority of economists that, given sufficient time, the entrepreneur can vary any production coefficient within limits.

There remains the final possibility that some of the production coefficients are fixed and others variable. Pareto, the leader of the important group adhering to this view, has suggested numerous examples of partial fixity of production coefficients:* the amount of pig iron that can be secured from iron ore is limited by the amount of ore utilized, and similarly the amount of chocolate is fixed by the amount of cocoa. (Such services are frequently called *limitational*, since they put an upper limit on the amount of product.) As a variant of this approach, Pareto has suggested that two or more productive services may be in fixed relationship to each other, rather than to the product. As an example, a delivery truck may require one and only one driver; yet the combination can deliver a variable amount of goods.

In the long run (i.e., when the entrepreneur has sufficient time to make any changes he desires), Pareto's objections to the validity of variable production coefficients seem unconvincing. Within limits the amount of iron extracted from iron ore can be and is varied, and similar statements can be made about the other examples of this type. The fact that some waste is always involved in the use of a productive service is sufficient to insure some variability of the production coefficients — and that is enough. Within shorter time periods the entrepreneur does not have the same freedom in varying production coefficients, and then special complications arise which will be examined in Chapter 9.

HOMOGENEITY OF PRODUCTIVE SERVICES

Each of the productive services to which reference has been made so frequently is homogeneous, and this leads to a problem that can no longer be postponed. Homogeneity may be defined with respect to either physical characteristics of productive services or their products. We may classify agricultural lands, for example, according to the chemical and mechanical properties of their soils, or we may define as identical all areas of land which can produce (with appropriate cooperating productive services) 100 bushels of corn.

---

* See Pareto, Vilfredo, *Cours d'économie politique*, Pichon, Paris, 1897, Vol. II, § 714, 717; also *Manuèl d'économie politique pure*, 2nd ed., Giard, Paris, 1927, especially pp. 326 ff.

The second alternative is unworkable: if all productive services were classified according to their productivities, an acre of land might be equivalent to a man-week of a certain kind of labor and to eight hours' use of a tractor; so all of these would have to be considered as identical. There would be no problem of distribution or costs, or rather these problems would be begged.

The classification of productive services on the basis of physical characteristics, whereby complete interchangeability for purposes of production becomes the criterion of homogeneity, avoids the foregoing difficulty only to create others. Interchangeability usually depends on the use to which a group of productive services is put: bricklayers and carpenters are different classes if they are engaged in building houses, but they are homogeneous from the viewpoint of an army drill sergeant. It follows that productive services can be defined only with respect to a specific problem; there is no universally valid classification.

Productive services can be classified as narrowly as one desires; one may treat of laborers, or musicians, or players of stringed instruments, or violinists, or first violinists, or concertmasters, or good concertmasters. Professor Chamberlin has pointed out that the fineness of the classification affects the divisibility of the service:

> Now the number of units of each factor will vary inversely as the number of factors into which the whole is classified. There are many more "laborers" in a large retail establishment than there are "bookkeepers," and therefore a bookkeeper, although a very small part of the total number of workers employed, is relatively a more appreciable part of the office staff, and a still more appreciable fraction of the corps of bookkeepers. The number of units is also much smaller for one concern than for a large number of concerns, so that a bookkeeper (or a "laborer") is a relatively smaller part of the total number of competing bookkeepers (or of "laborers") in a large city, than of the staff of any one firm.[*]

He concludes that "the larger the number of factors, the less finely they are divisible, for to make the number of factors very large *involves* making the number of units of each one very small." [†]

This is not, of course, a proof that productive services are indivisible in small firms, since that conclusion would follow only if

[*] Chamberlin, Edward, *The Theory of Monopolistic Competition*, 3rd ed., Harvard University, Cambridge, 1938, p. 203.
[†] *Ibid.*, p. 204.

the units were assumed to be indivisible.* What this argument does suggest, however, is that, if the units of a productive service are of finite size, then the smaller the number of these units in a firm, the greater may be their indivisibility relative to those of other productive services. Suppose that a particular commodity is produced by two services, A and B, and 1 unit of A produces 20 units of product and 1 unit of B produces 45 units of product, per unit of time. Then if 2 units of A are used with 1 of B, 11 per cent of B's "capacity" is unutilized; if 22 units of A are used with 10 of B, then only 2.2 per cent of B's "capacity" is wasted.†

The reader has probably observed that the foregoing discussion has been couched exclusively in terms of anonymous productive services rather than the classical "factors of production," land, labor, and capital. There are two reasons for this terminological change. The first reason is negative: there is little economic significance in grouping productive services together under a few general heads. The differences within these broad classes are usually greater than the differences between the classes.‡ This is not to deny that there are economically important differences between various productive services, but these differences vary relative to, and therefore must be stated specifically with respect to, the problem in hand.

The second reason for using the concept of services rests on a simple but fundamental point in the theory of capital. A productive service may be yielded by a durable or by a nondurable resource. Examples of services from nondurable resources are the heat from burning coal and the services of fragile tools. Shelter from buildings and the supporting power of a bridge are illustrations of services that can be secured for relatively long periods of time from the same resources. It is clear that to carry on production entrepreneurs require only services, which, if they come from durable capital goods, can always be hired even though it is usually convenient to own them. But the present value of a capital good is equal to the discounted value of its future incomes (services); the

---

* If the units of a productive service are infinitesimal in size, then to subdivide the service will not reduce the number of units in any subclass — half of infinity is infinity!

† This phenomenon is called *balance of processes* by E. A. G. Robinson. See *The Structure of Competitive Industry*, Nisbet, London, 1935, pp. 32 ff.

‡ For a penetrating discussion of this point, see Frank H. Knight, *Risk, Uncertainty and Profit*, London School Reprints of Scarce Works, No. 16 (1933), pp. 123 ff.

value of a service need not be discounted since, by definition, it does not continue over a sufficiently long period of time to make the discount factor appreciable.

RECOMMENDED READINGS

1. Wicksteed, P. H., *The Commensense of Political Economy*, Routledge, London, 1933, Bk. I, Ch. 9.
2. Davenport, H. J., *The Economics of Enterprise*, Macmillan, New York, 1935, Chs. 6, 8.
3. Knight, Frank H., *Risk, Uncertainty and Profit*, London School Series of Reprints of Scarce Works, No. 16 (1933), Ch. 4.
4. Knight, Frank H., "Fallacies in the Interpretation of Social Cost," *Quarterly Journal of Economics*, XXXVIII (1924), 582–606, reprinted in *The Ethics of Competition*, Harper, New York, 1935.
5. Robbins, L., "Remarks on Certain Aspects of the Theory of Costs," *Economic Journal*, XLIV (1934), 1–18.

CHAPTER 8

THE LAWS OF RETURN AND THE COST CURVES

The laws of return describe the characteristics of the production function. These laws are necessarily generalizations which contain no precise quantitative results, and in fact their usefulness in economic theory turns on their applicability to all important forms of productive activity. The quantitative relationships between the productive services and the product are therefore stated in ordinal terms, such as *increasing* and *greater than*, rather than cardinal terms, such as *increase by 10 per cent.*

The study of the laws of return may be broken down into two parts. The first branch, known as the *law of variable proportions,** is concerned with the behavior of the total product when only one productive service is varied in quantity. The second branch, here labeled the *law of returns to scale of plant,* considers the general problem of the effect on the product of variations in the quantities of all of the productive services. These two branches of the laws of return will be taken up in turn.

I. THE LAW OF VARIABLE PROPORTIONS

The law of variable proportions may be stated as follows: *If the quantity of one productive service is increased by equal increments, the quantities of the other productive services remaining fixed, the resulting increments of product will decrease after a certain point.†*

The formal and very general statement of the law may be supplemented in certain respects:

1. The law relates to quantities per unit of time.

2. The law is essentially technological, indicating only the relationship between inputs of physical things (e.g., man-hours, acre-

---

* And also as the *law of proportionality, diminishing returns,* etc.

† For a continuous production function, $P = \phi(A, B, C, \ldots)$, after a certain value A_0,

$$\frac{\partial^2 \phi}{\partial A^2} < 0.$$

For equal finite increments,

$$\phi(A + \overline{\Delta A}, B, C, \ldots) - \phi(A, B, C, \ldots) > \phi(A + 2\overline{\Delta A}, B, C, \ldots) - \phi(A + \overline{\Delta A}, B, C, \ldots).$$

year) and the outputs of physical things (e.g., bushels of corn, tons of coal).

3. Since the law is technological, it is of no *direct* assistance in determining how much of a variable productive service should be used with a given amount of other productive services. There is no sense in the frequent assertion that one should stop applying additional units of a productive service once the point of diminishing returns has been reached.

4. The units of the variable productive service are homogeneous. The presence of diminishing returns is not due to the employment of less and less efficient men, for example, but because men of equal ability are being employed less efficiently. It may be added that diminishing returns are not due to the mistakes of entrepreneurs; it would arise even in an unfortunate world populated only by omniscient technicians.

1. *AVERAGE VS. MARGINAL RETURNS*

The law of variable proportions is frequently stated in terms of average returns rather than (as above) in terms of marginal returns. The distinction between the two definitions will be developed by use of a numerical example.* Table 6 portrays a hypothetical schedule of total products resulting from various inputs of a variable productive service. The relations between total, average, and marginal products have already been developed in Chapter 4.

We may state the law of proportionality in terms of either average or marginal products, but the two statements must be distinguished. In Table 6, marginal product begins to decrease with the application of the fifth unit of the variable service, whereas average product begins to decrease only with the seventh unit. Both of these points of diminishing return are pertinent to economic

---

* Analytically, the distinction is between stating that the marginal product will decrease, i.e.,

$$\frac{\partial \left[\dfrac{\partial P}{\partial A}\right]}{\partial A} < 0,$$

and that average product will decrease, i.e.,

$$\frac{\partial \left[\dfrac{P}{A}\right]}{\partial A} < 0.$$

analysis, but grounds will be advanced later for preferring the statement of the law in terms of marginal products.

TABLE 6

(1) Units of Variable Service	(2) Total Product	(3) Average Product	(4) Marginal Product
0	0	0	0
1	5	5	5
2	13	$6\frac{1}{2}$	8
3	23	$7\frac{2}{3}$	10
4	38	$9\frac{1}{2}$	15
5	50	10	12
6	60	10	10
7	68	$9\frac{5}{7}$	8
8	75	$9\frac{3}{8}$	7

II. *THE PROOF OF THE LAW*

The law of variable proportions is one of the few pillars of economic analysis that has been accepted by most economists since its first formal statement, at the beginning of the nineteenth century. This unusual agreement has rested on two essentially different types of proof.

The more popular line of proof is a priori: it rests on the attempt to deduce the law from self-evident propositions. There are numerous variants of this approach,* but it will suffice to consider only one. This particular proof is a *reductio ad absurdum* from the assumption that average and marginal products are increasing. The argument may be illustrated by the schedule of returns on a 10-acre plot of land (Table 7); the schedule premises, as the reader can easily verify, both increasing marginal and increasing average returns.

The proof continues:

If 2 men working on 10 acres will produce 22 units, then 1 man working on 5 acres will produce 11 units,

* For an excellent critical analysis of the more popular proofs, see K. Menger, "Bemerkungen zu den Ertragsgesetzen," and "Weitere Bemerkungen zu den Ertragsgesetzen," *Zeitschrift für Nationalökonomie*, VII (1936), 25–56, 388–396.

and continuing the process,

> if 10 men working on 10 acres will produce 190 units, then 1 man working on 1 acre will produce 19 units.

But this line of analysis leads to the preposterous conclusion that one man can produce more, the less land he works, as Table 8 clearly exhibits. Since the assumption of increasing marginal returns (as in Table 7) leads to results so contradictory of all experience in the real world, it follows that increasing returns is impossible.

TABLE 7

Units of Variable Service	Total Product
1	10
2	22
3	36
4	52
5	70
6	90
7	112
8	136
9	162
10	190

TABLE 8

Acres of Land Cultivated by 1 Man	Total Product
10	10
5	11
1	19
1/100	1,009
1/1,000,000	10,000,009

This proof, which is only of an extensive genus, is unfortunately question-begging. It can in fact be demonstrated that if

> $2x$ men working on $2y$ land will produce $2z$ units,

when x men working on y land will produce z units,

and certain other mathematical conditions are fulfilled, then there
must be diminishing returns.* This and similar proofs are essentially tautological. In the present case, there is little advantage in
assuming that the production function is of the type just described,
rather than explicitly assuming diminishing returns.

The second line of proof of diminishing returns is empirical: no
one has discovered any important exceptions to the doctrine. But
this is not equivalent to saying that the law of variable proportions
is a rough generalization of experience: diminishing returns seems
to be as exceptionless — under certain conditions — as any fundamental law of physics — which also holds only under certain
conditions. Occasionally someone has collected statistics indicating that the law of variable proportions is invalid, but such data
have always been inadequate, or they have been misinterpreted,
or they have failed to satisfy the conditions of the law.

As an example of quantitative verification, we may cite the
famous experiment at Rothamsted, where a variable amount of
nitrogen (in a mixture of ammonium nitrate and ammonium sul-
phate) was applied to similar plots of land (see Table 9). There is
a large number of such agricultural illustrations available.† A
second type of illustration of diminishing returns is provided by net
rentable area as a function of the height of office buildings (see
Table 10). In this case the decreasing marginal product is due
primarily to two factors: building setbacks are required by zoning
laws, and an increasing proportion of the space must be devoted to
elevators and other facilities.

TABLE 9‡

Pounds of Fertilizer	Bushels of Wheat Secured	Marginal Product
0	18.3	—
43	28.6	10.3
86	37.1	8.5
129	39.0	1.9
172	39.5	.5

* See Menger, *loc. cit.*

† See F. L. Patton, *Diminishing Returns in Agriculture*, Columbia University, New York, 1926; W. J. Spillman and E. Lang, *The Law of Diminishing Returns*, World Book, Yon-kers-on-Hudson, 1924.

‡ Taken from Patton, *op. cit.*, p. 34.

TABLE 10 *

Height of Building (stories)	Net Rentable Area (square feet)	Marginal Product [a]
8	513,420	——
15	803,102	41,383
22	983,806	25,815
30	1,165,862	22,757
37	1,313,346	21,069
50	1,491,259	13,686
63	1,653,342	12,468
75	1,791,924	11,548

[a] Marginal product = increase in net rentable area/increase in number of stories.

III. *QUALIFICATIONS OF THE LAW*

Although the law of variable proportions has a very strong empirical basis, it is subject (as is every other scientific generalization) to certain restrictions:

1. To repeat, the law holds only if certain of the productive services are held constant in quantity while the remaining productive service is varied.†

2. More important, the law is applicable only to the case where the proportion in which the productive services may combine is variable — hence the title of *variable proportions*. An example from chemistry will serve to illustrate this restriction of the scope of the law. According to the theory of valence, chemical elements combine only in certain fixed ratios. A stable compound of hydrogen and oxygen, for instance, is water (H_2O), which results from the combination of two molecules of hydrogen with one of oxygen. If,

---

* Based on W. C. Clark and J. L. Kingston, *The Skyscraper*, American Institute of Steel Construction, New York, 1930, p. 40.

† It should be noted that to hold the quantities of B, C, D, ... constant is not equivalent to removing their influence on the marginal productivity of A. The marginal product of A is

$$\frac{\partial \phi(A, B, C, \cdots N)}{\partial A},$$

which is clearly a function of B, C, D, ... In general the behavior, as well as the size, of the marginal product of A will depend upon the quantities of other productive services, i.e.,

$$\frac{\partial^2 \phi}{\partial A \partial B}, \quad \frac{\partial^2 \phi}{\partial A \partial C}, \cdots$$

are not zero.

then, one starts with a certain number of molecules of oxygen, and adds units of hydrogen, under ideal laboratory conditions one will secure a constant marginal product (water) until all of the oxygen is utilized, and thereafter the marginal product of hydrogen will be zero.

3. Another, and more subtle, qualification is closely related to the foregoing point. Its specific nature can best be brought out by use of an example. Assume that a crew of 10 men with 10 shovels digs 50 yards of ditch per day. If now an 11th man is added to the crew, what will be the marginal product of 11 men? Of course the answer turns on the equipment of the 11th man. If he secures a shovel, then he will produce, let us say, 5 yards per day. But how much of this is due to the man and how much to the shovel? From the economic viewpoint this is an extremely important question. The entrepreneur cannot make intelligent decisions regarding the employment of any one productive service unless he can isolate the marginal product of that service. Several possibilities are open:

a. There may be only one type of shovel suitable for this kind of work. Then one of two things may be done: First, the man may be equipped with another shovel. This is a case of rigidly fixed proportions, exactly like that between hydrogen and oxygen. It will be impossible to allocate the increased product between the laborer and his equipment. Second, the 11th man may be used to spell off other workers, to fetch (as D. H. Robertson has suggested) pails of beer, or for similar purposes. He will then add some product, but considerably less than if he were also fully equipped. This may be termed a case of partially fixed proportions.

b. The second major alternative, however, is the one implicit in the law of variable proportions. In general there is not only one type of equipment that the 11th man may use. The entrepreneur may substitute 11 smaller shovels for the 10 previous large ones. If the 11 smaller shovels have the same cost (say, $100) as did the previous 10, then the investment in equipment has remained unchanged, and the additional product of the 11th man is attributable only to that man. This is a special case of the general requirement that the productive services which are held fixed in quantity must be readapted in form to the changing quantity of the variable service.

4. The law of variable proportions holds only in the absence of

any new inventions, improvements in organization, and the like. It asserts that, given the state of the arts, the product will behave in a certain way when the quantity of one productive service is varied.

We must hasten to add, however, that in assuming that there are no improvements of the techniques of production, we do not say that there can be no changes in the techniques. At any given time there is an *array* of possible techniques available for the production of any commodity. Which specific technique is chosen depends upon what productive services are used, and this in turn depends upon the relative prices of the productive services. To use the pre-

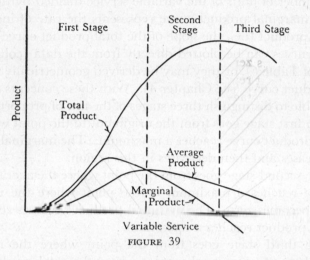

FIGURE 39

vious example, we do not exclude the possibility of using shovels of different sizes or, for that matter, steam shovels, but we do exclude shovels which are operated by the rays of the sun.

IV. *GEOMETRICAL EXPOSITION OF THE LAW*

Since the law of variable proportions is technological, and since techniques vary widely between different plants, industries, and times, it is not surprising that there is no graphical illustration of the law that is universally applicable. The hypothesis most widely accepted by economists is that of Professor Knight,* which is reproduced in Figure 39. It need scarcely be emphasized that only

* See Frank H. Knight, *Risk, Uncertainty and Profit*, London School Reprints of Scarce Works, No. 16 (1933), p. 100, n.

the ordinal relationships in this figure purport to be of general significance.

The fundamental curve in this figure is the total product curve, which corresponds to column (2) of Table 6.* The total product curve is continuous because it is assumed that the units of the variable service can be made as small as desired. As the figure suggests, the total product will usually first increase at an increasing rate, then at a decreasing rate until it reaches an absolute maximum, and finally decrease to zero.

The average product curve represents the total product of any given number of units of the variable service divided by that number; the marginal product curve represents the rate of increase of the total product (i.e., the slope of the total product curve). Both of these curves can be plotted directly from the data (columns (3) and (4) of Table 6), or they may be derived geometrically from the total product curve (see Chapter 4). With these concepts in mind, it is possible to distinguish three stages of the law of proportionality:

1. The first stage goes from the origin out to the point where the average product curve reaches a maximum. The marginal product first increases and then decreases in this region.

2. The second stage goes from the point where the average product curve reaches a maximum to the point where the marginal product becomes zero. The marginal product becomes zero when the total product reaches a maximum.

3. The third stage goes from the point where the marginal product becomes zero to the point where the total product (and hence the average product) becomes zero; the marginal product is negative in this region.

It is obvious that under no sensible conditions will an entrepreneur ever operate in the third stage, for then he is literally wasting the variable productive service. If the variable service is free, therefore, the entrepreneur will go to the end of the second stage. On the other hand, if the fixed service is free, the entre-

---

* The one difference between the graph and the table is that in the former it is assumed that a very small amount of variable service will yield no product. This is not an indispensable condition, but it does appear to be realistic. One day's labor per year on the entire area of a 160-acre farm will not yield any product. It will be shown later that if a small amount of the variable service yields no product, then it requires only a finite amount of the variable service to reduce the total product to zero; if the total product curve begins at the origin, then it requires an infinite amount of the variable service to reduce the total product to zero.

preneur will maximize the return per unit of variable service — that is, he will operate at the beginning of the second stage. The second stage, where the marginal product is less than the average product but still positive, is the only economically significant region.

Another specific hypothesis concerning the law of variable proportions has had considerable vogue among agronomists. This particular thesis is that if the first unit of the variable service produces X, the marginal product of 2 units will be $9/10\,X$ (or some other proper fraction of X); the marginal product of 3 units will be $9/10 \times 9/10\,X$; and similarly, 20 units will have a marginal product of $(9/10)^{19}\,X$.* It follows that, if this hypothesis is true, there exists only the second stage represented in Figure 39: the marginal product would decrease from the outset, but never reach zero. This theory seems less general than that portrayed in Figure 39 and will not be utilized in the subsequent analysis.

v. *REVERSIBILITY OF THE LAW OF VARIABLE PROPORTIONS*

It is important to note that the law of variable proportions is, as its very title indicates, symmetrical with respect to both or all productive services. When the number of units of the variable service is increased (or decreased), the ratio of variable to fixed services increases (or decreases) but *pari passu* the ratio of fixed to variable services decreases (or increases). The declining marginal product of the variable service can be attributed either to an increasing quantity of the variable service relative to the fixed service or to a decreasing quantity of the fixed service relative to the variable service. As a corollary, the first and third stages of the law are complementary: the total product declines in stage three because of the excess of the variable service (relative to the fixed service), and the average product decreases as one moves to the left in stage one because of the excess of the fixed service relative to the variable service.

* More generally, let r be the ratio between successive marginal products. Then if the marginal product of one unit is B, the total product will be
$$S = B(1 - r^n)/(1 - r)$$
where n is the total number of units applied. Von Thünen first employed this hypothesis in *Der isolierte Staat*, 3rd ed., Fischer, Jena, 1930, pp. 495 ff. It attained considerable popularity due to Mitscherlich and Spillman, who call it the "law of the soil" and "the law of the diminishing increment," respectively. The formula fits statistical data from agricultural experiments with some accuracy. See Spillman and Lang, *op. cit.*, especially Part I.

vi. *THE TRANSITION TO COST CURVES*

The law of variable proportions has now been explored sufficiently to permit a transition to the cost curves of the individual firm. The fundamentally new element in the discussion will, of course, be the introduction of prices of the productive services. The transition is made here only for the case of competition — that is, the prices of the productive services are constant because the firm does not buy enough of any service to affect its price.

TABLE 11

Units of Variable Service	Units of Fixed Service	Total Product	Total Variable Cost	Total Fixed Cost	Total Cost
0	10	0	0	$30	$30
1	10	5	$ 5	30	35
2	10	13	10	30	40
3	10	23	15	30	45
4	10	38	20	30	50
5	10	50	25	30	55
6	10	60	30	30	60
7	10	68	35	30	65
8	10	75	40	30	70
9	10	81	45	30	75
10	10	86	50	30	80
11	10	90	55	30	85
12	10	93	60	30	90
13	10	95	65	30	95
14	10	96	70	30	100

The transition to cost curves is made in Table 11, which is based on the data in Table 6. The price of the variable service is assumed to be $5, and $3 is the price of the fixed service. It is then merely a matter of multiplication to secure total variable cost (units of variable service times $5) and total fixed cost (units of fixed service times $3).

These various schedules of total costs could be employed in analyses of the output of a firm, but it is customary to use average and marginal costs instead. The schedule of these latter costs, derived from Table 11, are presented in Table 12. The derivation may be outlined in summary form:

1. Average variable cost is total variable cost for any output (total product) divided by that output. Thus, when output is 75, total variable cost is $40, so average variable cost is $.53.

2. Average fixed cost is total fixed cost divided by output. For an output of 75, average fixed cost is $.40.

3. Average cost is the sum of the average fixed and average variable costs, or, what amounts to the same thing, it is total cost divided by output. For an output of 75, average cost is $.53 + $.40 = $.93.

4. Marginal cost is defined as any increase in total cost divided by the corresponding increase in output. Total cost increases from $30 to $35 when output increases from 0 to 5. Hence marginal cost equals $5/5 = $1.

For those who are interested in a precise statement of the relationship between the productivity curves and the cost curves, the following algebraic notes will be of interest:

1. Let AVC be average variable cost, AP average product, TVC total variable cost, V the quantity of the variable service, and Q output. Then

$$AVC = \frac{TVC}{Q} = \frac{V \times p_v}{Q} = \frac{V}{Q}p_v = \frac{p_v}{AP}$$

2. Average fixed cost depends on the productivity curves only indirectly by way of the number of units of the fixed service. It is always a rectangular hyperbola when drawn as a curve.*

3. Let MC be marginal cost and MP marginal product. Then

$$MC = \frac{\text{increase in total cost}}{\text{increase in } Q} = \frac{\text{increase in } V \times p_v}{\text{increase in } Q}$$

$$= \frac{\text{increase in } V}{\text{increase in } Q}p_v = \frac{p_v}{MP}$$

* Let F be the quantity of the fixed service, p_f its price, AFC average fixed cost, and AC average cost. Then $AFC = Fp_f/Q$ and $AC = (p_v + Fp_f/V)/AP$.

The foregoing cost schedules are presented in their customary graphical form in Figure 40. The continuous cost curves, of course,

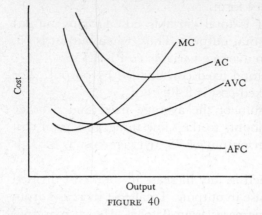

Cost

MC

AC

AVC

AFC

Output

FIGURE 40

premise infinite divisibility of the variable productive service and of the product, but on the other hand, divisibility of the fixed services would alter the marginal and average variable cost curves somewhat.*

These cost curves are usually called *short-run* cost curves, because in a short period of time the entrepreneur cannot freely vary the salaries of executives, taxes, insurance, interest on investment, and similar outlays, and these are therefore fixed costs representing fixed productive services. Other expenditures, such as those on day labor, power, and materials, do vary much more directly with output and may therefore be considered to be variable costs representing variable productive services. This conventional view will be accepted temporarily, but in the next chapter certain qualifications to which it is subject will be pointed out.

II. THE THEORY OF RETURNS TO SCALE OF PLANT

The second major stage in the analysis of the theory of production concerns the theory of returns to scale of plant. This is a vastly more

* The regions of decreasing marginal and average variable costs are the result of increasing marginal and average products respectively. These products increase, to recall, when the ratio of variable to fixed productive services is very small. If the fixed service is divisible, some of it can be left unutilized and the marginal and average products of given small quantities of the variable service will rise. (In other words, if applied to less of the fixed service, the given small quantity of the variable service will fall in the second stage [Figure 39], whereas if this quantity is applied to more of the fixed service, it will fall in the first stage.) Hence, if the fixed service is divisible, no entrepreneur will operate in a region of falling average variable costs, and these cost curves should be redrawn so that they are horizontal up to the beginning of the second stage (see problem 5 of this chapter).

The nature of the modifications in the cost curves when the variable services are relatively indivisible is suggested in George J. Stigler's "Note on Discontinuous Cost Curves," *American Economic Review*, 1940, 832–835.

complicated problem than that of the law of variable proportions, so it will be analyzed first for a special case which is useful as an introduction to more complicated types, as well as because this case is important in its own right.

TABLE 12

Output	Average Variable Cost	Average Fixed Cost	Average Cost	Marginal Cost
0	0	∞	∞	—
5	$1.00	$6.00	$7.00	$1.00
13	.77	2.31	3.08	.63
23	.65	1.20	1.85	.50
38	.53	.79	1.32	.33
50	.50	.60	1.10	.42
60	.50	.50	1.00	.50
68	.51	.44	.95	.63
75	.53	.40	.93	.71
81	.56	.37	.93	.83
86	.58	.35	.93	1.00
90	.61	.33	.94	1.25
93	.65	.32	.97	1.67
95	.68	.32	1.00	2.50
96	.73	.31	1.04	5.00

I. THE FIRST APPROXIMATION: CONSTANT RETURNS

The first approximation is as follows: when all of the productive services are increased in a given proportion, the product is increased in the same proportion.* The rationale of this assumption will be examined subsequently;† here three of its implications will be noted.

First, it must be emphasized that the case of constant returns does not contradict the law of variable proportions. It is one thing to

* Symbolically, if $P = \phi(A, B, C, ...)$, then
$$\lambda P = \phi(\lambda A, \lambda B, \lambda C, ...),$$
where λ is any arbitrary constant.

† The important and interesting history of the use of this assumption (which is associated with the name of Euler because this mathematician first discovered the third corollary to be discussed in the text) in the history of economics is summarized in George J. Stigler, *Production and Distribution Theories*, Macmillan, New York, 1941, Ch. 12.

say that the average or marginal product of *one* productive service decreases when the amount of that service is increased; it is quite another thing to say that, when *all* of the productive services are increased in the same proportion, the product will increase in that proportion. The law of variable proportions states that if two productive services A and B yield a product of P, then $2 A$ and B will yield a product of less than $2 P$. The first approximation concerning returns to scale of plant states that if A and B yield P, then $2 A$ and $2 B$ will yield $2 P$.

The second aspect is of crucial importance: when the production function is of this type, it is a matter of complete indifference which size of plant the entrepreneur may build;* every size is just as efficient as every other size. If entrepreneur X produces only half as much as rival Y, then X uses only half the productive services that Y requires. If, further, X and Y pay the same prices for these productive services, then X's total cost of production will be half that of Y, and the average costs of the two entrepreneurs will be equal.†

The final property of constant returns to scale of plant is of paramount importance in the theory of distribution: the sum of the marginal products of the productive services, each multiplied by the quantity of that service, is equal to the total product. A rigorous proof of this theorem requires the use of the calculus;‡ here an algebraic illustration will be given.

Consider the production function, $P = \sqrt{AB}$, where P is product and A and B are quantities of two productive services. It can be

---

* *Plant* is here meant to include all productive services whose quantities cannot easily be changed in short periods of time.

† In mathematical analysis this indeterminacy of the size of plant appears when the secondary conditions for a maximum are examined. It is known that

$$\left(\frac{\partial^2 P}{\partial A^2}\right)\left(\frac{\partial^2 P}{\partial B^2}\right) > \left(\frac{\partial^2 P}{\partial A \partial B}\right)^2$$

is a condition for a maximum (or minimum), but all linear homogeneous production functions (i.e., cases of constant returns) fail to satisfy this condition. See J. L. Mosak, "Interrelations of Production, Price, and Derived Demand," *Journal of Political Economy*, XLVI (1938), 772 n.

‡ If $P = \phi(A, B, C, ...)$ and $\lambda P = \phi(\lambda A, \lambda B, \lambda C, ...)$ then

$$P \equiv \frac{\partial P}{\partial A} \cdot A + \frac{\partial P}{\partial B} \cdot B + \frac{\partial P}{\partial C} \cdot C + ...,$$

as can be seen by differentiating the second equation with respect to λ. A more general theorem is given below, page 141, note.

shown at once that there are constant returns to scale. If $A = B = 100$, $P = \sqrt{100 \cdot 100} = 100$, and if $A = B = 200$, $P = \sqrt{200 \cdot 200} = 200$ — hence doubling each of the productive services doubles the product.

The illustration of the theorem now follows: Let $A = 101$ and $B = 100$, so $P = \sqrt{101 \cdot 100} = 100.49876$. The marginal product of A (i.e., the amount one unit of A adds to the total product) can be measured by subtracting from 100.49876 the total product of 100 units of A and of B: the marginal product of A is $.49876$. When B is increased from 100 to 101 and A held at 100 units, it is found that the marginal product of B is also $.49876$. The theorem states that

(marginal product of A) $\times$ (units of A)

$+$ (marginal product of B) $\times$ (units of B) = total product.

This is approximately true in the present example, for

$$.49876 \times 100 + .49876 \times 100 = 99.752,$$

whereas $P = \sqrt{100 \cdot 100} = 100$. The slight discrepancy (1/4 of 1 per cent) is due to the fact that the units of A and B are relatively large; if A and B were each increased in turn from 900 to 901, the discrepancy would be only 1/36 of 1 per cent.

II. *THE COST CURVES UNDER CONSTANT RETURNS*

With the aid of the apparatus of cost curves developed in a preceding section, it is possible to translate the case of constant returns to scale of plant into cost curves. The derivation rests on the fundamental fact that if the total product doubles when the quantities of the productive services are doubled, then the minimum average cost remains unchanged — again assuming that the prices of the productive services remain unchanged. Thus, 8 units of the variable service and 10 of the fixed service yield a product of 75 (Table 11) with an average cost of $.93 (Table 12), so 16 units of the variable service and 20 units of the "fixed" service will yield a product of 150, with the same average cost.

A few average cost curves, each appropriate to a different amount of the "fixed" productive service, are given in Figure 41. On the assumption that we can vary the "fixed" service by very small amounts, it is possible to draw sets of these curves as close together as we desire. The line AB is then drawn tangent to all of the

U-shaped curves at their minimum points. Since, by hypothesis, the size of plant has no effect on average costs, line *AB* is horizontal.*

It is clear that the entrepreneur will not operate the plant represented by AC_1, if output is to be *OD*. For then he could reduce his average costs *FG* by building a larger plant of the size represented by AC_2. Because it takes time to depreciate one plant (AC_1) out of existence and to build another (AC_2), the line *AB*, which represents all of the entrepreneur's preferred positions when he has had sufficient time to make complete adjustment of plant to output, is called the *long-run* average cost curve.

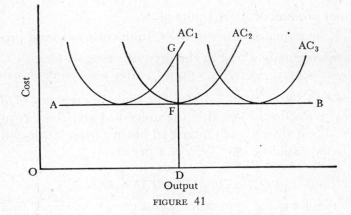

FIGURE 41

III. *VALIDITY OF THE FIRST APPROXIMATION*

Is it ever true that when all the productive services are increased in a certain proportion, the product is increased in like proportion? Our problem, in other words, is to discover the empirical validity of the production function based on constant returns to scale of plant.

From a certain general viewpoint, constant returns is a very plausible generalization. For does it not assert that if a given house is built on one lot, with equal productive services a duplicate

---

* An algebraic demonstration may not be amiss. Let π be average cost, and p_a and p_b the prices of *A* and *B* respectively. Then

$$P\pi = Ap_a + Bp_b.$$

Under constant returns, $\lambda P = \phi(\lambda A, \lambda B)$, hence

$$\lambda P\pi = \lambda Ap_a + \lambda Bp_b,$$

so π is independent of λ, the scale of plant.

house can be erected next door? This sort of reasoning is not precise, but it does possess some plausibility — enough, in fact, that we may rephrase the question and ask what, if any, cases it does not fit.

Two general categories of phenomena have been suggested to upset the first approximation, at least in many cases. The first arises out of *indivisibilities* of productive services. To illustrate, suppose a single line of railroad track can handle efficiently only 200 trains per day. Should the traffic increase beyond 200 trains per day, the railroad may do one of two things. First, it may put on more sidings, run longer and heavier trains, and expand loading and unloading facilities. But this solution will become more and more expensive if traffic continues to increase, until the company will be forced to resort to the second alternative. This latter alternative is to lay another line of track. But then, supposing traffic stands at 300 trains per day, the two tracks are used relatively lightly; so the cost per train is high. Increases of traffic up to 400 trains per day will be accompanied by falling average costs.

In more general terms, it may not be possible to increase all of the productive services in a given proportion. Some productive services will usually be indivisible relative to others, so that the indivisible services are underworked or overworked at most outputs. Many illustrations of this phenomenon will be given in the subsequent section on increasing returns to scale of plant.

There is, moreover, a second reason for the failure of the first approximation. This latter reason arises out of what may be termed, for lack of a better phrase, the human factor in the production function. Two examples may serve to clarify this point.

The division of labor or, more properly, the specialization of labor, refers to the concentration of individuals on specific parts or processes of production. The shoemaker may make the entire shoe, or (quite aside from the use of machinery) he may restrict himself to cutting soles. The expertness resulting from concentration on only one process (which is due to practice, natural adaptation, and other factors beyond our present interest) * frequently and within limits, leads to this result: 10 shoemakers each making only one part of a shoe can produce more than 10 shoemakers each making complete shoes.

* See the classic description of the manufacture of pins in Adam Smith, *The Wealth of Nations*, Modern Library ed., Random House, New York, 1937, pp. 7–8.

A second example of this problem of the "human factor" relates to management and control, the entrepreneurial functions. Empirically there is strong evidence that when the number of men in a plant is doubled, the supervisory, coordinating, and decision-making staff must be more than doubled.* The larger unit is more unwieldy and cumbersome, and there are real costs involved in overcoming these characteristics.

This last-mentioned case may easily be translated into terms of indivisibilities. One could speak of management as an indivisible productive service, so that as the firm grows in size, the coordinating and decision-making faculties are used more intensively subject to diminishing returns. It is possible, but somewhat artificial, to consider the previous case of specialization of labor as also representing an indivisibility. Assuming that each of 10 processes involved in making shoes requires an equal amount of time, then why cannot the single shoemaker spend one day on each of the processes, and do as much work that day as the specialist who always works on this one process? Because, among other reasons, with this reduced practice his proficiency will be less. But this can be restated: the shoemaker has only so much ability to learn (from instruction and practice), and the more he learns of one process, the less he learns of the others. This single unit of learning ability, then, is cultivated subject to diminishing returns.†

Although from a formal viewpoint almost all deviations from constant returns can be subsumed under indivisibilities, such classificatory problems are unimportant relative to the fact that constant returns is not a necessary characteristic of the production function. We will pass now to the direct consideration of the indivisibilities as they affect returns and hence costs.

iv. *INDIVISIBLE PRODUCTIVE SERVICES*

Indivisible services, by their very nature, lead to alternating stages of increasing and decreasing returns to scale of plant. To

---

* To the extent that they can be increased; some things, like the ultimate authority to make decisions, can be given to more executives in a firm only at the cost of loss of unity and expedition.

† It follows that if a man were to specialize primarily on one process, and yet make the whole product, he would produce less than if his training were more general. Once a man concentrates all of his learning ability (which includes all of his working time) on one specialized task, no further gains can be secured from specialization.

return to our previous example, one line of track may be most efficiently utilized when there are 200 trains per day. Until this output of transportation services is reached, other productive services will have to be added as traffic grows, but there will not be an increase of trackage. Therefore one need not and cannot double all productive services when the traffic increases from 100 to 200 trains per day: the track will not be changed.* But if traffic increases to where 300 trains are run daily, half a track cannot be added. The railroad must either overcrowd the single track or build another track which, at least for a time, will not be utilized fully. Hence for train loads of less than 200 (or 400 or 600), the railroad will be operating subject to increasing returns; for loads of more than 200 (or 400 or 600) the railroad will be operating subject to decreasing returns.

We shall list some of the major indivisibilities which affect the scale of operations of the firm: †

1. Indivisibility of Machinery. Perhaps the most popular of all reasons advanced to explain increasing returns to scale of plant is that only when production reaches a certain rate is it possible to use complicated machinery. If a concern made only 10 automobiles a year, almost all parts would have to be made by hand. If 100,000 automobiles are made, it is possible to make casting molds for engine blocks, to use an assembly line, and to exploit other specialized machines.

One may ask at once, however, why smaller machines cannot be used by smaller plants. One of several replies may be given to the inquiry:

a. It may be impossible to construct smaller (or less durable) machines for a given type of work. Once a pattern is made for automobile fenders, it is necessarily available no matter how many fenders are pressed. At most the difference between the cost of making a pattern for 1,000 cars and 100,000 must be trivial. This is a perfectly valid explanation, but the narrow scope of its applicability must be recognized. In the overwhelming number of cases, machines may be made in a large variety of sizes. Frequently only one or a very few sizes are made, as with boxcars, but this practice

---

* Ignoring, for simplicity's sake, the fact that items such as ballast, rails, and bridges must be improved when traffic increases.
† On this subject, see the references to this chapter.

is usually explicable on some other grounds (such as the advantages of standardization).

b. More generally, therefore, the reply will be that small machines are much more expensive relative to their output. And, in turn, two reasons are given for this:

(1) At times, it is just a physical datum that larger machines require (relative to output) less material. There are several classic examples of this. The contents of a boiler increase as the cube of its dimensions, but the enclosing metal increases only as the square of its dimensions (ignoring differences in thickness of walls). Similarly, the capacity of a boat increases as the cube of its dimensions; the water resistance increases only as the square. Every building has one roof, no matter how many stories.

(2) Small machines are very uneconomical in their demands on labor, in both construction and operation. The fitting together of the parts of a 10-horsepower motor does not require 10 times the labor necessary to fit those of a 1-horsepower motor. Similarly, a truck requires 1 driver, whether it has $\frac{1}{2}$-ton or 2-ton capacity.

Granting these points, it must be emphasized that in general there is a limit to the advantage of size. A quotation from Professor J. M. Clark will illustrate the point:

> There is a story of a man who thought of getting the economy of large-scale production in plowing, and built a plow three times as long, three times as wide, and three times as deep as the ordinary plow and harnessed six horses to pull it, instead of two. To his surprise, the plow refused to budge, and to his greater surprise it finally took fifty horses to move the refractory machine. In this case, the resistance, which is the thing he did not want, increased faster than the surface area of the earth plowed, which was the thing he did want. Furthermore, when he increased his power to overcome this resistance, he multiplied the number of his power units instead of their size, which eliminated all chance of saving there, and since his units were horses, the fifty could not pull together as well as two.*

Beyond a certain point, larger machines become less flexible, involve undue interruptions for repairs, cannot cope with fluctuations of output, and suffer from many other limitations.

But if economies of machinery do not continue forever, we may say that diseconomies need never set in. If larger machines become

*J. M. Clark, *The Economics of Overhead Costs,* University of Chicago, Chicago, 1923, p. 116.

less efficient, a firm always has the alternative of using more machines of smaller size. The point where gains from larger machines stop is, of course, dependent on the industry in question. In railroading, a 4-track system may be the limit; in the corn belt a farm of 640 acres can use most existent agricultural machinery.

2. *Marketing Indivisibilities.* Examples of marketing indivisibilities are:

a. A salesman may be able to handle a full line of goods, rather than a single product, with no significant increase of costs, and, indeed, the various products may advertise one another.

b. Advertising cannot always be carried on in just one region. By expanding to national size, a firm can utilize more fully the coverage it secures from advertising in national periodicals.

c. It is possible for a large firm to maintain a purchasing department which buys expertly according to specification.

3. *Financial Indivisibilities.* These are usually of lesser importance, but examples are:

a. The investigating and managing costs of a loan do not increase proportionally with its size; so larger loans (of equal safety) may be secured on slightly better terms.

b. Securities issued in small quantities cannot be listed on exchanges, thus hampering slightly the acquisition of long-term funds.

4. *Research Indivisibilities.* This point is too familiar to require illustration. The cost of discovering a new product is not affected by the scale on which it will be produced. A large concern, moreover, can take advantage of the principle of insurance, since research is notoriously uneven in its yield.

v. *SPECIALIZATION AND MANAGEMENT*

The gains arising out of specialization of labor are so well publicized that they require no elaboration here. The individual laborer gains in proficiency owing to concentration on one task and saves time in shifting tools and positions (although in offset the materials must now be brought to him).

As a firm expands, the entire time of more men can be devoted to single processes, with consequent increases of efficiency. Two limitations on this tendency may be noted, however. First, the output of a laborer will generally increase more when he is reduced from three tasks to two, than when he is reduced from two to one

This follows from the fact, already noticed, that intensive utilization of the learning ability of a man is also subject to diminishing returns. Second, once a man is fully occupied with one task, further expansion of output will secure no economies in that process; at best merely another man will be put beside the first to do similar work.

What is true of the laborer is even more true of the entrepreneur. The ability to administer and to make decisions, which is one of the most diverse of all "natural" endowments of men, can be utilized fully in a large plant, where most (but not all) of the details and routine may be delegated.

But on the other side, the growth of a firm puts heavier and heavier burdens on the management. Quite aside from the difficult problem of expansion itself, large groups are much harder to coordinate than smaller units. For management, and control in general, inherently face a problem: the final authority to make decisions cannot be subdivided or delegated. Large units are, in fact, confronted by a dilemma. At one extreme all authority may be delegated. Then there will be no unity of policy or uniformity of performance. At the other extreme, all decisions may be made by a final center. This system involves bureaucracy in its worst form: "red tape," hopeless delay, decisions based on diluted memoranda. Between these two extremes the large firm attempts to steer a middle course, but it never achieves that compactness, flexibility, and singleness of purpose which are possessed by every well-managed medium-sized firm. The growing difficulty of coordination and decision-making eventually stops the growth of every firm.

vi. *THE TRANSITION TO COST CURVES*

If the foregoing analysis be accepted, there are usually two stages in the behavior of output when all of the productive services are increased. Up to a certain point the output may be increased without a proportional increase of all productive services, owing to the economies considered above. After a certain point, management costs increase more rapidly than output, offsetting the diminishing economies secured in other departments of the business.*

This situation is portrayed by several "short-run" cost curves in Figure 42. The line AC_1 is the average cost curve for a certain amount of the "fixed" services (which are, of course, variable in the

---

* A more detailed analysis of economies of scale is made in Chapter 11.

long run), AC_2 is the curve for a larger amount, and AC_3 represents an even larger amount. When the plant represented by AC_1 is expanded to that represented by AC_2, the output is doubled with

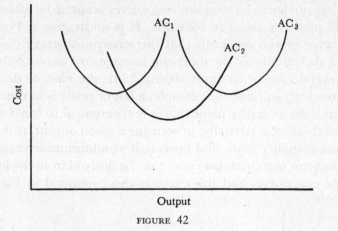

FIGURE 42

less than a doubling of all services; hence minimum average costs fall. The expansion from AC_2 to AC_3 involves decreasing returns to scale of plant; so minimum average costs rise.

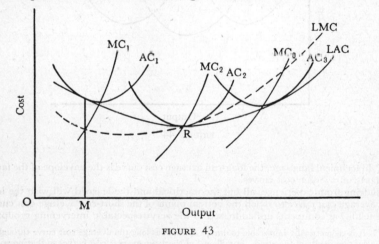

FIGURE 43

In order to secure a better description of the behavior of costs when the size of plant changes, we utilize the concept of long-run average costs. *Long-run average cost* is defined as the lowest possible average cost of producing any output when the entrepreneur has adequate time to make all desired adjustments. It follows from this definition that no portion of the long-run average cost curve can ever lie above any portion of a short-run average cost curve. It turns out that the long-run average cost curve is tangent to the whole set of short-run average cost curves secured by varying the "fixed" plant by small increments. It is illustrated in Figure 43. It deserves special emphasis that the long-run average cost curve touches the minima of the short-run average cost curves only in the very special case of constant returns.* In the case of decreasing long-run average costs, for example, a larger plant is so much more efficient than a smaller plant that it is economical to build a larger plant and utilize it partially, in securing a given output, rather than to build a smaller plant and operate it at minimum average costs.

A long-run marginal cost curve may be derived from the long-run average cost curve, and this curve is also contained in Figure 43.

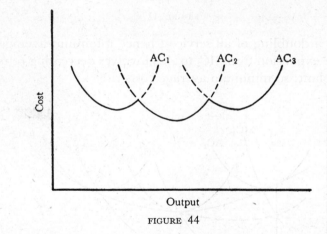

FIGURE 44

* In technical language, the long-run average cost curve is the envelope of the family of short-run average cost curves.

Judging from experience, all but the uncritical and the learned will wish the long-run average cost curve to touch the bottom points of the short-run average cost curves. The following comments are addressed to the very respectable intervening group:

  i. It is geometrically impossible to draw a continuous long-run average cost curve through the bottom points of thousands (or millions) of short-run average cost curves so that no portion of the former curve ever lies above any portion of a short-run average cost curve. Try it.
 ii. Suppose only three sizes of plant were possible (because the "fixed" factor comes in only three sizes): then the solid curve would be the long-run average cost curve. Now draw more and more short-run average cost curves between these three, always retaining nonoverlapping sections as the long-run average cost curve. Eventually one gets the curve in Fig. 43.
iii. The slope of the long-run average cost curve must be negative in a falling region, but the slope of a short-run average cost curve must be zero at the minimum point. Hence a falling long-run curve cannot be tangent to the minimum point of the short-run curve.

It represents the cost of an additional unit of output when all productive services vary. Long-run marginal costs can be greater than or less than short-run marginal costs. On the one hand, the full adaptability of all services tends to make long-run marginal costs lower; on the other hand, long-run marginal costs are affected by the payments for all productive services, whereas short-run marginal costs depend only on the cost of the variable services. Which factor is decisive is a question, of course, of where one is operating a given short-run plant. It may be added that the short- and long-run marginal costs are equal where the short- and long-run average cost curves touch.* Thus, at output M (Figure 43), SMC equals LMC below the point at which $SRAC$ touches $LRAC$.

One difference between this case and that of constant returns to scale deserves mention: it was demonstrated that in the latter case, the sum of the marginal products of the various productive services times their respective quantities is equal to the total product. This is true at any output. The theorem is still applicable, but only at the minimum point (or minima) on the long-run average cost curves, such as that at point R in Figure 43.† In the region of

* It was shown in Chapter 4 that any marginal quantity (M) is related to the corresponding average quantity (A) by the equation
$$M = A(1 + 1/\eta),$$
where η is the elasticity of the A curve. At the point where $SRAC = LRAC$, their elasticities (slope and position) are equal, so $LRMC = SRMC$.

† We may employ in proof an elegant demonstration in E. Schneider, *Theorie der Produktion*, Springer, Vienna, 1934, pp. 19–21. If $P = \phi(A, B, C, ...)$, then

$$dP = \frac{\partial P}{\partial A}\, dA + \frac{\partial P}{\partial B}\, dB + \frac{\partial P}{\partial C}\, dC + \cdots \tag{i}$$

Increase all of the productive services in a constant proportion λ, so

$$\lambda = \frac{dA}{A} = \frac{dB}{B} = \cdots. \tag{ii}$$

Substitute (ii) into (i) and divide by λP,

$$\frac{dP}{\lambda P} = \frac{1}{P}\left[\frac{\partial P}{\partial A}\cdot A + \frac{\partial P}{\partial B}\cdot B + \frac{\partial P}{\partial C}\cdot C + \cdots\right]. \tag{iii}$$

But the left side of (iii) is the relative change of product resulting from an equal relative change in the quantities of all productive services, and may be called the *elasticity* of the production function (e). Then,

$$P\cdot e = \frac{\partial P}{\partial A}\cdot A + \frac{\partial P}{\partial B}\cdot B + \frac{\partial P}{\partial C}\cdot C + \cdots \tag{iv}$$

If $e > 1$, then we have increasing returns (or decreasing long-run average costs), and the product is less than the sum of the marginal products times the quantities of the respective productive services. If $e < 1$, the opposite holds. Finally, if $e = 1$, so there is constant returns (and constant average costs, as is true at the minimum point on the long-run average cost curve); then the statement in the text is true. But then (iv) is an equation true only for certain values of the variables; in note ‡, page 130, the relationship was an identity.

decreasing long-run average costs, the sum of the marginal products times the quantities of the productive services is greater than the total product, and vice versa in the region of rising long-run average costs.

III. EXTERNAL ECONOMIES

Certain factors beyond the control of a firm may also affect its costs. Following Marshall, these are called *external economies* or *diseconomies*, according as they serve to decrease or to increase the firm's production costs. An extensive analysis of external economies is not necessary at this point,* but a brief discussion may serve to indicate the nature of these influences on the firm's costs.

The simplest case of an external economy arises when the production function of a firm contains as an implicit variable the output of the industry. On the side of diseconomies, the most popular example is that of several companies pumping oil from the same pool; the more oil one company secures, the less (or the greater the cost of) the output of the other firms. As a parallel external economy, we may cite the case of adjacent coal mines, where the greater the amount of water other firms pump from their shafts, the less the remaining firm need remove.

A second and more general type of external influence is provided by changes in the prices of productive services due to changes in the size of the industry. One building contractor may hire all of the carpenters he wishes at the ruling (constant) wage rate. If the building trade expands in that locality, however, wages may rise in order to secure a larger supply of carpenters. Figure 45A describes the industry: when the demand of the industry rises from D_1 to D_2 the wage rate rises from OM to ON. The individual firm, whose purchases are too small to affect the price of the service, faces corresponding supply curves given in Figure 45B. The quantities measured along the base of Figure 45B are only a very small fraction of those measured along the base of Figure 45A.

The effect of external economies or diseconomies on the cost curves of the firm cannot be traced without resort to the production function. If wages are 50 per cent of the cost of building and wages rise by 10 per cent, it does not follow that building costs rise by 5 per cent. The entrepreneur will substitute other services for labor,

* See Stigler, *Production and Distribution Theories*, pp. 68 ff., and references there cited.

since labor has become more expensive relative to other productive services, and the rise in building costs will be less than 5 per cent. On the other hand, there must be some increase in costs, or the entrepreneur was not employing the various productive services in the best combination before the rise of wages took place.

When the prices of "fixed" services rise, the short-run marginal cost curves of established firms will not be affected, since they depend only on variable costs. The "fixed" costs must be written up, but this does not affect their short-run output and price, as will

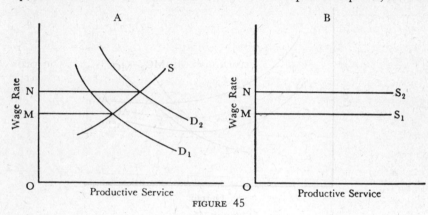

FIGURE 45

be shown in the next chapter. The sole effect, to repeat, will be a rise of the average fixed and average cost curves.*

When the existing plants are worn out and are replaced by new plants, the marginal cost curve of the new plant will be above the former marginal cost curve, for the following reason: The "fixed" service has risen in price relative to the variable services; so more variable and less fixed services will, be used to produce any given output. But with a smaller amount of the fixed service, a given quantity of the variable service will have a smaller marginal product (with a higher marginal cost). The situation is summarized in Figure 46. The original marginal and average cost curves are represented by solid curves. The same marginal cost curve holds until a new plant is built, but the average cost curve immediately shifts to AC_1 when the price of the fixed service rises. Once a new

* The new curves will not be parallel to the old. Total fixed cost rises by (say) $1,000, so average fixed and average costs rise by $1,000/output, and this decreases as output increases. The unchanged marginal cost curve intersects the new average cost curve at its minimum point.

plant is built, the costs become the broken curves, AC_2 and MC_2.*
These relationships hold for all "short-run" average cost curves, so
the increased price of the "fixed" service ultimately leads to an upward shift of the long-run average and marginal cost curves.

The other possibility is that the price of the variable service rises.
The formal explanation runs in the same general terms: the first
effect of the price rise is a corresponding rise of the average variable,
average, and marginal cost curves.† Once a new plant is built, the
entrepreneur will increase relatively the quantities of the (cheaper)

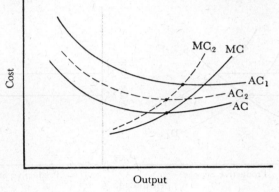

FIGURE 46

fixed services, which will offset in part the increased cost of the
variable service. Again the long-run average and marginal cost
curves will rise. The graphical illustration (Figure 47) is as follows:
AC_1 and MC_1 are the original curves; AC_2 and MC_2 are the curves
immediately after the price of the variable service increases; and
AC_3 and MC_3 are the curves after the entrepreneur has built a new
plant which incorporates relatively more of the fixed services.

RECOMMENDED READINGS

1. Cassels, J. M., "On the Law of Variable Proportions," *Explorations in Economics*, McGraw-Hill, New York, 1936, pp. 223–236.
2. Clark, J. M., *The Economics of Overhead Costs*, University of Chicago, Chicago, 1923, Chs. 4–6.
3. Marshall, A., *Principles of Economics*, 8th ed., Macmillan, London, 1920, Bk. IV, Chs. 8–13; Bk. 5, Chs. 3–5.

* If new firms enter the industry — and this would be a possible cause of the rise
in the price of the fixed service — they would construct the plant represented by AC_2.

† Since there are usually many variable services, the entrepreneur will modify the
proportions between them in such a way as to minimize the immediate increase of costs.

4. Robinson, E. A. G., *The Structure of Competitive Industry*, Nisbet, London, 1935.
5. Viner, J., "Cost Curves and Supply Curves," *Zeitschrift für National-ökonomie*, III (1932), 23–46.

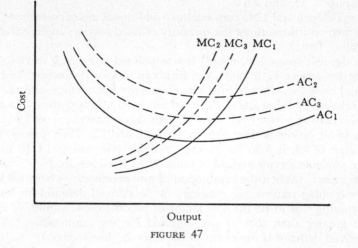

Output

FIGURE 47

PROBLEMS

1. Verify all of the relationships (see Chapter 4) between average, marginal, and total costs in the following example. Total fixed cost is $100. Compute and plot average fixed, average variable, marginal, and average costs from the above data.

Output	Total Variable Cost	Output	Total Variable Cost
1	$10	13	$101
2	19	14	113
3	27	15	126
4	34	16	140
5	40	17	155
6	45	18	171
7	50	19	188
8	56	20	206
9	63	21	225
10	71	22	245
11	80	23	266
12	90	24	288

2. Assign a price to the variable productive service and construct the product curves (see page 127).
3. Taking the marginal cost curve of a firm to be its supply curve (this will be proved in the next chapter), compute the elasticity of supply at outputs 9, 15, and 22.
4. Use Tables 6 and 12 to construct two additional sets of cost curves based on two and three times the quantity of fixed services underlying these tables. Plot.
5. In the text (page 128, note*) it was pointed out that if the fixed productive service is divisible, the firm can reduce its average and marginal costs (or, what is equivalent, increase the average and marginal products) by using less of the fixed service if it is operating in a region of increasing average returns. Find the lowest average cost for outputs up to 60, on the basis of data in Tables 6 and 12. (The answer, for an output of 13, is $.50 for average variable cost, using 13/10 units of the variable service and 6 1/2 units of the fixed service.)
6. Appraise: "When the production of any commodity obeys the law of diminishing returns, the elasticity of the derived demand for labor — assuming this to be the sole factor of production — would, of course, be greater than that of the demand for the commodity." (Note: derived demand is irrelevant to the error in this passage.)
7. If there are only two productive services (A and B), under constant returns they are related as follows:

$$MP_aA + MP_bB = P,$$

where MP_a is the marginal product of (variable) A and MP_b is the marginal product of (fixed) B. Reproduce Figure 39 of the text and draw in the MP_b curve on the basis of this relationship. (Remember that B is constant, say, equal to unity.)

CHAPTER 9

PRICING UNDER COMPETITION

The foregoing chapters have provided us with the complete apparatus for the analysis of pricing under competitive conditions. The requisites for such an analysis, to summarize, are: market demand curves and demand curves for individual producers, the nature of costs, and the cost curves of individual firms.

The entire analysis rests on one fundamental thesis: *Every supply curve is a cost curve* — although of course not vice versa. The very definition of the economic problem indicates that this should be so. Individuals seek to allocate scarce means among competing ends in such a way as to attain these ends as fully as possible. Therefore economic behavior is a choice between alternative allocations of given means, and the foregone alternatives are the *costs* of the alternatives which are chosen. To have meaning, a supply curve must be a cost curve.

One of Marshall's greatest contributions to economics was the discovery that the pricing problem should be treated primarily from the viewpoint of *time*. He distinguishes three fundamental time periods in pricing: *

1. Market price — the price of a commodity during a period in which its supply is fixed.
2. Short-run normal price — the price of a commodity during a (longer) period in which the rate of production (per unit of time) is variable, but in which there exists a fixed plant.
3. Long-run normal price — the price of a commodity during the period in which the rate of production is completely variable, a fixed plant no longer existing.

These periods will be defined with greater precision in the subsequent discussion.

* See A. Marshall, *Principles of Economics*, 8th ed., Macmillan, London, 1920, Bk. V, Ch. 5. Marshall added a fourth concept, *secular price*, but this was essentially a historical category.

Certain preliminary observations, however, are in order. First, this classification is not complete: it would be possible, and for certain purposes it would be necessary, to use a much finer classification.* Some of the possible refinements will be considered later, but for immediate purposes the broad outline is sufficient. Second, the time periods are defined in terms of economic forces, and refer to operational time (time measured by operations), not to clock time. The "short-run normal" period is considerably less than a year in airplane production; it is perhaps 20 years in the case of an apple orchard.

Finally, all of these prices are theoretical concepts, not statistical averages. The average price of wheat over a 30-year period is not its long-run normal price. As a matter of fact, if there were no changes in long-run cost or demand conditions during this period, the average of the prices of the last few years of the period would be closer to the long-run normal price than would the 30-year average, for the early years would probably represent a less complete adjustment of price to these demand and cost conditions. But long-run demand and cost conditions do not remain fixed for 30 years; new inventions, a changing population, a foreign tariff, or other developments are certain to lead to a new long-run normal price before the previous one is reached. This is not to question the value of the concept of normal price: it tells us the direction of future movement of price, and if we have all of the relevant facts, it tells us when, and at what rate, the normal position will be reached.

I. MARKET PRICE

The market price of a commodity is its price during a period within which the stock of the commodity is fixed. The standard case is where a stock of goods is accumulated periodically, as with agricultural products at the end of a crop year. (Inventory movements are better handled in connection with short-run normal price.) In this and succeeding sections we will consider first the individual or entrepreneur, and then the market as a whole.

* Thus Professor Knight has criticized Marshall's classification because it failed to begin with *speculative price*, the momentary price established in organized markets by professional traders (see Frank H. Knight, *The Ethics of Competition*, Harper. New York, 1935, pp. 170–171). Some elements of this problem will be introduced in our discussion of market price.

1. *THE INDIVIDUAL SUPPLIER*

The individual will treat the current market price as given. This, to recall, is a specific assumption of competition: no individual buys or sells enough of a commodity to exert a perceptible influence on its price. The supply curve appears to the buyer (and the demand curve appears to the seller) as a horizontal line. One can buy or sell all he wishes at the ruling price.

What are the costs of production of a stock of goods already in the seller's possession? It is tempting to reply that the costs are the sums of money which were previously paid for the stock of goods, but is this really a sensible answer? Is the money spent in the past *now* an alternative to holding the stock of goods? It is apparent from this question that past outlays cannot directly influence present alternatives, and hence present costs. If I "bought" Brooklyn Bridge for $500, that is not its present cost — or foregone alternative — to me, and similarly, if I bought wheat at $1.00 a bushel, that is not its present cost to me. To insist on recovering historical costs is irrational, and people who obstinately insist on doing so must be phenomenally lucky to avoid the bankruptcy courts.

There are only two alternatives to selling a stock of goods in a given market at whatever price is offered for it. One may sell in other markets, or rather in other geographical regions of the market. This is indeed the method by which prices are equalized within a market area — its nature is self-evident. The other, and usually the more important, alternative is to hold the goods off the market until some future time when better prices are expected. The cost of goods sold today is primarily the amount the seller expects he could receive tomorrow. If a definite price, say $1.00, is expected for wheat six months hence, the least the seller will accept now is $1.00 minus the (marginal) cost of holding wheat six months.*

The bases of expectations of future price movements have already been discussed in part (see pages 95 and following). In the case of sellers, two general types of factors seem to underlie anticipations. The first type may be termed *extrapolative*. If the price of wheat has been rising, many people will deem this a sufficient reason for expecting the movement to continue. Or if other prices have been

---

* In the case of a buyer with the same expectation, the most that will be paid is $1.00 plus an amount which measures the (marginal) gain from immediate possession.

rising, the speculative fever is communicated to wheat. The second type may be termed *analytical*. Some contemporary or probable future change in cost or demand conditions is expected to dictate a higher or lower price in the future. A foreign war is expected to favor exports, or weather reports suggest a short crop.

The individual seller rarely expects a unique price to rule at a future date; rather there is a range of possible prices, each with a specific probability. Instead of expecting wheat to be $1.00 a bushel in six months, the seller expects that

> there is 1 chance in 10 that it will be $ .50
> there are 2 chances in 10 that it will be   .75
> there are 3 chances in 10 that it will be   1.00
> there are 3 chances in 10 that it will be   1.10
> there is 1 chance in 10 that it will be   1.20

The mean expected price (or mathematical expectation) is $1/10 \times$ $.50 + 2/10 \times \$.75 + 3/10 \times \$1.00 + 3/10 \times \$1.10 + 1/10 \times$ $1.20 = \$.95$. Let us name this mean expected price minus the holding costs the discounted price. If holding costs are $.05, the discounted price is $.90.

The current price may be $1.00. What will the seller do? He will sell his entire stock of 10,000 bushels, and he may even sell short for future delivery. The precise extent of his short sales will be determined as follows: the gain from the sale of an additional bushel is the present price minus the discounted price. In a competitive market this gain is constant since the individual cannot influence either of these prices. The marginal cost of short sales is the return that would be secured in alternative uses of the last increment of money tied up in short sales. These alternative uses might be investment in government bonds, or paying off a mortgage, or expanded personal consumption. This marginal cost rises with increased commitments of funds (because as more money is devoted to trading in wheat, the marginal rates of substitution of prospective wheat profits for other uses of money rise). The seller will stop at the point where the marginal cost of the funds is equal to the present price minus the discounted price. Before this point (of short sales) $1.00 will yield more in short sales than elsewhere; beyond this point it will yield less.*

* For a more detailed proof that the rule, marginal cost equals price, is the proper criterion for maximum profits, see page 157.

On the other hand, if the current price is $.80, a discounted price of $.90 is equivalent to the expectation that the price will rise. Hence the seller will hold all of his stock, and will in fact buy on margin to an extent determined as before. That is, the gain from buying a bushel on margin is discounted price minus present price, and the marginal cost is the amount that the expenditure of the present price would yield in alternative uses. He will buy on margin up to the point where marginal cost equals the gain.

We may summarize the argument up to this point in graphical terms (Figure 48). At a present price above the discounted price ($.90), the seller will dispose of his entire stock (*OA*) and sell short, and he will sell more, the greater the present price — this is represented by *RS*. At a present price below $.90, he will hold his stock and buy on margin, and he will buy more the lower the present price. This purchase may be viewed as a negative sale and is represented by *MN*.

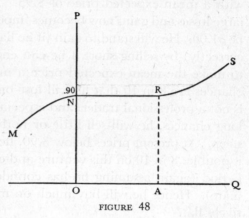

FIGURE 48

But this simplified analysis must be modified in certain respects. It makes a difference whether the seller thinks the expected price is $.95 with a distribution such as

        1 chance in 10 that it will be $ .90
        8 chances in 10 that it will be   .95
        1 chance in 10 that it will be   1.00

or whether the chances are 1 in 10 that the future price will be $.50, $.60, $.70, $.80, $.90, $1.00, $1.10, $1.20, $1.30, $1.40. The greater the dispersion of the distribution, the less money he will venture on this deal. If we use the customary statistical measure of dispersion, this amounts to saying that the amount of money he will venture will vary inversely with the standard error of the probability distribution. In terms of Figure 48, the more dispersed the probabilities of future prices, the steeper the curves *MN* and *RS* will be. Conversely, if a seller were absolutely certain that the future price was to be $.95, *MNRS* would become a horizontal line (whose length would be twice his total capital expressed in units of the commodity).

Moreover, the behavior of the seller will be affected by the skewness of the probability distribution (given its standard error). Suppose the probability distribution of future prices to be as follows:

> 1 chance in 10 that the price will be   0
> 1 chance in 10 that the price will be $ .54
> 8 chances in 10 that the price will be 1.12,

with a mean expected price of $.95.   The seller's attitude toward large losses and gains now becomes important.   Let the present price be $1.00.   He will stand to gain (if he has appraised the probabilities correctly) by selling short if he can engage in enough transactions to make the mean expected price a meaningful concept.   But the chances are 8 in 10 that he will lose on this one transaction.   If he is not a professional trader, and especially if he does not like to take long chances, he will sell little or nothing — *RS* will become very steep.   At present prices below $.90, however, his assurance of gain is double: 8 in 10 on this venture and certainty over a long enough period (again assuming he has confidence in his probability estimate).   Hence he will buy much on margin — *MN* becomes relatively flat.

Let us assume, conversely, the following distribution, which has a mean expected value of $.95:

> 4 chances in 10 that the price will be $ .05
> 3 chances in 10 that the price will be   .10
> 1 chance in 10 that the price will be 1.00
> 1 chance in 10 that the price will be 3.00
> 1 chance in 10 that the price will be 5.00

Again it will pay to buy on margin if the present price is less than $.90, but the chance of loss is great.   On the other hand, there is a small chance for enormous gain (if the price goes to $3.00 or $5.00), and this will attract many people (witness the popularity of lotteries).   Conversely, it will pay to sell short at present prices above $.90, but there is a small chance of enormous loss which repels many individuals.   Probably *MN* will become flatter and *RS* steeper, although it all depends on people's attitudes toward large but improbable gains and losses.

By a very similar analysis it is possible to derive the demand curve for a commodity. So far as speculative demand is concerned, it would be adequate. But if the demand is that of consumers, or of producers (e.g., flour millers), the dominant element in the demand is contained in the usual demand analysis (Chapter 5) or in the marginal productivity theory (Chapter 10), respectively. Speculative elements are important in dating purchases, rather than in determining them, if such a distinction can be drawn.

ii. THE MARKET

In the case of the market, an additional element is introduced: the expectations of various sellers (and buyers) will vary considerably. Individual estimates of future will differ considerably because of differing knowledge of relevant facts — we are all familiar with the myth of how the Rothschild fortune blossomed out of early dispatches containing news of the outcome of the Battle of Waterloo. Moreover, temperaments are important; every large market contains its Casper Milquetoasts as well as its heavy plungers. The combination of these factors insures a wide range of anticipations in the market at any one time.

This diversity of expectations does not per se offer any theoretical difficulties, but a concomitant factor does complicate our problem enormously. No trader's expectations are completely independent of those of other traders in the market, and in certain very speculative markets a trader's expectations are primarily guesses as to what other traders expect.* Any realistic explanation of the behavior of such markets becomes primarily an essay in social psychology — and at times in abnormal psychology. Those interested in attempts to handle this interdependence of expectations, which is too complicated to be treated here, will find some references in a footnote.†

Once the individual demand and supply curves are given, the formal determination of market price is very elementary, so much so as to be the common property even of those whom Cannan deemed least informed on economics, "city editors and that very ignorant

* See J. M. Keynes, *The General Theory of Employment, Interest, and Money*, Harcourt, Brace, New York, 1935, Ch. 12.

† See A. C. Pigou, *Industrial Fluctuations*, Macmillan, London, 1927, Pt. I, Chs. 6, 7; F. Lavington, *The Trade Cycle*, King, London, 1922, Ch. 4; O. Morgenstern, *Wirtschaftsprognose, eine Untersuchung ihrer Voraussetzungen und Möglichkeiten*, Springer, Vienna, 1928.

person, the man on the street." The demand and supply curves are the horizontal sums of the respective curves of the individuals in the market — they are given in Figure 49.* The price will be AR; the quantity sold OA. At a higher price the quantity supplied would exceed the quantity demanded, and the competition of sellers would force the price down. Conversely, at prices less than AR, the quantity demanded would exceed the quantity supplied, and the competition of buyers would force the price up. In less formal terms, AR represents the consensus of the market. It is the only price which equates the amount sold by those who believe that the price will not rise (by more than holding costs) with the amount purchased by those who believe that the price will rise (by more than holding costs).

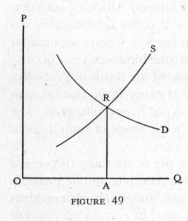

FIGURE 49

This bit of analysis is so obvious that at times its import is not realized. Market price can be looked upon as a device which rations a limited supply in two directions: first, it allocates the supply over the period of time in question; all of the wheat is not consumed in the first six months after it is harvested. Second, it allocates the supply among buyers at any given time, so that all who are willing to buy at that price can secure the quantities they desire. In a well-organized market it performs these functions efficiently and economically, and so impersonally that many individuals do not realize that such problems exist. But when prices are abandoned, as when prices are fixed by government during a war, everyone is impressed with the complexity of the priority and rationing schemes which must be instituted to perform these functions. Indeed, in each such period it seems necessary to relearn the elementary lesson that in the absence of a free price system, other forms of market control are required.

The experiences in World War II provide innumerable examples of the difficulty in achieving by conscious direction the many-sided

* Our individual supply curve became a demand curve at certain prices (section MN of Figure 48). It is convenient to add this section in as a portion of the demand. The RS section representing short sales is really a part of the future's market; as an approximation, however, it may be taken to influence the current price equally.

balancing that is required of a price system. If the prices are frozen at the levels of a certain period, as they almost invariably are, every peculiarity of that period is perpetuated. A fresh vegetable may not have moved in accustomed quantities to a particular city because of a transport strike; the relatively high price in that city means that it will receive an unusually large share of the vegetable for the duration of the price ceilings, and competing markets relatively less. Or growth of the city due to expansion of war industries will lead to lower per capita supplies because price ceilings make it impossible for this city to increase its bids against other cities which have lost population. Again, it is only when prices are fixed that one is implored at one season to consume a commodity in the largest possible amounts, and a few months later warned of a "shortage."

It should be observed in this connection that errors in price-fixing are in part corrected and in part concealed by the operation of rationing, which is in effect a second price system. If the depopulated city has not sufficient "points," goods will be more easily procured in that city than in a city which has grown rapidly (where coupons are in extreme cases only hunting licenses), but there will be no obvious piling up of supplies.

Even if silver money were to be completely replaced by a colored plastic wampum, it should be evident that prices would persist. In substance, prices are merely the terms of acquisition. Things which are scarce obviously must be more difficult to acquire than those which are plentiful, and the difficulties of acquirement represent the true prices. There is no difference in principle — although a perceptible one in efficiency — between paying twice as much for one commodity as another and waiting twice as long in a queue.

II. SHORT-RUN NORMAL PRICE

Short-run normal price emerges when the firm has a definitely fixed size of plant and the industry has a fixed number of firms. "Plant" is a generic concept: it includes all productive services whose quantities are temporarily fixed for the firm. The most obvious illustration is specialized equipment (buildings and machinery) owned or leased for definite periods by the firm. Any other productive services (e.g., insurance) which are contracted for considerable periods of time are also a part of plant, and custom dictates that the firm retain executives and certain types of laborers even when reduced output would make them temporarily dispensable.

Of course the "short-run" period merges into the "market" period at one end and into the "long-run" period at the other. Two later sections, on inventories and quasi-long-run phenomena, will be devoted to some of the relations between these periods. For the time being, however, it will greatly simplify the analysis if we treat the short run as a very rigid concept, and consider all costs to be either completely fixed or completely variable.

I. *THE INDIVIDUAL SUPPLIER*

The short-run cost curves of the firm have already been developed in the preceding chapter. To determine the output of a firm, we must also know its demand curve and the purpose for which it is operated. We shall assume, with respect to purpose, that the entrepreneur seeks to maximize money profits.* The demand curve is a *datum* at this point in the analysis. At a given time there is a ruling price for a commodity in a competitive market. Since the products of all firms are homogeneous, no firm can sell any amount above the ruling price, but it can sell any amount within its productive capacity at the ruling price. Price is constant to the firm.

TABLE 13

Output	Price	Average Cost	Total Receipts	Total Cost	Net Profit	Marginal Cost
11	$14	$16.40	$154	$180	− $26	—
12	14	15.85	168	190	− 22	$10
13	14	15.50	182	201	− 19	11
14	14	15.20	196	213	− 17	12
15	14	15.07	210	226	− 16	13
16	14	15.00	224	240	− 16	14
17	14	15.00	238	255	− 17	15
18	14	15.06	252	271	− 19	16

* It would be possible to include objectives, such as a desire for an easy life, by use of the indifference curve apparatus. See B. Higgins, "Reply," *American Economic Review*, XXX (1940), 349–350, and literature cited.

It is a matter of simple arithmetic to determine the maximum profit output, once the costs and the demand curve of the firm are known. The data given in Table 13 will serve as an illustration. In this particular case price is less than average cost at any output, so losses must be incurred. But at an output of 15 or 16, losses are at a minimum; hence the entrepreneur will operate at one of these outputs. To be specific, let us always take the larger output (16) when two yield equal profits or losses.

Instead of going through such computations each time, it is easier to follow a general rule: <u>the entrepreneur maximizes profits</u>

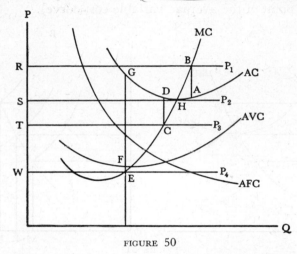

FIGURE 50

(or minimizes losses) at the output whose marginal cost equals price. This is evidently true at output 16. The reason for the rule is fairly obvious: marginal cost is the amount an additional unit of output adds to total cost; price is the amount it adds to total receipts. As long as price exceeds marginal cost, the entrepreneur will expand output, since then he will be adding more to total receipts than to total costs. When marginal cost exceeds price, he will contract output, for then he will be reducing total receipts less than he reduces total cost.

The graphical determination of output is analogous (Figure 50). At price P_1, the firm will operate at output RB and make profits of AB per unit; at price P_2 the firm will operate at output SH, with zero profits; and at price P_3, the firm will operate at output TC, with losses CD per unit. At price P_4, however, a new element enters. If the firm operated at *WE*, its losses would be *EG* per unit, but if the plant were closed down, its losses would equal only total fixed costs, or *WE* times *FG*. More generally, the competitive firm will never produce at a price less than minimum average variable cost, for then the "out-of-pocket" costs are not completely covered — it is cheaper to close down.

Let us define the supply schedule of a competitive firm; it is a list of quantities that will be supplied at all possible prices. Since the firm always operates where marginal cost equals price, the short-run supply curve of a firm is its marginal cost curve (above the minimum point of the average variable cost curve).

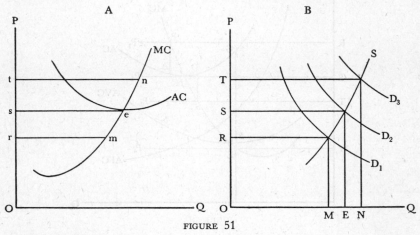

FIGURE 51

II. *THE MARKET*

The market demand curve has already been derived (see Chapters 5 and 6). If the tastes and incomes of consumers are specified, and if the prices of substitutes are constant, there exists a unique set of quantities of a commodity which will be purchased at various prices.

In the short run, when the size of plants is fixed, the number of firms must also necessarily be fixed. The short-run supply curve of the industry is then merely the (horizontal) sum of the supply curves of the individual firms. The determination of short-run normal price then follows readily: it is the price which equates quantity supplied to quantity demanded, where quantity supplied is, for each firm, established by equating marginal cost to price. The graphs for one firm and the industry are given in Figure 51.

If D_1 is the demand curve, price will be R, and the firm will operate
at rm; with D_2 as the demand curve, price will be S, and the output
of the firm se; with D_3 as the demand curve, price will be T, and
output of the firm tn.

If the price of the fixed service rises when the industry expands its
output from OM to ON, it will be necessary to redraw the average
cost curve of each firm at a higher level, but the marginal cost
curves of the firms and hence the supply curve of the industry will
remain unchanged.* But if the price of the variable service rises
as the industry expands, the average variable cost curve, and hence
the marginal cost curve, of each firm must be redrawn. This effect
has already been analyzed (see page 144). The net effect is to make
the short-run supply curve of the industry steeper than it would
otherwise be.

III. LONG–RUN NORMAL PRICE

Long-run normal price rules after a period sufficiently long to
permit an entrepreneur to build a plant any size he wishes (including zero, i.e., leave the industry). There are long-run periods of
expansion and of contraction, and these two will seldom be equal in
length. Thus it may take 20 years to expand an orchard by growing
new trees; it will take only a week to chop down the existing
orchard. Conversely, it requires only a few years to build a dam
for a hydroelectric unit, but the dam will last for generations.

I. *THE INDIVIDUAL SUPPLIER*

The full range of long-run alternatives open to the firm are represented by its long-run average cost curve (Figure 52). Let us assume
that RP_1 is the price line (demand curve) and SAC_1 the currently
operated plant. The firm's short-run output is of course RQ, for
here marginal cost is equal to price. If the long-run average cost
curve declines continuously, the firm will expand its plant and make
enormous profits. In fact, no matter how much the firm expands,
its (average and total) profits will increase. Eventually it will become so big that it cannot sensibly ignore the effect of its output on
price, and the demand curve will turn down (TN in Figure 52).
But the industry is then organized into one or a few firms, and
monopoly or oligopoly replaces competition. *Decreasing long-run*

* See Chapter 8, page 143.

average costs and competition are incompatible. Eventually the long-run average cost curve must rise or competition will disappear.

We will henceforth assume that diseconomies of large-scale production set in soon enough to insure numerous firms and therefore competition. But in the long run the firm will build a larger plant — either SAC_2 or SAC_3 (see Figure 53). If the price were expected to stay at RP_1, the firm would expand to the output RQ, where long-run marginal cost equals price. This would be a position of maximum profits, for at smaller outputs a unit increase of output

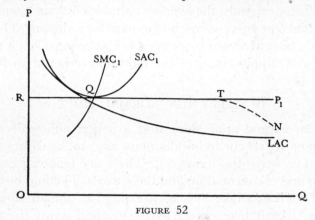

FIGURE 52

would add more to total receipts than to total costs, and at larger outputs a unit decrease of output would reduce total costs more than total receipts.

But it would be impossible for the price to remain at RP_1 in the long run. It follows from our very definition of costs that in the long run average cost must equal price. Costs are the amount that these productive services could earn elsewhere. If price exceeds average cost, resources earn more in this industry than elsewhere; so new firms will enter the industry, and their additions to output will eventually force the price down to minimum long-run average cost. On the other hand, if price were less than minimum long-run average cost, firms would leave the industry because the productive services could earn more elsewhere. In long-run competitive equilibrium, therefore, the firm will operate at price DD_1, plant SAC_2, and output C. At this price and output, long-run marginal cost = long-run average cost = short-run marginal cost = short-run average cost = price.

Since there is only one price for a homogeneous product under competition, this argument must assume that the minimum long-run average costs of all firms in the industry are equal. But why should any firm have lower costs than its rivals? The reply is probably that some firms have superior productive services — better managers, better location, or some such advantage. For example, the superior resource, say, unusually well-located land, might save $.01 per unit of output on transportation costs, or a

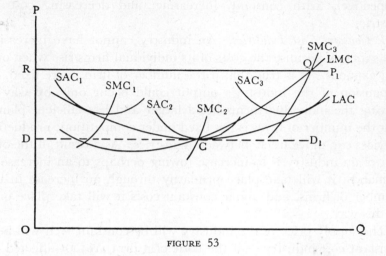

FIGURE 53

total of $10,000 per year. But then any entrepreneur in this industry would offer $10,000 more rent per year for this plot than for other plots. (Actually he might offer only $500 more at first, but competition would force the rental offer up to the saving in transportation costs.) Therefore the firm which secured the resource would have to pay a higher rent, and its costs would equal those of other firms — i.e., it would have lower transportation costs but higher land costs. If the firm owns the superior resource, correct accounting will dictate a write-up of the capital value of the resource. All firms will have equal minimum long-run average costs. But they need not be of equal size, and most probably the firm with more efficient resources will be larger.*

* It is shown in Chapter 10 that in equilibrium the marginal productivities of all productive services must be proportional to their prices. Since the price of a superior service is higher, its marginal productivity must be higher. This higher marginal productivity is secured by using more of the other factors of production — the output of the firm is larger.

II. *THE MARKET*

The derivation of the long-run supply curve of the industry hinges on the theorem just proved: that each firm will be operating at minimum long-run average cost, and this cost will equal the price. In addition, we shall require a knowledge of external economies and diseconomies, which were taken up in Chapter 8. It will be convenient to break the analysis down into three parts, dealing respectively with constant, increasing, and decreasing cost industries.

1. Constant Cost Industries. An industry cannot have increasing costs merely because the costs of its individual firms rise when output expands. It is true that if the number of firms were fixed, an expansion of the industry's output could occur only by way of having the individual firms build larger and less efficient plants. But the number of firms is not fixed under competition; productive services can move freely between industries. As a result, if the output of an industry is to increase (owing perhaps to an increase of demand), it will take place primarily through an increase in the number of firms, and under constant costs it will take place only in this way.

The supply price of the industry will be constant — it will be a constant cost industry — if the costs of a firm are not affected by the number of firms. Aside from technical external economies (which are not very important and may be disregarded here), the method by which the number of firms affects one firm's costs is through the prices of the productive services. In a constant cost industry, the number of firms has no effect on the prices of productive services. There is only one condition under which this is true: prices of productive services will not be affected by the size of the industry when the industry uses only a small fraction of the total supply of each productive service. The hairpin industry uses little steel, little skilled labor, and little machinery; hence it can probably expand in size without driving up the prices of productive services. The housing industry uses much skilled labor and much of certain materials, so if it expanded, prices of services would be sure to rise. The former industry must approach constant costs, the latter increasing costs.

The relationship between the cost curves of a firm and the supply curve of the industry are exhibited in Figure 54. At first, the industry is in equilibrium, with demand curve D_1, short-run supply curve S_1 (the sum of the marginal cost curves of the firms), price R, output Rt for one firm, and output RT for the industry. Now assume that the demand suddenly rises to D_2. The immediate effect is for the price to rise to S, where the quantity demanded equals the (short-run) quantity supplied. But each firm is now making profits; so new firms enter the industry. As each additional firm enters, the short-run supply curve shifts slightly to the right, since it is now the sum of a larger number of short-run marginal

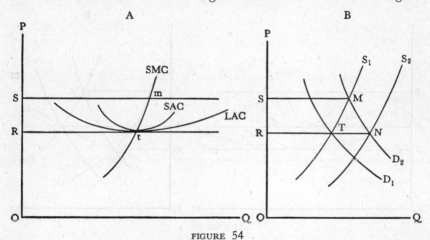

FIGURE 54

cost curves. Eventually the short-run supply curve will become S_2, and the price will have fallen to R again.* Since profits have disappeared, the industry is again in long-run equilibrium. The long-run supply curve of the industry is made up of such points as T and N, and it is of course a horizontal line.

2. *Increasing Cost Industries.* The formal analysis of an increasing cost industry begins in exactly the same way as for a constant cost industry. Let D_1 and S_1 be the demand and short-run supply curves of the industry, with price R, and output Rq for the firm and RQ for the industry (Figure 55). The industry is clearly in long-run equilibrium. Again let the demand curve shift up to D_2, with an immediate rise of price to S and large profits for each firm. New firms will enter the industry, attracted by these profits.

* If all of the firms have minimum average costs at the same output, the number of firms will increase by TN/Rt.

At this point a new element enters if this is an increasing cost industry. The prices of certain of the productive services will rise as the demand for them increases. Such price rises will be necessary to attract the additional quantities of the productive services away from other industries (and localities). Two phenomena will explain the necessity for higher prices. First, the additional units of the productive services may be less suitable for employment in this industry, and then their cost to the industry rises in terms of productivity, even if their price does not rise. Second, as other industries lose labor and restrict output, the remaining quantities of

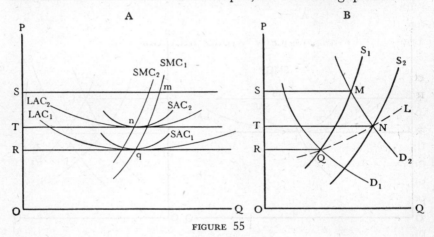

FIGURE 55

productive services become more valuable because they have higher marginal products and their products command higher prices.*

Therefore, as the number of firms increases, the costs of each firm will rise, and this is shown by the higher cost curves in Figure 55A. There will be two forces working on the short-run supply curve (S_1). On the one hand, the increased number of firms will shift it to the right; on the other hand, each individual marginal cost curve shifts to the left. The former influence must dominate.†

---

* This is likely to be true even if the increased demand (D_2) is merely a shift from other products, for rarely will the former object and the new object of consumer demand require the same resources in the same proportions.

† This can be proved as follows: If the entrance of one new firm raised (i.e., shifted to the left) the sum of the marginal cost curves of the existing firms by as much as the output of the new firm, then the new firm must have drawn all of its productive resources from the firms already in the industry. But all of the productive services of the industry cannot be absolutely fixed in supply. Hence the new firm will hire some new services, and its output will more than offset the restriction of output of the existing firms.

Eventually this short-run supply curve will arrive at S_2, with price T, and at this price the new minimum average costs are just covered. The industry is again in long-run equilibrium. The long-run supply curve of the industry is made up of points like Q and N, and they are points on a rising curve (L).

3. *Decreasing Cost Industries.* A brief word may be added on decreasing cost industries, more for the sake of comprehensiveness than because this category is likely to be important. An industry will operate subject to decreasing costs if on balance the prices of productive services fall when this industry expands. Two main reasons exist for falling supply curves of productive services. First, this industry may buy from another decreasing cost industry. There is nothing logically wrong with this explanation, but it smacks of lifting (or rather, lowering) oneself by one's bootstraps. Second, this industry may buy from a monopoly — and it is perfectly possible for a monopoly to operate in a region of decreasing average costs, as will be shown later. But even this alternative is not too attractive, since it does not necessarily follow that because the demand curve of a monopolist shifts to the right, he will cut his price (unless, of course, the price is regulated, as with public utilities). The situation of decreasing costs must be rare in competitive industries; its geometrical analysis can be left to the reader.

4. *Sraffa's Case.* As the foregoing discussion suggests, it is always possible to draw an unambiguous supply curve for a competitive industry, but Sraffa has pointed out that "the" demand curve may not exist.* Suppose that increasing cost industry A expands its output, owing perhaps to a fall in costs (because of a technological improvement), and as a result hires more productive services. The prices of these services will rise, and industry B (which also uses these services) will experience an upward shift of its cost curves. Industry B must raise its selling price, and if its product is a close substitute for or complement to that of industry A, the latter's demand curve will shift. Hence the demand curve of industry A will depend indirectly on the output of industry A, and a new demand curve will have to be drawn for each output. Illustrations of this double (cost and demand) relationship between commodities are

* See Sraffa, Piero, "The Laws of Returns under Competitive Conditions," *Economic Journal*, **XXXVI** (1926), 535–550; also "Sulle relazioni fra costo e quantita prodotta," *Annali di Economia*, **II** (1925–26), 277–328.

common in agriculture, for instance, in the case of different kinds of wheat.

IV. INTERPERIOD RELATIONSHIPS

The foregoing classification of prices as market, short-run normal, and long-run normal, is of course a great simplification of reality. As such it has important uses, but it may be of interest to indicate some of the interperiod relationships which operate to diminish the sharpness of the Marshallian classification. Certain aspects of the theory of inventories will be discussed first, for inventories are an important channel through which adjacent short-run periods influence one another. Thereafter the more detailed relationships between short- and long-run periods will be examined.

1. *INVENTORIES*

Inventories are perhaps the most important link between the prices and outputs of adjacent short periods of time. Since dates and periods are so important in this matter, it is necessary to define them more precisely. Suppose that the short-run normal period of production of a commodity — the period within which plant is fixed — is one year. The firm may make its production plans by months, and within each month it will adhere to the plan made at its beginning unless its expectations concerning future prices and costs are badly shaken by new developments. Our theory will apply to its decision on the first of any month to produce more or less than it sells in that month (i.e., whether to build up or run down inventories). And even between short-run normal periods, when it decides to expand or contract its plant, inventories will play a part in the transition.

In a stationary economy inventories would be carried only because of discontinuities in production or sales. Wheat stocks would have to be carried through crop years since the rate of consumption is more stable than the rate of production, and conversely, it would be cheaper to produce and store some electric fans during the winter because of the high marginal costs entailed by concentrating production in the spring and early summer. Except to the extent that production or consumption was influenced by unexpected factors (droughts and cold summers, respectively, in our examples), however, stocks would vary little from year to year.

But most short-run analyses are uninteresting under stationary conditions; the real complications in inventory analysis arise out of uncertainty. The entrepreneur does not know the precise dates on which he will sell specific products.* Otherwise purchases would be coordinated with sales, and only a minimum of stock would be on the shelves at any one time. This minimum would be governed by the cost of ordering and delivering the goods in the case of dealers, and by the additional cost of sporadic production in the case of producers.

This factor of uncertainty, however, would not lead to rapid or wide fluctuations of inventories. The relevant gains from having a stock of a commodity are things such as customer good will, elimination of the expense of many small orders, and the extra cost of a nonuniform rate of production. The costs of inventories are interest on investment and storage costs. These factors usually do not fluctuate greatly; so inventories themselves would be stable except for periodic fluctuations due to seasonal influences.

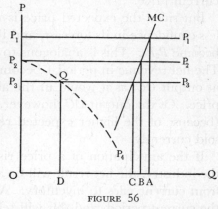

FIGURE 56

A second factor in inventory decisions is much more variable: the anticipated prices and costs in the next planning period. If the selling price is expected to rise, it will be profitable to build up present inventories; if costs are expected to decline, it will be profitable to let inventories run down. Since expectations of future prices are frequently, and sometimes radically, revised, this is the dominant factor in temporary fluctuations of inventories.

The detailed process of determination of inventory size may be explained with reference to Figure 56.† (The analysis is restricted to future price expectations for simplicity; the expectation of a

---

* As a result, his own orders to replenish supplies are uncertain in size and date. Uncertainty extends backward through the production process. However, there will be some cancellation: one grocer's tardiness in buying may be offset by another's unusually early purchases.

† See E. S. Shaw, "Elements of a Theory of Inventory," *Journal of Political Economy*, XLVIII (1940), 465–485.

change in costs could easily be introduced.) The present price is P_3; the mean expected price next "month" is P_1; and the discounted price (expected price minus storage costs) is P_2. Marginal costs are expected to be the same in both months.

At this point we must recapitulate what was said before on the effect of dispersion and skewness of the distribution of probabilities of various future prices.

If the net expected price were certain, the firm would produce quantity OB in period 1 and OA in period 2 and sell all of the output $(OA + OB)$ in the second period. It would be absurd to sell now when the future price was certain to exceed storage costs plus current price.

But since the expected price is not certain, the firm will place less confidence in its forecast, and the net expected price curve will become P_2P_4. This is analogous to the falling of MN in Figure 48. The net revenue in period 1 becomes P_2QP_3, and the firm operates at output OC, as it would in the absence of an anticipated rise in price. Of the output OC, however, OD will be held until period 2 (because of the higher expected return per unit) and DC will be sold currently.

If the anticipation of a price rise is held generally throughout the industry, the net result will be a substantial diversion of output from current sales to inventory. As a result, the price will rise in the current period, and this will tend to restrict inventory growth. Prices in the next period, on the other hand, will be decreased because of the unloading of inventories. In the limiting case of perfect knowledge, the price will rise in period 2 only by an amount sufficient to cover the carrying costs of inventory.

ii. *A RE-EXAMINATION OF THE SHORT RUN* *

We may begin with a somewhat more critical analysis of the short-run cost curves of a competitive firm. The third assumption underlying the law of variable proportions is that the "fixed" productive services can be adapted in form to the varying quantities of the variable services; in our previous example 10 shovels could be changed into 11 of equal total value (see page 122). In the short run, however, the fixed services are usually fixed in form as well as

* This section is essentially a summary of portions of the article, George J. Stigler, "Production and Distribution in the Short Run," *Journal of Political Economy*, XLVII (1939), 305–327.

in quantity; full adaptability can usually be secured only by wearing out a plant and then replacing it with a new plant of the desired form.* Hence in the short run there will usually be imperfect adaptability, and this phenomenon calls for certain modifications in the theory of short-run cost curves.

The effect of imperfect adaptation on the shapes of the cost curves depends upon the extent to which the fixed services are divisible. If the plant consists of 100 identical machines, each of which can be used only with one laborer, a fixed quantity of raw materials, etc., then a machine will be dropped from use each time output falls by

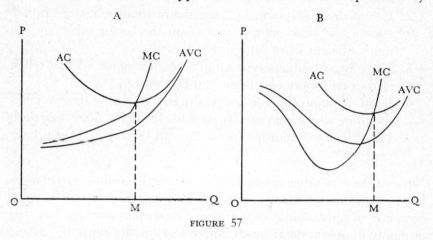

FIGURE 57

1 per cent of "capacity." This is a case of short-run constant returns; so the marginal and average variable costs will be constant up to the point where all of the machines are used, and thereafter output from the plant cannot be increased. If there is some adaptability, the curves will look like those in Figure 57A. If the plant is indivisible and possesses no adaptability whatever, the marginal and average variable cost curves would become vertical lines since only one output would be possible. With partial adaptability the curves would take on the shapes shown in Figure 57B.

There would be nothing to add to this discussion of imperfect adaptability if the entrepreneur could be certain that he would always operate at output OM. But if he anticipates fluctuations of price and output, as is almost always the case, he will seek a more

* There are exceptions like agricultural land, which can be combined efficiently with varying amounts of plowing, seed, etc., within relatively wide limits.

flexible production plan. The reason for seeking flexibility is that at outputs much less than or much in excess of *OM*, the firm is very inefficient in the use of fixed or variable services. The entrepreneur will deliberately build a plant which is more flexible in the sense that it is relatively efficient over a considerable range of outputs — at the cost, however, of being less efficient at "capacity" (i.e., output *OM* in Figure 57). Some devices which may be used to increase flexibility are:

1. Inventories, except in the case of goods which cannot be stored.
2. Use of divisible plant, i.e., use many small machines rather than a few large ones, even though the larger machines are more efficient when fully utilized.
3. Use more variable services and a smaller plant, so that when output falls more cost items can be reduced.
4. Build a plant capable to producing several different commodities whose outputs are not likely to fluctuate together. (The theory of multiple products will be discussed in a later chapter.)

None of these or other methods of achieving flexibility is free, however, so the entrepreneur must make some compromise between economy of operation at outputs near minimum average cost and economy of operation at much larger and smaller outputs.

So far we have assumed that there is a unique short-run normal period, but there are two important reasons why there is no clear-cut distinction between short and long periods. In the first place, "plant" is really a portmanteau concept. It includes some productive services which are fixed for only a short period — for instance, an insurance policy may have only three days to run. At the other extreme the fixity may be almost permanent, as when a factory site is leased for 99 years. Normally the individual elements of plant will be fixed for a whole array of periods. The longer the short-run period, the greater will be the number of costs that become variable. Any particular classification of costs between fixed and variable is valid only for one specified time period.

But, secondly, it is unrealistic to view plant replacement or expansion as purely a technological or legal phenomenon (i.e., when a machine wears out or a contract expires). Of course technological factors are important for they affect the cost of changing the size of plant; it is more efficient to build a large plant *de novo* than to achieve the same size by piecemeal additions to a smaller plant. If for some reason the entrepreneur becomes convinced that his plant is too large or too small, he will generally make alterations in that plant. The extent and time of the alterations will be governed by the cost of making them and by the gains which will accrue from possessing a plant of more appropriate size. The short-run alterations may be in either direction, but usually it is easier to expand than to contract a plant, for the technical rate at which a plant wears out is a more serious obstacle in the latter case. The net effect of a plant expansion is to shift the marginal cost curve to the right in the relevant regions; it is impossible to say in general whether it will become more or less elastic.

The upshot of this discussion is that one cannot distinguish between fixed and variable costs in any period of time only on the basis of technological and legal limitations on the entrepreneur's control over costs. In addition one must know his expectations with respect to future costs and selling prices. Costs which may be rigid if the price of a product is $10 will probably become variable if the price rises to $25 and is expected to remain at that level for some time.

RECOMMENDED READINGS

(See also references to Chapter 8.)

1. Marshall, A., *Principles of Economics*, 8th ed., Macmillan, London, 1920, Bk. V, Chs. 5, 8–13, 15.
2. Knight, Frank H., "Cost of Production and Price over Long and Short Periods," *Journal of Political Economy*, XXIX (1921), 304–335, reprinted in *The Ethics of Competition*, Harper, New York, 1935.
3. Hart, A. G., *Anticipations, Uncertainty and Dynamic Planning*, University of Chicago, Chicago, 1940.

PROBLEMS

1. Utilizing the costs given in problem 1, Chapter 8, draw the total cost curve of the firm. On the same graph draw the total revenue curve, on the assumption that the price is $16. Ascertain the output at which total revenue is most in excess of total cost, i.e., where net profit is maximized. Prove that this method is equivalent to equating marginal cost to price. (Remember that marginal cost is the slope of the total cost curve; see page 48.)

2. A general problem in pricing. (This is a summary of a problem given by Professor Henry C. Simons, in *Economics 201: Materials and Problems for Class Discussion*, University of Chicago, Chicago, n.d.)

This problem relates to an industry consisting of 1,000 firms which produce a completely standardized product. The industry is highly competitive. Each firm owns and operates one plant, which is of the most efficient size. (This is equivalent to saying that the short-run average cost curve lies at the bottom of the long-run average cost curve.) All firms have identical costs, and these costs are given in problem 1, Chapter 8. The demand curve is given by

$$pq = \$255,000.$$

The first task is to make out a demand schedule, and incorporate it in your solution as Appendix 1.

Part i

1. Draw the supply curve (i.e., the sum of the marginal cost curves) and demand curve of the industry on the same graph (Figure 1). Read off the equilibrium price and quantity. Prove that the answer is correct by comparing quantities supplied and demanded at (*a*) a price $1.00 higher, (*b*) a price $1.00 lower.
2. Draw the cost and demand curves of the individual firm on the same graph (Figure 2). Accompany these graphs with detailed textual explanation of their construction.

Part ii

Congress now unexpectedly imposes a tax of $4 per unit on the manufacture of this commodity. The tax becomes effective immediately and remains in effect indefinitely. Assume
   a. No changes in the economic system other than those attributable to the tax.
   b. None of the changes due to the tax has any effect on the prices of productive services used by this industry. (This assumption will be dropped later.)
1. Draw the new supply curve and the demand curve of the industry (Figure 3). Read off the new equilibrium price.
2. Draw the new cost curves and demand curve of the individual firm (Figure 4). Explain the details of the construction of these graphs.
3. Why can the price not remain as low as $15?
4. Why can the price not rise to and remain at $19?
5. Precisely what would happen if the price remained for a time at $16?
6. At precisely what level would the price become temporarily stable? What does it mean to say that this is an equilibrium level?
7. Suppose the short-run equilibrium price to be $17. How would you answer the query:

"I don't see why every firm should produce 15 units per day when the price is $17. It would make just as much if it produced only 14, for the 15th unit adds just as much to expenses as it adds to revenues." Precisely what would happen if some firms produced 14 units per day and others 15 units?

8. Would short-run equilibrium be reached at a higher or lower price (and with larger or smaller output) if the elasticity of demand were lower (less than unity)? If it were higher (greater than unity)?

9. What would happen if demand had an elasticity of zero? An elasticity of infinity?

Part iii

As Figure 4 will reveal, the new minimum average cost is $19. The short-run equilibrium price was $17; hence this industry becomes unattractive as an investment, relative to other industries. As plants are worn out, therefore, they will not be replaced; plants will be junked sooner; and even maintenance will be reduced. To simplify the problem, we assume:

  a. Each plant has a life of 1,000 weeks.
  b. The plants in the industry are staggered so that, at the time the tax was imposed, there is one plant 1 week old, one plant 2 weeks old, etc.
  c. At the time the tax was imposed, 20 plants were so near completion that it is impossible to divert them to other uses. These are completed at one-week intervals.

Hence for 20 weeks the price will stay at $17, and then rise gradually as entrepreneurs fail to replace worn-out plants.

1. What will the situation be at the end of the 25th week? (Answer in terms of "greater than" or "less than.")

2. When 120 weeks have passed (900 plants left), will the price be above or below $18? Explain carefully.

3. How many weeks must pass (how many plants must be scrapped) before the price rises to $18? Explain precisely.

4. Will the output per plant increase or decrease as the number of plants declines?

5. When 220 weeks have passed (800 plants left), will the price be above or below $19?

6. How many plants must be scrapped before the price rises precisely to $19?

7. What would the price be if the number of plants declined to 750? What would be the output per plant? What would happen to the number of plants?

8. What happens to the short-run supply curve of the industry as the number of plants diminishes? Draw, on the same graph (Figure 5), the supply curve when there are 1,000 firms and 800 firms. Compute elasticities of supply for these two curves at a given price.

9. How could the process of adjustment, and the final equilibrium, be different
   a. If the elasticity of demand were greater than unity?
   b. If the elasticity of demand were less than unity?
      (The significant points are: (1) price, (2) output per plant immediately after the tax is imposed, and (3) number of plants and total output at the new long-run equilibrium.)

Part iv

Finally, the prices of the productive services will be affected by the purchases of the industry. Some of the services will be specialized: Larger quantities can be secured only at higher prices, and smaller quantities can be secured at lower prices. Assume that all of these services are "fixed," and that all variable services are unspecialized (i.e., any quantity can be secured by the industry at a constant price).

1. Will the short-run effects of the tax be any different than they were in Part 2? Explain in detail.
2. How will the long-run adjustment differ? Will the final price be more or less than $19, and the daily output more or less than 13,421? Again explain in detail.
3. Suppose that a special and scarce kind of land is required for production of the taxed commodity, and that this land is not used (or within practicable limits usable at all) in the production of any other commodity, and that all other resources are completely unspecialized. What is likely to be the effect of the tax on the price of the use of such land (on its rent)?
4. Suppose that this special and scarce land is also used in one other industry. Will the rent of this land fall more or less, if the demand for the product of this second industry is elastic or inelastic?

CHAPTER 10

PRICING OF PRODUCTIVE SERVICES UNDER COMPETITION

The pricing of productive services differs in only one important respect from the pricing of consumers' goods. Entrepreneurs, or firms, sell consumers' goods and buy productive services (which include products of other firms); consumers of course buy consumers' goods, and in their capacity as owners of productive resources, sell productive services. Because of this circular relationship between the markets for consumers' goods and productive services, a good deal of the theory of pricing of productive services has already been implied in the preceding chapters, and the present chapter can be viewed as a systematization and elaboration of familiar subject matter from a different viewpoint.

It must be observed that the prices of productive services, and not the prices of productive resources, are under study at this point. Our problem is to explain rent per year, for instance, and not the value of an acre of land. The valuation of productive resources which yield income over a considerable period of time requires an interest rate because future services must be discounted. The theory of the interest rate, and the consequent valuation of productive resources, is taken up at a later point.

We shall begin with the study of the demand curve of a firm for a productive service, and then extend the results to a whole economy. Thereafter supply factors will be considered.

I. THE DEMAND OF THE FIRM

In explaining consumer demand it was necessary to postulate an objective of consumer choice to satisfy wants as fully as possible. Similarly, in explaining the demand of a firm for a productive service, we require an objective for the firm's activity. By almost universal agreement this objective is held to be the maximization of net profits. Given this objective, the laws of return, and the prices of productive services and the product (these prices are independent of the firm's activities under competition), the demand for a productive service is easily established.

The derivation of the demand schedule for a service is illustrated by the hypothetical data in Table 14. Columns (4) and (7) represent market prices, and columns (1), (2), and (3) are based on the law of variable proportions. Total cost, column (5), is equal to the cost of the variable service, column (4) times column (1), plus the cost of the fixed services, which is assumed to be $20. Net profit reaches a maximum at an input of 6 or 7 units of the variable productive service, and again, to be specific, let us take the larger quantity.

Rather than follow such a laborious arithmetical procedure each time, a fundamental rule may be derived and utilized. A unit of a productive service adds an amount to total cost equal to its price; it adds an amount to total receipts equal to its marginal physical product times the price of the product. An employer will continue to add units of a service as long as they add more to receipts than to costs — in other words, as long as the value of the marginal product is greater than, or equal to, the price of the service. Thus, at 7 units of the service, the value of the marginal product is equal to the price of the service, $20.

We emerge with the fundamental principle: the demand curve of a competitive firm for a productive service is equal to the curve of the value of the marginal product of that service. Since, as was shown above (page 124), a competitive firm always operates in the region of diminishing marginal product for each productive service, the demand curve for a service must fall throughout the effective region.

This analysis assumes that the quantities of all of the productive services except one have already been established, but this assumption is easily dropped. Suppose there are three productive services, A, B, and C. The following equations must hold (where MPP is marginal physical product, p is the price of the product, and p with a subscript is the price of a service):

$$MPP_a \times p = p_a$$
$$MPP_b \times p = p_b$$
$$MPP_c \times p = p_c$$

TABLE 14

(1) Quantity of the Productive Service	(2) Total Physical Product	(3) Marginal Physical Product	(4) Price of the Service	(5) Total Cost of the Service	(6) Total Cost	(7) Price of the Product	(8) Total Receipts	(9) Net Profit	(10) Value of the Marginal Product
1	60	60	$20	$20	$40	$0.50	$30	– $10	$30
2	130	70	20	40	60	.50	65	5	35
3	210	80	20	60	80	.50	105	25	40
4	280	70	20	80	100	.50	140	40	35
5	340	60	20	100	120	.50	170	50	30
6	390	50	20	120	140	.50	195	55	25
7	430	40	20	140	160	.50	215	55	20
8	460	30	20	160	180	.50	230	50	15
9	480	20	20	180	200	.50	240	40	10
10	490	10	20	200	220	.50	245	25	5

These three equations are sufficient in number to determine simultaneously the quantities the firm will employ of each of the productive services, A, B, and C. By simple manipulation, moreover, these equations yield a famous theorem, for

$$\frac{MPP_a}{p_a} = \frac{MPP_b}{p_b} = \frac{MPP_c}{p_c}$$

That is to say, *the marginal physical products of all productive services must be proportional to their prices.*

I. TOTAL PRODUCT EQUALS SUM OF DISTRIBUTIVE SHARES

A mathematical proof has already been given of the fact that the total product will be exactly sufficient to remunerate the productive

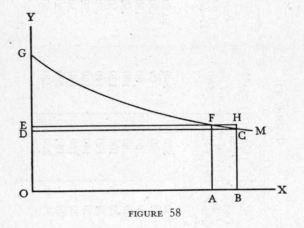

FIGURE 58

services if they are paid the values of their respective marginal products, in competitive equilibrium (page 141, note). Since this theorem is of considerable importance, it is worth while to supplement this with a geometrical demonstration.* The proof is based on Figure 58. Let there be N identical farms in an economy, each tilled with an equal number of laborers. OX represents labor per farm, and OY (and M) the marginal product of labor. If OB labor is applied to a farm, the total product of the farm will be $OBCG$ (see proposition 1, page 46). If labor is paid its marginal product, BC will be the wage rate, $OBCD$ the total wage bill, and the residual, GCD, will be the rent per farm. (This is the method by which rent

* The proof is due to S. J. Chapman. See "The Remuneration of Employers," *Economic Journal*, XVI (1906), 523–528.

is isolated in the Ricardian theory.) Our task is to prove that this residual is precisely the marginal product of land. Once this is shown, it may be concluded that if both land and labor are paid their marginal products, the total product will be exhausted.

The total product of this hypothetical economy is $N \times OBCG$. Now let another farm be added, the total supply of labor remaining constant. The resulting change in the product of the economy is, by definition, the marginal product of land. Each farm will now have less labor (OA), because each has ceded a small amount of labor to the $(N + 1)$th farm. (Obviously $N \times AB = OA$.) The total product of the economy with $(N + 1)$ farms is

$$(N + 1) \times OAFG = N \times OAFG + OAFG.$$

The former product of the economy with N farms was

$$N \times OBCG = N \times OAFG + N \times ABCF.$$

The increase in the total product of the economy due to the $(N + 1)$th farm is therefore

$$N \times OAFG + OAFG - N \times OAFG - N \times ABCF$$
$$= OAFG - N \times ABCF$$
$$= GFE + OAFE - N \times ABCF.$$

But $N \times ABCF = N \times ABHF - N \times FHC$, and $N \times ABHF = OAFE$. Hence the marginal product of $(N + 1)$ farms is

$$GFE + N \times FHC,$$

and the last term ($N \times FHC$) approaches zero as N increases (i.e., as the size of a unit of land decreases). Hence the marginal product of land is equal to rent determined by the residual method, which was to be shown.

II. QUASI RENTS

Up to this point it has tacitly been assumed that long-run equilibrium conditions were under consideration, for the entrepreneur was free to use each productive service in any desired quantity. In the short-run normal period, however, this is not true; certain product services (and resources) are relatively fixed in quantity. These "fixed" services are usually subsumed under the heading of "plant," although it has been pointed out that this usage involves some violence to the everyday meaning of *plant*.

In the short run these productive services will not be reduced in quantity even if they are unprofitable in existing quantities. In general they are highly specialized,* so that the next most profitable alternative uses are so low as rarely to come into consideration.† On the other hand, it usually requires considerable time to expand the amount of such productive services, and hence high returns may continue for some time before increased supplies force down their prices to long-run normal levels. These returns to temporarily specialized productive services are called *quasi rents*.‡

The total quasi rents of a firm are easily illustrated by the usual short-run cost curves of the firm. These are reproduced in Figure

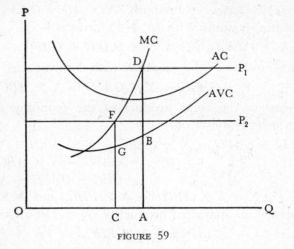

FIGURE 59

59. If the price is P_1, the firm will operate at output OA. The return to the "fixed" services will be BD per unit of output, and $OA \times BD$ are total quasi rents. If price is P_2, output will be OC, and total quasi rents are $OC \times GF$.

This procedure is sufficient to determine total quasi rents, but no

---

* This is an empirical observation, not a corollary of the definition of *fixed* services. If common day labor were hired under annual contract, it would become a "fixed" service, yet it would have alternative uses which yielded products equal to those fixed in the contract.

† The chief of these competing uses are two: possible production in the future, and scrap value. In the case of a material resource, the foregone alternative (or cost) is postponable depreciation (but not obsolescence).

‡ Marshall, who first formulated the theory of quasi rents, defined them as total returns to temporarily specialized services *minus* costs of maintenance and replacement (*Principles of Economics*, 8th ed., Macmillan, London, 1920, p. 426 n.). This definition, unlike that in the text, permits quasi rents to be negative. It is not consistent with our general theory of rents in the sense of noncost outlays (see *supra*, pages 104–105), nor can Marshall's quasi rents easily be illustrated in the conventional cost diagrams of the firm.

such simplicity attaches to the imputation of this total to the various constituent elements of plant. One of several alternative techniques of imputation must be used for this latter purpose. First, if the elements of plant join in variable proportions, it is possible to apply the marginal productivity theory. For example, a farmer may use a varying amount of land (the total of which is temporarily fixed by lease) to secure a given amount of wheat, so land rent may be separated out of total quasi rents. Second, the various elements of plant may combine in fixed proportions — e.g., each machine may require a fixed amount of floor space. Fixity of proportions is probably exceptional in the long-run normal period, but in the short run (and this is the only case in which quasi rents arise) the scope for fixity is very considerable. And here a dichotomy enters.

On the one hand, the elements of plant may be used in other firms and industries in different (although presumably fixed) proportions. Then it is possible to impute separate quasi rents to each element by the use of the principle that under competition the quasi rent of a productive service will be uniform throughout the economy. Suppose 6 units of plant element X and 3 of Y yield total quasi rents of \$75 in industry A and 5 of X and 4 of Y yield \$70 in industry B. In equations,

$$6 X + 3 Y = 75$$
$$5 X + 4 Y = 70$$

Solving these equations, $X = \$10$ and $Y = \$5$. This approach (which is due to Walras) can of course be used for any number of productive services.*

Or alternatively, the various elements of plant may combine in the same fixed ratio in all uses. Since all possibility of variation is absent by hypothesis, there is no scope for imputation of quasi rents. Indeed the combination of elements must be treated as a single productive factor, whether the "elements" are two kinds of machines or the right and left arms of a laborer.

III. THE DETERMINANTS OF DEMAND

The determinants of the demand for a productive service are implicit in the foregoing discussion, but it may be worth while to summarize them explicitly. They are four in number.

* For a more detailed discussion, see George J. Stigler, *Production and Distribution Theories*, Macmillan, New York, 1941, pp. 166 ff., 237 ff.

1. The demand price for a given quantity of a productive service will generally be higher, the greater the quantities of cooperating productive services. This almost self-evident rule follows from two considerations: the price of the product being given, the demand price is proportional to the marginal physical product, and the marginal physical product is greater, the more of the other productive services used in collaboration. The possible exception may be noted: if some of the other services are close substitutes, they amount in effect to an increase in the quantity of the service under consideration, and hence (by the law of diminishing returns) reduce its marginal product.

2. The demand price for a unit of a productive service is lower, the more of the service is employed. This follows from the law of diminishing returns.

3. The demand price for a productive service will be greater, the more valuable the finished product in whose production it is used, for the demand price equals the marginal physical product times the price of the product.

4. Finally, the demand price of a given quantity of a productive service is higher, the more productive the service — i.e., the state of technology is a determinant. An increase in carpenters' productivity, for example, causes a rise in the marginal productivity curve of carpenters' services.

II. THE DEMAND OF THE INDUSTRY AND THE ECONOMY

As is usually the case in such matters, the demand curve of an industry for a productive service is the horizontal sum of the demand curves of the individual firms. This is all that need be said on the level of formal definition, but a certain complication in carrying out the addition is to be explained. In the analysis of the individual firm it is permissible (and indeed necessary) to treat the selling price of the product as constant, for the firm's output does not exert a perceptible influence on price. If the quantities of the services B, C, D, ... are given, a unique marginal productivity curve of A is determined. If this marginal physical product of A is multiplied by the constant price, a single demand curve for the service A is established. But when all firms of an industry vary their outputs, the price of the product must necessarily change. There is thus a different demand curve of the firm for every possible price.

It is not possible completely to explain away this difficulty without moderate use of algebra (which is given below), but the following remarks may suggest the nature of the solution. Let us assume that an industry is in short-run equilibrium: each firm is operating at the output which maximizes net profits (marginal cost = price), and it is producing that output as cheaply as possible (the marginal physical products of the various productive services are proportional to their prices), and the quantity supplied by the industry per unit of time equals the quantity demanded. Suppose now that the price of one of the services (A) falls, perhaps because of the adoption of a new process in its manufacture. Each firm will increase the use of this service, with the following results:

1. The output of the industry will increase, and the price of the finished product will fall.
2. The cheapened service will be substituted in part for the other services, which may lead to
   a. A rise in the price of A, but the price will not return to the previous level.
   b. Decreases in the prices of the other productive services (as a rule; see section 3 below).

Eventually the industry will attain a new short-run equilibrium position. The price of the product will be lower; the use of service A will be increased; and the use of the other services may be either increased or decreased (depending upon the elasticity of demand for the product, the extent to which A can be substituted for the other services, and the direction and extent of changes in the prices of the other services). If the original price of A was $10 and the quantity demanded by the industry 10,000 units, and the new price and quantity demanded are $9 and 12,000, these are two points on the industry's (short-run) demand curve for A.

A similar complication arises when the demand curves of various industries are summed to secure the demand curve of the economy. The demand curve of one industry will depend upon the demand curves of other industries. For example, a reduction in the cost of producing automobiles will lead to a lower price and increased sales, so the industry's demand for steel will increase. This demand of the automobile industry, however, cannot simply be added to the previous demand of the railroads, for the fall in the price of automobiles will lead consumers to shift from train to automobile transportation, thereby reducing the railroads' demand for steel. In general, the change in total demand will be less than the sum of the changes in demands of industries producing substitutes, and the changes in total demand will be greater than the sum of the changes in demands of industries producing complementary goods.

ALGEBRAIC STATEMENT

A more precise explanation of the construction of an industry demand curve is possible if use is made of the conditions of equilibrium. The following conditions, or equations, are at our disposal:

1. In the short-run normal period the number of firms is constant; in the long-run normal period it is determined by the equation,   average cost = price.

2. Sum horizontally the demand curves of the individual firms, and then the demand prices of the various productive services must equal their supply prices.*

   $$MPP_a \times p = \text{supply price of A}$$
   $$MPP_b \times p = \text{supply price of B}$$
   $$MPP_c \times p = \text{supply price of C}$$
   $$\cdots \cdots \cdots \cdots \cdots \cdots$$

3. The demand curve for the product is given, and it is utilized in the relationship,

   quantity demanded = quantity supplied.

If there are n productive services, we have $(n + 2)$ equations, sufficient in number to determine the $(n + 2)$ unknowns: n quantities (or prices) of the productive services demanded, the number of firms, and the price of the product of the industry.†

Since these equations describe the basic forces which govern the input, output, and price of product of an industry, it would require a complicated discussion to examine fully their content. Never-

---

* That is, find the intersection of the demand and supply curves for each of the productive services used by the industry. The supply curve is discussed in section 3 of this chapter. The summing of the demand curves does not affect the form of the left side of these equations, but now MPP_a, for example, is a function of the total quantity of A (and B, C, ...) demanded by the industry, not of that demanded by the firm. (If there are technological external economies, then the demand for a service is also a function of the size of the industry.)

† The output of the industry is of course known once the quantities of the productive services employed are known, since the former is determined by the latter (i.e., the production functions are unique).

theless some elaboration may be useful. Suppose that an industry expands output owing to an increase of demand. Some of the effects of the increase in demand are as follows:

1. In the short-run normal period, it will be profitable to expand the rate of production from existing plants. This can be viewed as either

    a. The expansion of output to the point where marginal cost equals the higher price, or

    b. The hiring of additional productive services until the values of their marginal physical products fall (owing to diminishing returns) until they again equal the prices of the services.*

2. As the quantities of the services employed are increased, some will probably rise in price (see section 3). Their use will accordingly be economized, and the cheaper services will be substituted for them. This shift will temper the rise of prices of very scarce services and probably increase prices of moderately scarce resources. These price changes make the marginal cost curve shift upward (see page 144), and hence serve to restrict the expansion of output.

3. With the passage of time new firms will enter the industry, and established firms will be able to vary the quantities of the "fixed" services. (These two changes need not be simultaneous, of course.) The selling price of the product will fall, profits will decline and eventually disappear, and scarce variable services will be economized in the established plants by substituting more of the fixed services if the latter's prices do not rise.

---

* That these two views are identical can be demonstrated. Let $P = \phi(A, B)$ be the production function, and define total cost as

$$\pi = Ap_a + Bp_b.$$

Writing P and π in differential form,

$$dP = \phi_a dA + \phi_b dB, \tag{i}$$
$$d\pi = p_a dA + p_b dB. \tag{ii}$$

Dividing $d\pi$ by dP we have

$$\text{marginal cost} = \frac{d\pi}{dP} = \frac{p_a dA + p_b dB}{\phi_a dA + \phi_b dB}$$

$$= \frac{p_a}{\phi_a} = \frac{p_b}{\phi_b}$$

But the second set of conditions of equilibrium state that

$$\phi_a p = p_a, \quad \text{and} \quad \phi_b p = p_b.$$

Hence these last equations imply that the firm is operating where marginal cost equals price.

The summing of the demand curves of various industries for a given productive service follows an analogous procedure. The demand curve of the automobile industry for steel, in the example used above, depends upon the prices of both automobiles and railroad transportation. Once this fact is introduced into the equations, the difficulty is overcome.

III. THE SUPPLY CURVE OF A PRODUCTIVE SERVICE

The supply curve of a productive service will be considered only with reference to labor, the most important productive factor in an economy, but the discussion will also be applicable to other factors with appropriate alteration of terminology and (not too much) change of emphasis. This exposition will be essentially a selective summary of what is really a very large and complicated subject, but it may be useful to follow a fairly systematic approach.

Three broad questions may be treated briefly. First, the number of human beings will be taken as constant. In the early nineteenth century the theory of population was a fundamental part of economics; in recent times the population problem has generally been delegated to sociologists, especially in America. In part this abandonment by the economists reflected a proper realization that economic factors alone supply a very inadequate explanation of population movements, but the abandonment has nevertheless been too complete. There is no doubt that economic factors are important: no satisfactory explanation of the decline of population growth, for instance, could exclude the simple fact that children add more to family expenses than to family income. On the other side, a change in the rate of increase of population has extremely important economic effects. Two may be cited: A decline in the rate of increase will raise the average age of the population, with consequent changes in relative demands for, e.g., elementary education and wheel chairs. Second, the housing industry (which is everywhere an important investment industry) may contract very sharply, and this would bring about a whole host of changes throughout the economy.

The second question, the proportion of the population that works, is quantitatively of the same order of importance as the size of population. Between 1930 and 1940 there was a decline from 84.1 to 79.7 per cent in the number of males over 14 who were "gainfully employed" (roughly, working or seeking work); this meant a difference of two and a half million workers. As another example, the proportion of women over 14 who are gainfully employed has risen from an eighth to a fourth since the Civil War, and this change has increased our working force by over six million. Such long-run developments are due primarily to changing social attitudes, but at a given time it appears that higher average annual earnings lead to a decline in the proportion of those who work. The proportion of males between about 20 and 60 and of females between 18 and 25 who work is relatively fixed, but when earnings are high, children go to school longer, men retire earlier, and fewer women work outside the home.* The theoretical analysis which will be given later to explain the determination of hours of work is appropriate also to this case.

The third question, the occupational and geographical distribution of those who work, is a subject on which the economist has considerable to say.† The distribution among occupations is the resultant of many forces. Nature herself places some limitations — only a small portion of the human race could ever become physicists or self-supporting tenors. But, as with consumer preferences, these limits are broad. The more specific explanation is that wages are at equilibrium when the net advantages of different occupations between which individuals can move are equalized for people of equal efficiency. (It should be remembered that the consideration of monopolistic elements has been deferred.)

What are these net advantages? They consist of the net money income of an occupation plus any nonpecuniary advantages or minus any such disadvantages.‡ Some of these advantages are a part of our cultural heritage, e.g., the preference for white-collar work, the prestige of the medicine man, and the contempt for the prostitute. But many are more narrowly economic in nature.

Of these economic determinants, only a few will be mentioned. Cost of education or training is sufficient to explain much, and it

* See E. H. Schoenberg and P. H. Douglas, "Studies in the Supply Curve of Labor," *Journal of Political Economy*, XLV (1937), 45–79.

† See Marshall, *op. cit.*, Bk. VI, Chs. 3–6; A. C. Pigou, *The Economics of Welfare*, 4th ed., Macmillan, London, 1932, Part III, Ch. 9; and S. Kuznets and M. Friedman, *Incomes from Independent Professional Practice*, 1929–1936, National Bureau of Economic Research, *Bulletins* 72–73 (1939).

‡ The determination of net income is not easy; see Marshall, *op. cit.*, pp. 552 ff.

explains even more when allowance is made for the time devoted to training.* Similarly, costs of movement are obviously important in explaining geographical wage differentials. The mean expected income must also be interpreted in light of the dispersion about it. The attitude toward the chance of large gains is highly variable, however: there is no shortage of postmen, although they cannot possibly advance much in rank or pay; nor is there any shortage of movie extras, who are lured by the infinitesimal probability of achieving enormous incomes. Similar remarks could be made concerning the stability of earnings.

In an expanding economy, the supply of labor of an industry can contract relative to the economy merely by recruiting fewer young workers, it can contract absolutely at a rate of perhaps 3 to 5 per cent a year merely by refraining from replacing those who die or retire, and this rate of contraction can easily be doubled by transferences of adult laborers to other industries.† The mobility of laborers between allied occupations is much greater than between industries as a rule, in part because intermediate ranks of skilled laborers are usually filled by promotion from lower ranks in the same industry. It deserves emphasis that relative wage rates ‡ play a fundamental part in such movements. In normal times the occupational pattern of wages is relatively stable; so movements between occupations escape attention (especially since American statistics are very poor in this field). When this pattern is greatly distorted, as in a war economy, the great flexibility of the occupational distribution becomes much more apparent.

The number of hours a laborer will work per week is determined by the relative attractiveness of money income and working, on the one hand, and of leisure, on the other. The formal analysis is easily presented by means of indifference curves. In Figure 60 leisure is measured along OX up to point R, which represents the total number of hours in a week; money income and other amenities of working are measured along OY. When the wage line is AR, the

* Kuznets and Friedman estimate that the annual earnings of a physician must exceed those of a dentist by approximately 17 per cent to compensate for the postponement of income and shorter working life of the physician due to the extra three years of training.

† See H. Makower, J. Marschak, and H. W. Robinson, "Studies in the Mobility of Labour," *Oxford Economic Papers*, No. 4 (1940), pp. 56–58.

‡ Or more accurately, probable annual earnings, to allow for the employment prospects.

wage rate per hour is OA/RO, and when the wage line rises to BR, the wage rate becomes OB/RO. By the usual argument the laborer will work MR hours at the lower wage rate and NR hours at the higher rate, for in each case he is then on the highest possible indifference curve. As the figure is drawn, the individual works less at the higher wage rate. Marshall believed that such a result would occur only in the case of "the more ignorant and phlegmatic of races and of individuals," and that the opposite was true in the case of "those whose mental horizon is wider, and who have more firmness and elasticity of character" (i.e., Englishmen). Most

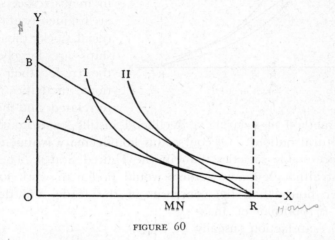

FIGURE 60

economists now believe that Figure 60 is typical also of Anglo-Saxons; in the absence of such an attitude it would be difficult to rationalize the long decline in the hours of labor.

The simplified analysis could readily be modified to handle certain complications. For instance, the compulsory time-and-a-half for overtime alters the wage line beyond, e.g., 40 hours. Beyond this maximum (TR in Figure 61) an hour of labor earns 50 per cent more, so the slope of the wage line increases correspondingly. In our particular graph this does not lead to an increase of hours (for P is on the highest indifference curve the laborer can reach), but this is of course only one possible result. Qualification could also be made for the fact that laborers prefer to work 5 days a week for 7 hours rather than 7 days a week for 5 hours.

In many occupations the hours of the individual laborer are not very flexible, of course. It should be observed, however, that usually some flexibility is attained by devices such as absenteeism and vacations between jobs (the quitting rate in a flourishing industry is frequently 5 per cent a month). But flexibility should not be judged only from the individual laborer's viewpoint. The workers in a given occupation are usually similar in many respects. They are frequently of the same racial stock; their friendships are largely within the trade; their recreational activities are interrelated; and their common method of securing a livelihood instills some homogeneity of cultural outlook. Of course this homogeneity is much greater in more stable societies than in the United States. The upshot is that although many workers would prefer to work longer or shorter hours than the consensus of the trade, the deviations from a position of maximum satisfaction usually are not large.

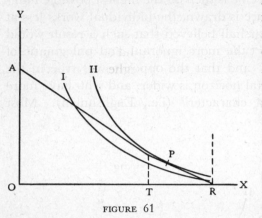

FIGURE 61

We turn finally to the supply curve of labor to an industry. (The supply curve to the firm is a horizontal line under competition.) If only one industry uses a particular kind of skilled labor — unskilled labor is used by many industries — the supply curve

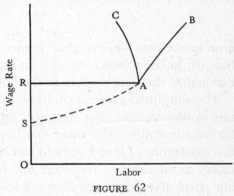

FIGURE 62

may take numerous shapes, as is suggested in Figure 62, depending upon the supply curves of the individual laborers. No wage rate below OR will secure laborers if this is the rate paid to laborers in another occupation to which these men can transfer.* In general *RAB* is the more probable supply curve, at least in the long run, because higher wages will attract laborers from other occupations.

If two or more industries use the labor of this type, the supply curve to one industry cannot have a negative slope. As one industry increases its employment of labor, the wage rate must rise because of two factors. First, the reduced numbers of laborers in other industries have higher marginal physical products, and second, the reduced output of these industries leads to higher selling prices. Both factors tend to increase the demand prices of these other industries. In the limiting case where an industry uses only a small fraction of the supply of labor of a given type, its demands will have no perceptible influence on the wage rate — it will be a constant (labor) cost industry.†

RECOMMENDED READINGS

1. Marshall, A., *Principles of Economics*, 8th ed., Macmillan, London, 1920, Bk. V, Ch. 6; Bk. VI, especially Chs. 1, 2.
2. Knight, Frank H., *Risk, Uncertainty and Profit*, London School Reprints of Scarce Works, No. 16 (1933), Ch. 4.
3. Robertson, D. H., "Wage Grumbles," in *Economic Fragments*, King, London, 1931, pp. 42–57.
4. Chapman, S. J., "Hours of Labour," *Economic Journal*, XIX (1909), 353–373.
5. Hicks, J. R., *The Theory of Wages*, Macmillan, London, 1932.
6. Rowe, J. W. F., *Wages in Practice and Theory*, Routledge, London, 1928.

Douglas' — Theory of Wages c 12. 3.
Clark JB — Dist of Wealth.

PROBLEMS

1. The total product secured on a farm varies as follows with the number of laborers employed:

Laborers	Product
1	10
2	21
3	33

---

* This is a simplified case, of course. Some of the workers will prefer to practice this occupation even though they could earn more in other lines — this is represented by *SA*. Other factors like inertia and cost of shifting support this qualification.

† Except in this case it will be an increasing (labor) cost industry. In none of these cases, not even if the supply curve is *RAC*, will the industry have decreasing labor costs. The falling section *CA* represents a willingness of laborers to work more if the wage rate falls, not an insistence on lower wages as more men are demanded. An increase in demand raises the wage rate, decreases the supply of labor, and increases even more the costs of the industry.

If 3 laborers are hired, the marginal product is 12; if each laborer is paid at this rate, the total wage bill is 36, which exceeds the total product. Explain.

2. Let there be 1,000 each of three kinds of farms, the production schedules of which are as follows:

Laborers	Type of Farm		
	A	B	C
1	100	90	80
2	195	176	159
3	285	258	237
4	371	336	314
5	453	410	390
6	532	481	465
7	608	549	539
8	682	614	612
9	754	676	684
10	824	736	755

a. If there are 8,000 laborers, determine the rent of each type of farm and the wage rate.

b. Determine the same quantities with 20,000 laborers.

c. Destroy one farm, allocate its laborers to other farms, and measure the decrease in product. What is the relation of this product decrease to the rent of land?

3. Assume that in a certain colony there are 1,000 ten-acre farms suitable only for growing wheat and 800 ten-acre farms suitable only for grow-

Price of Cotton	Quantity of Wheat Demanded (bushels)	Quantity of Cotton Demanded (pounds)
$.10	100	600
.20	100	580
.30	100	560
.40	100	540
.50	100	520
.60	100	500
.70	100	480
.80	100	460
etc.	etc.	etc.

ing cotton. There are 10,000 laborers, who can work on either type of farm. The colony is on the wheat standard, so the price of one bushel of wheat is by law $1.00. The relative demands for cotton and wheat are given in the schedule at the bottom of page 192.

(The equation is $c = 620 - 2p$, where c is demand for cotton and p is its price in cents.) Observe that these are *relative* demands; the total quantities demanded depend upon, and in fact are at equilibrium equal to, the income or product of the colony.

The physical production functions for a firm of each variety are given in the following schedule:

Number of Laborers	Bushels of Wheat	Pounds of Cotton
1	50	280
2	125	700
3	195	1100
4	260	1480
5	320	1840
6	375	2180
7	425	2500
8	470	2800
etc.	etc.	etc.

Determine: (*a*) the annual wage, (*b*) the rent of each type of farm.
4. Analyze the effects on wages and rents of
   a. Labor supplies of 8,000 and 15,000 men.
   b. A decrease of 25 per cent in the relative demand for cotton.
   c. The discovery of 200 more cotton farms.
   d. An increase in the productivity of labor on wheat farms of 10 bushels per laborer.
5. Rent was measured as a residual in problem 3. Compute the rent of wheat farms by the marginal productivity method, i.e., by measuring the effect on total product of reducing the number of wheat farms by one.
6. Suppose, under conditions of problem 3, all of the men were on wheat farms when the cotton farms were discovered, and the cost to a laborer of moving to a cotton farm was equivalent to an annual difference of earnings of $20. Determine the new equilibrium rents and wages.
7. Determine the new allocation of labor, and consequently the wage rate and rents, if a new invention makes it possible to convert a cotton farm into a wheat farm (or vice versa) at a cost equivalent to a rent of $10 per farm.
8. Derive the demand schedule of a farm of either variety for labor.
9. Derive the demand schedule of all wheat farms for labor.

PART III

THE THEORY OF IMPERFECT COMPETITION

CHAPTER 11

THE NATURE AND BASES OF IMPERFECT COMPETITION

The theory developed in Part II was restricted to conditions of perfect competition. The basic requirements for perfect competition, it will be recalled, are three: (1) all economic units (i.e., households, firms, owners of resources) are so small as to exert no perceptible influence on prices; (2) there are no social restrictions on the mobility of resources or on prices; and (3) all individuals possess complete knowledge. When we turn to imperfect competition, it would seem natural to abandon these assumptions individually and in combination and study the resulting changes in prices and outputs. This approach would insure complete analysis of all possible economic situations. Unfortunately, it is impracticable.

The impracticability arises out of two circumstances: variety and ignorance. By variety is meant the literally infinite number of possible deviations from perfect competition which may occur. For example, a laborer may be discouraged in varying degree from entering a given occupation by citizenship requirements, initiation fees of $1 or $3,000, equally varied apprenticeship rules, or a seniority system. Similarly with respect to the size of firm, there is an unlimited number of combinations of number and size of firm which violate the condition that the firm have no influence on prices.

But variety alone is not fatal — it would usually be possible to establish sensible classifications which would reduce the problem to much more manageable proportions, and in fact this has been done in good part. But the second and more fundamental obstacle of ignorance is less easily surmounted. Our factual knowledge of imperfect competition is considerable but it is, on the whole, so fragmentary as to present the isolation and analysis of all important forms. Consider the famous problem of two firms A and B comprising an industry (i.e., duopoly). Will A and B conspire together,

will A attempt to drive B out of the industry, will A assume that
B insists on a certain share of total sales, or will A assume that B
will be slow in following price cuts? There are many other possibilities, and unfortunately we do not possess the factual knowledge
to select for detailed study those cases which are empirically important.

It deserves emphasis that this ignorance is primarily an ignorance
of relevant assumptions, not of the techniques which are appropriate
in exploring the assumptions. Doubtless there are many empirical
situations so complex that our analytical tools cannot cope fully
with them, but the more urgent need is for factual knowledge.*
Until this knowledge becomes available — and this is a slow, accre-
tionary process — the detailed content of the theory of imperfect
competition will remain in large degree intuitive.

The remainder of this chapter is devoted to certain topics of
orientation. This material can be viewed as either a detailed statement of the author's *Weltanshauung* which underlies the selection
of content in subsequent chapters or a survey of the major factors
underlying the important departures from perfect competition. It
is hoped that the two views are not unrelated.

I. THE MOTIVATION OF MONOPOLY†

Postponing consideration of inevitable or "natural" monopolies
(based primarily on economies of large-scale production), where
motivation is unimportant, two fundamental purposes in reducing
competition are evident. They are the desire for monopoly gains
and desire for power.

The first motive, desire for monopoly gains, is obvious enough.
Monopoly gains may be defined (tautologically) as gains which are
incompatible with the existence of a considerable number of independent and freely competing firms. The gains are of various
types, and they may accrue to several distinct groups involved in the
production process.

---

* Compare the discussion of economies of scale, *infra*, p. 206.

† "Monopoly" will be used loosely in this chapter to denote any firm or combination
of firms, or individual or combination of individuals, which possesses sufficient power
over output and prices to establish a market situation departing materially from competition. (Even in this loose sense monopoly is not equivalent to imperfect competition.)
This everyday usage will be replaced by a more precise set of concepts in the next
chapter.

The first group that is attracted by monopoly gains is the entrepreneurs — entrepreneurial gains have been the classic incentive
for combination. It would be wrong to interpret "gains" in the
narrow sense of returns on investment in excess of the competitive
rate. On the contrary there is much evidence for the proposition
that a more important source of monopoly is the threat or existence
of "excessive" competition which does not permit all of the firms in
an industry to earn competitive rates of return.* These factors have
been attributed to most mergers and combinations.

The second group which has reaped considerable gains from the
suppression of competition consists of the investment bankers. The
estimated $62,500,000 cash reward to the syndicate headed by
J. P. Morgan doubtless played some part in the merger that resulted
in the United States Steel Corporation, and the same force contributed to monopoly in other industries.† The historical importance of this factor is suggested by the fact that the two great
periods of mergers (1897 to 1903, 1925 to 1929) were also periods
in which the stock market was extremely buoyant. In the future,
however, the limitations placed on promoters' flights of fancy by
increased regulation of the security markets will probably reduce
sharply the part played by promotional profits in the growth of
monopoly.

The third class of beneficiaries of diminished competition has
been the organized labor groups. Labor unions have pursued
policies identical with other monopolies'. They have restricted
numbers by various entrance requirements (e.g., long apprentice-
ships, large initiation fees); they have suppressed substitutes (such
as machine-mixed concrete) and enlarged the demand for their
services (as by requiring union musicians to turn phonograph

* The "excessive" competition, it need scarcely be remarked, is not perfect: as a rule
the productive resources in the industry are relatively immobile so adjustment to new
conditions such as declining demand or technological improvements would require a
long time (e.g., coal, agriculture).

† In one paradoxical case this factor temporarily diminished monopoly. When W.
B. Ward was approached by Pittsburgh bakers who wished to raise the price of bread,
their representative reported: "Moreover, he [Ward] did not see how he could raise the
price so soon after the forming of the Continental [Baking Company], as he would in all
probability soon have the Government on his heels, and furthermore, what he was after
was volume, as he needed volume to sell his stock and that he was more concerned at
that time with selling stock than he was with baking. He was 'banking,' not 'baking.'"
Federal Trade Commission Report, *Competition and Profits in Bread and Flour*, Washington,
1928, p. 117.

records at radio stations). More important — basic indeed to their existence — they have consistently strived for higher wage rates. A survey of certain features of the marketing of labor services will be given in Chapter 15.

It is worth adding that monopoly in the labor market often leads to the suppression of competition among employers. The most important example is found in the bituminous coal industry, where legally enforced minimum prices were established to protect incomes of some mine operators and the union's wage structure. In many local markets labor unions frequently prevent price competition by refusing to supply labor to price cutters and in some cases independent employers have been driven out of business.* Such practices are of course based primarily on the belief that price competition is incompatible with the maintenance of high wage rates.

The second motive in forming monopolies is the desire on the part of industrial leaders to head great enterprises. This motive has ancient antecedents in noneconomic callings, as Plutarch's Life of Pyrrhus testifies:

> When Pyrrhus had thus retired into Epirus, and left Macedonia, he had a fair occasion given him by fortune to enjoy himself in quiet and to govern his own kingdom in peace. But he was persuaded, that neither to annoy others, nor to be annoyed by them, was a life insufferably languishing and tedious. . . . His anxiety for fresh employment was relieved as follows. [Then follows a statement of his preparations for making war against Rome.]
>
> There was then at the court of Pyrrhus, a Thessalonian named Cineas, a man of sound sense, and . . . who had devoted himself to Pyrrhus in all the embassies he was employed in . . . and he continued to heap honours and employments upon him. Cineas, now seeing Pyrrhus intent upon his preparations for Italy, took an opportunity, when he saw him at leisure, to draw him into the following conversation: "The Romans have the reputation of being excellent soldiers, and have the command of many warlike nations: if it please heaven that we conquer them, what use, Sir, shall we make of our victory?" "Cineas," replied the king, "your question answers itself. When the Romans are once subdued, there is no town, whether Greek or barbarian, in all the country, that will dare oppose us; but we shall immediately be masters of all Italy, whose greatness, power, and importance no man knows

---

* See Corwin Edwards, "Public Policy Toward Restraints of Trade by Labor Unions: an Economic Appraisal," Supplement to *American Economic Review*, March, 1942, pp. 432–48.

better than you." Cineas, after a short pause, continued, "But, after we have conquered Italy, what shall we do next, Sir?" Pyrrhus, not yet perceiving his drift, replied, "There is Sicily very near, and stretches out her arms to receive us, a fruitful and populous island, and easy to be taken. . . ." "What you say, my prince," said Cineas, "is very probable; but is the taking of Sicily to conclude our expeditions?" "Far from it," answered Pyrrhus, "for if heaven grant us success in this, that success shall only be the prelude to greater things. Who can forbear Libya and Carthage, then within reach? . . . And when we have made such conquests, who can pretend to say that any of our enemies, who are now so insolent, will think of resisting us?" "To be sure," said Cineas, "they will not; . . . But when we have conquered all, what are we to do then?" "Why, then, my friend," said Pyrrhus, laughing, "we will take our ease, and drink, and be merry." Cineas, having brought him thus far, replied, "And what hinders us from drinking and taking our ease now, when we have already those things in our hands, at which we propose to arrive through seas of blood, through infinite toils and dangers, through innumerable calamities, which we must both cause and suffer?"

This discourse of Cineas gave Pyrrhus pain, but produced no reformation. . . .*

The captains of industry also wish to become field marshals. It is impossible to rationalize the continued labors of an established multimillionaire in terms of the personal expenditures which can be made from a larger income; one must introduce considerations of power and prestige.† This factor has been especially important in American business because politics, the church, and the army — historically the three leading fields for the ambitious and the aggressive — were throughout a long period of our history subordinate to industry and commerce in the rewards offered to the successful.

One would normally expect new rivals to be attracted by whatever gains a monopoly secures, and frequently, of course, competition emerges. Such competition will not develop, however, if the economies of large-scale production are substantial, for then the market cannot support numerous firms (see page 159). Hence we shall first discuss economies of scale; then certain controls over the entrance or competitive position of new firms will be considered.

* Quoted in a related context by F. H. Knight, *The Ethics of Competition*, p. 32n.

† Thus Professor Taussig observed: "The instinct for domination plays a considerable part, I believe, in the movement for combination. . . . They [the industrialists] will talk of the economies from large-scale operation and consolidation, of the wastes of competition, of better service, lowered prices, and what not. But in truth the schemes for overpowering combinations are to a great degree mere manifestations of megalomania." *Inventors and Money Makers*, Macmillan, New York, 1915, pp. 92, 93.

II. THE ECONOMIES OF LARGE–SCALE PRODUCTION

The most popular explanation of large-scale business and hence of industrial monopoly is that large concerns are more efficient than small concerns. A brief survey has already been made of types of economies of large-scale production (see page 134), but it is now appropriate to examine the question critically and in more detail. Two theoretical restrictions on the size of economies of scale may first be considered.

1. THEORETICAL PROPOSITIONS

The first proposition is: the total cost of producing any output must be greater than or equal to the total cost of any smaller output. This is demonstrable in formal terms: if output x_1 exceeds output x_0 and if the total cost of x_1 is less than that of x_0, a firm wishing only x_0 would produce x_1 and throw the excess $(x_1 - x_0)$ away. Hence the effective cost of x_0 cannot be greater than that of x_1. In less formal terms, a larger output surely requires more of some productive services and, within small variations of output, less of none. The proposition can be rephrased: the elasticity of the long-run average cost curve is numerically greater than unity.

The second proposition is not easily stated in terms which are both precise and concise; a somewhat loose statement is that the economies of scale increase at a diminishing rate. It was argued above (see page 133) that all economies of scale could be viewed as arising from indivisibilities, and it is from this fact that the second proposition is deduced.* It follows that the indivisible productive processes will have different ' capacities," i.e., rates of output at which average cost of the service is minimized.† As the size of plant expands, the firm will add additional units of the process of lowest "capacity," since there is no gain in increasing the size of this process. Hence after one unit of the process of lowest capacity is fully used, no further economies of scale can arise in this section of the plant. The same conclusion is true of other processes once output exceeds the "capacity" of one unit of these processes. As output expands fewer and fewer processes contribute to the economies of scale; the economies of scale increase at a decreasing rate.

---

* It is tautological that economies of scale rest on indivisibilities, for an indivisible productive service is defined as one which is not equally efficient in all sizes (measured in terms of output).

† For a discussion of the meanings of capacity, see p. 275.

This argument will become more concrete after examining the numerical illustration in Table 15. The only necessary assumption is that all of the productive processes are not of equal "capacity"; all other properties of the figures here chosen can be altered without affecting the qualitative results.

TABLE 15

Process	"Capacity"	Cost of Process	Average Cost for Output of				
			10	50	100	1,000	2,000
I	10	$ 30	$ 3.00	$3.00	$3.00	$3.00	$3.00
II	25	25	2.50	1.00	1.00	1.00	1.00
III	70	100	10.00	2.00	2.00	1.50	1.45
IV	100	30	3.00	.60	.30	.30	.30
V	300	40	4.00	.80	.40	.16	.14
VI	500	30	3.00	.60	.30	.06	.06
VII	1,000	40	4.00	.80	.40	.04	.04
VIII	2,000	50	5.00	1.00	.50	.05	.03
Average Cost			34.50	9.80	7.90	6.11	6.02

The computation of average cost is simple: for example, process III has a "capacity" of 70 so 15 units of III are required for an output of 1,000, and average cost = $(15 \times \$100)/1,000 = \$1.50$. The example greatly exaggerates the economies of scale which would arise in this case,* but the conclusion is clear: increasing output from 10 to 50 decreases average costs by $24.70, increasing output from 50 to 100 decreases average costs by only $1.90. Similarly, increasing output from 100 to 1,000 decreases average costs by $1.79, whereas an additional increase in output to 2,000 lowers average costs by only $0.09.†

The long-run average cost curve based upon this numerical example is given in Figure 63.‡ The shape of the curve is of course

* The decrease in average costs is exaggerated for two reasons:
1. The large "capacity" processes simply would not be used in a small plant, — a cheaper method would surely be found to perform these tasks.
2. The cost of a process is usually dependent on output, e.g., process VI would probably cost less with 200 units of output than with 500.

† Minimum average cost ($5.987) would be reached at an output equal to the lowest common multiple of all "capacities" (42,000).

‡ The derivation cannot be made solely on the basis of the data in Table 15, quite aside from the qualifications mentioned in the next to last footnote. Suppose an output

very irregular, and this is why the proposition is not easy to state. But the general course of the curve clearly illustrates our second generalization, and if costs are computed for various multiples of the "capacity" of a suitably chosen process it will be seen that average costs fall at a decreasing rate which ultimately approaches zero.

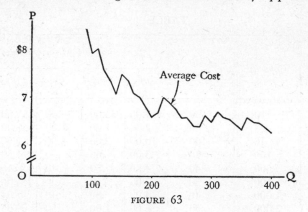

FIGURE 63

It deserves mention that in all probability this example exaggerates the range of increasing returns because managerial costs have not been taken into consideration.

II. *FIRM VS. PLANT*

It has tacitly been assumed up to this point that every economic unit (firm) owns and operates only one technological unit (plant), and this simplification must now be reconsidered. For present purposes it is not necessary to explain all cases of multiple-plant firms, but only those cases in which a firm is producing identical or very similar products in several plants.*

There appear to be only two important reasons why a firm should utilize two or more plants in producing identical or closely related commodities or services. The first explanation is that it is expensive to move the product to buyers (e.g., cement, bricks) or that the buyer is unwilling to travel any distance (e.g., retail chain stores). The second explanation is that the plants were acquired by merger. A third, but much less common, explanation is that beyond a cer-

of 400 is desired — one must know whether it is cheaper to use 5 or 6 units of process III. The figure is constructed on the assumption that the "capacities" are technological maxima.

* Later we shall take up vertical integration (p. 209) and multiple plants producing diverse products (Ch. 16).

tain size a plant would become so cumbersome that it is more economical to produce additional output from a second plant. In each case the question arises, what are the advantages of joint ownership of a series of plants over individual ownership? The following are the economies most frequently cited.

First, a multiple-plant firm can secure larger quantity discounts. It must be recognized that such discounts confer a material advantage on large purchasers, but the advantage should not be exaggerated. To cite two of the most important costs, there are no quantity discounts on labor and, with rare exception, there are only two rates (carload and less-than-carload) in railroad transportation. To the extent that discounts are based on actual savings in handling large orders, a large plant should be able to secure discounts virtually as large as those of a group of such plants. Moreover, unless the purchasing plans of the various plants are very closely coordinated — and this will usually entail costly rigidities in the organization — the various plants will not place orders or receive shipments simultaneously.

Of course quantity discounts frequently reflect the bargaining power of the large buyer, and then the multiple-plant firm will receive better prices than the one-plant firm. But these bargaining gains are not savings from the social viewpoint — they merely represent a redistribution of income between buyers and sellers. This does not alter the importance of such discounts but it may influence social policy with respect to mergers induced by such economies.

Second, a multiple-plant firm can unite certain of the "overhead" functions, in particular research, financing, legal work, and advertising. Little is known of the quantitative importance of these functions. The interest rate on commercial bank loans is much lower for large than for small firms,* but this is a very small part of

* A survey of rates charged by Federal Reserve member-banks in the spring of 1942 yielded the following pattern:

Borrowers' Assets	Interest Rate
Under $50,000	5.5
$50,000 to $500,000	4.5
$500,000 to $5,000,000	3.1
$5,000,000 and over	1.8
All	3.4

See G. L. Bach, "Interest Rates at Member Banks," *Federal Reserve Bulletin*, XXVIII (November, 1942), 1089–97.

the cost of doing business in most lines. Research and legal work are probably even less important: it may be hazarded that typically they account for less than 1 per cent of total costs. Usually it is not possible to centralize completely the overhead functions. Some research must be carried on in close touch with actual production processes — thus over 80 per cent of General Motors' engineering expenditures are on a plant basis, and probably less than $2.00 per car is normally spent on general research. Similarly, each plant must have a legal staff and a sales department, especially if the plants are widely separated. In the case of consumers' goods, however, the advertising economies may be very substantial if the product is marketed nationally.

Third, it has been suggested that certain plants can be kept at full operation and other plants, in which a maximum of flexibility has been built (page 168), can handle fluctuations in the rate of production. The advantages seem very limited. This plan conflicts with the savings in transportation costs. If the "buffer" plant were closed down, the foremen and skilled laborers might disperse, the morale of the workers would be poor, and if the plant was an important employer in the community in which it was located, the undesirable social implications of such instability of employment are obvious.

In general, therefore, once a plant of optimum size has been built, the additional gains to be secured by bringing additional plants under the same management are at best small. Theoretical considerations suggest that the chief purpose of merger must be to secure a monopoly position, and the history of combinations supports this presumption.

III. QUANTITATIVE STUDIES

The general discussion up to this point could yield no precise information as to the typical patterns of long-run average-cost curves — only quantitative studies can do this. Such studies, unfortunately, have not been made with sufficient care or in enough cases to permit of very detailed generalization.

The paucity of good quantitative studies is attributable to both the unavailability of data (for American business is reticent in such matters) and the difficulties in measuring the economies of scale. A few of the difficulties may be mentioned. The efficiency of a firm depends in part upon its ability to withstand wide business fluctuations and to adapt itself quickly to new technological developments and changes in demand, and none of these factors is adequately measured in a cross-section of average costs at any one time. The products of various companies are usually heterogeneous so interfirm comparisons may be misleading. If plants are widely separated, the relative importance of particular costs will vary and transportation costs must be considered. This list, which could of course be lengthened materially, explains both the scarcity and inconclusiveness of the empirical studies of economies of scale.

The studies which are available, however, tend to support the following statements in industries containing firms and plants of very different sizes:

1. In general large companies are more efficient than small companies, but the largest companies are not more efficient (and are frequently less so) than the large companies.
2. The quantitative differences between average costs of companies of various sizes are relatively small after a moderate size is reached.

These statements cannot be proved rigorously; the type of evidence on which they rest may, however, be illustrated. The average costs of bakeries of various sizes are presented in Table 16. It will be seen that the two generalizations made above hold in this case.*

The available evidence thus suggests the following behavior as being typical of the long-run average-cost curve: it falls fairly rapidly at first, flattens out and is virtually horizontal over a long range of outputs, and then rises gradually.† If this be true, one must look elsewhere for the explanation of the rise and persistence of most monopolies.

* For a collection of such material, see *Relative Efficiency of Large, Medium-Sized, and Small Business*, Temporary National Economic Committee Monograph No. 13, Washington, 1941.

† The weight of the human arm and the fact that most economists are right-handed have apparently had considerable influence on notions of the shape of demand and cost curves; for example, these must be the chief reasons why demand curves are drawn convex to the origin. One purpose of the extensive use of linear demand curves in this book is to combat this tendency.

TABLE 16

*COSTS OF WHOLESALE BAKERS**

Annual Plant Production (pounds per year)	Average Cost (in cents)			
	Ingredients	Manufacturing	Other	Total
Under 1,687,500	3.40	2.36	1.94	7.70
1,687,500 to 2,531,250	3.21	2.12	1.91	7.24
2,531,250 to 3,796,875	3.32	1.83	2.07	7.22
3,796,875 to 5,695,312	3.19	1.75	1.90	6.84
5,695,312 to 8,542,968	3.21	1.81	1.92	6.94
8,542,968 to 12,814,452	3.14	1.70	1.89	6.73
12,814,452 to 19,221,678	3.11	1.60	1.75	6.46
19,221,678 to 28,832,517	3.25	1.58	1.69	6.52
28,832,517 to 43,248,775	3.24	1.73	1.73	6.70

III. THE TACTICS OF MONOPOLY

Once a monopoly position has been attained, perhaps by merger or an early start in a new industry, certain tactics may be employed to advantage in preventing the entrance of new firms into the industry, or to prevent members of the industry from violating the price and output policies of the cartel. The most important of these techniques involve the assistance of government; they will be taken up in the next section. The private, and in some cases illegal, techniques will be considered at this point. They may be summarized under three heads.

First, the entrance of new firms may be estopped by control over indispensable resources or basic production processes. Thus the potential builder of a steel plant will find that almost all high-grade iron-ore deposits are owned by the major companies and that the price of iron ore sometimes rises but never falls. The potential manufacturer of telephonic equipment might be discouraged by the possibility that his products or processes infringe one of the 9,255 patents held (in 1934) by the Bell Telephone System. The term of a patent is limited to 17 years, but meanwhile a host of new patents on improvements will have been secured by the firm with the early

* Taken from *Competition and Profits in Bread and Flour*, Sen. Doc. 98, 70th Congress, 1st Sess., 1928, p. 301.

start.* In certain fields (e.g., petroleum), control over transportation facilities has been an important obstacle to the entrance of new firms. Similarly, the affiliation of powerful banking interests with a monopoly will not ease the financing problems of a potential competitor. This factor has occasionally come to the surface in national markets and there is wide scope for its operation in local markets.†

Second, the list of "unfair" trade practices is long enough to be a tribute to Yankee ingenuity.‡ The "muckraking" literature of the first decade of the century emphasized the importance of policies such as the following: localized price cutting; bribery and coercion of customers; bribery and coercion of sources of supplies; fake infringement suits; creation of dissent among employees; spreading rumors that competing products are inferior; and sabotage. The current reports of the Federal Trade Commission testify that these and similar practices are still with us, although they are now pursued with greater subtlety.

VERTICAL INTEGRATION

A third resource of monopoly is vertical integration, i.e., the ownership or control of plants which supply materials or markets for the finished product. Such integration can occur in the absence of monopoly so it will be useful to distinguish the various situations in which it may arise.

The most common explanation of vertical integration is that the profits of middlemen are eliminated. If these middlemen or producers are competitively organized, however, they are receiving only competitive rates of return for the indispensable services they render or the products they produce. Nor does it seem true generally that skill in the conduct of one kind of business implies the ability to operate other kinds of business with equal profit. This explanation is important only when monopoly exists or threatens to arise in the supply or market industries.

* The patent expires 17 years from the day it is granted, but by various devices a patent can be kept pending for considerable periods. The claim for a patent on the photographic recording of sound was in the patent office for 36 years before a patent was granted.

† It is estimated that 74.7 per cent of American cities having banks have only one bank, and an additional 18.3 per cent have only two banks — a situation which certainly expedites "stabilization" of local industries. See L. V. Chandler, "Monopolistic Elements in Commercial Banking," *Journal of Political Economy*, XLVI (1938), 1–22.

‡ "Unfair" in the sense of the common law; the current use of this word to characterize any move of a competitor which jeopardizes one's profits is in another category.

The other advantages often claimed for vertical integration are continuous operation (as in eliminating reheating in steel production) and the guarantee of supplies or demands. Except when new technological developments lead to redefinition of an industry, the former advantage does not appear to be very important, and the latter is provided also by competition. On the other hand, changing demands or technologies will usually soon disturb the quantitative relationships among stages of a productive process, and so make complete integration costly or impossible. For example, steel companies that produced the necessary amount of iron ore 20 years ago now have an excess because more scrap is being used.

The most important cause of vertical integration appears to be monopoly. Integration may be a defensive weapon when the markets for raw materials are monopolized or in danger of monopolization. Thus the Beryllium Corporation found that its attempts to expand the use of its products through price reductions were futile because the fabricating company wished to protect its own market in phosphor bronze. More commonly integration is a weapon of offense; two examples of its use may be cited.

In the struggle for outlets the retail market is frequently cartellized. The situation appears to be most acute when there are a few producers of close substitutes: in their endeavor to secure outlets without resort to price competition the producers establish their own retailing units or offer many special favors to exclusive dealers. This development is well illustrated by the petroleum industry: The major companies have entered retailing on an extensive scale and in addition they have used wider retail margins, free equipment, free painting, credit-card privileges, and threats of erecting competing stations to persuade independent retailers to handle only one major company's line of products. The same situation is highly developed in the motion-picture theater field and in automobile dealerships.

Again, if a firm is dominant in several of the production stages, it can manipulate the margins so as to practice price discrimination (see page 223) and to discourage the appearance of new rivals at any given stage. The bookkeeping losses incurred in one branch of the integrated firm may be more than offset by the profits in another, more sheltered branch, but the unintegrated rivals will not have this solace.

IV. STATE SUPPORT OF MONOPOLY

In this age of political cynicism it should not be necessary to belabor the point that governmental assistance can frequently be invoked to organize or support monopolies. In fact, some of the most important and the most persistent departures from competition rest on the powers of the state. The techniques of political intervention may be classified into five types.

i. *CONTROL OF ENTRY OF FIRMS*

The exclusion of potential firms or the suppression of existing competition may take several forms. For the sake of brevity only a few examples will be given of three leading types.

1. Geographical Barriers. The most important example of assistance to monopoly on a geographical basis is the protective tariff. Most of the nationwide monopolies have received some protection by this method. State barriers are gradually becoming equally familiar: they employ tax powers, highway controls, health and sanitation powers, and similar prerogatives in order to suppress out-of-state competition.* A typical municipal example of the same type is the refusal of health authorities to inspect dairy farms lying outside a given area.

2. Discrimination between Types of Organization. The most important example of discrimination between types of economic organizations is the antichain-store legislation, which customarily uses the taxing power to penalize competition with independent retailers. Thus in Texas a single store pays an annual tax of $1; each store beyond 50 in a chain pays $750. In Louisiana the tax on chain stores, which reaches $550 per store for over 500 stores, is based on the total number of stores in the chain. An analogous municipal development is the restriction on direct-selling to consumers, again pri-

---

* A few examples may be given. Taxation: in Alabama wine makers using 75 per cent or more of Alabama-grown raw materials pay an annual license fee of $25, others pay $1,000. Highway control: the itinerant merchant-trucker in Idaho or Washington annually pays a $300 license fee to every county in which he does business and also posts a bond of $500 with each county treasurer. Health and sanitation: when New York quarantined out-of-state cattle in 1932 to prevent the spread of Bang's disease, a milk cow could be imported only if it came from a herd which had shown three negative tests to the disease in the year preceding importation. No New York herd could meet this test. In many states the public institutions are compelled to buy local products, e.g., Colorado, Iowa, and numerous other states require institutions to buy locally mined coal; Nebraska requires purchase of local butter; and most states require that public printing be done within the state.

marily to protect local retailers. Considerable use is made of high
license fees but the most popular weapon has been the famous
Green River Ordinance, which reads in part:

> Section 1. The practice of going in and upon private residences in
> the town of Green River, Wyoming, by solicitors, peddlers, hawkers,
> itinerant merchants and transient vendors of merchandise, not having
> been requested or invited so to do by the owner or owners, occupant or
> occupants of said private residences, for the purpose of soliciting orders
> for the sale of goods, wares and merchandise, and/or for the purpose of
> disposing of and/or peddling or hawking the same, is hereby declared
> to be a nuisance and punishable as such nuisance as a misdemeanour.
>
> Section 5. It being deemed by the Town Council of the Town of
> Green River that an emergency exists, this ordinance shall be in force
> and effect from and after its passage and approval.

3. *Licensing of New Competitors.* The restrictive licensing of new
competitors is a direct and efficient method of "stabilizing" a trade.
Fields in which there is a well-established public interest, such as
banking or liquor retailing, have long been subject to such considerations.   In many occupations — thus plumbers, barbers,
morticians, and certified public accountants — a necessary license
of competence is granted — mayhap sparingly — by practitioners
of the craft.

II. *SUPPRESSION OF SUBSTITUTES*

Analogous to restrictions on new firms is the suppression of
commodities which are substitutes for those sold by articulate special
interests. The ceaseless efforts of the dairy industry to exterminate
the margarine industry provide innumerable examples, of which
three may be cited. The federal government imposes a tax of
10 cents per pound on margarine;* Montana requires a license
which costs $400 a year of each retailer who handles margarine;
and Missouri requires eating places to serve margarine in vessels
indelibly marked "oleomargarine" or "impure butter." In Texas
the maximum net weight of a truck is 7,000 pounds unless its route
does not overlap that of a railroad, in which case it is 14,000 pounds;
this example tends to refute the popular charge that railroad
management has not kept up with the times.

---

* From 1902 to 1931 the tax was 10 cents on "artificially" colored margarine and
¼ cent on uncolored margarine. Manufacturers began to use ingredients like peanut
oil and soybean oil which impart a "natural" yellow color, so in 1931 the law was
amended to tax all colored margarine 10 cents per pound.

III. *THE PREVENTION OF PRICE COMPETITION*

The prevention of price competition is found at all governmental levels. The limitations on price competition may be permissive or compulsory.

Permissive legislation enables a firm to fix the price of its product at later stages in the marketing process or authorizes cooperation of producers with accompanying waiver of the antitrust laws. The federal resale-price-maintenance legislation (the Miller-Tydings Amendment) permits a manufacturer to fix the retail price of commodities when this is authorized by the state in which the article is sold, and most states have given such authorization. Agricultural cooperatives, export associations, and coal marketing associations are partially exempted from the federal antitrust laws, and supreme court decisions have conferred almost complete immunity on labor unions.*

There are several important federal examples of legal prevention of price competition. Under the Bituminous Coal Acts, mine operators selling coal at less than administratively determined levels were fined $19\frac{1}{2}$ per cent of the receipts from such sales. The Walsh-Healey Act permits the Secretary of Labor to set minimum wage rates in plants eligible to bid on federal contracts, and this power has been used vigorously. The Fair Labor Standards Act ordains a minimum hourly wage eventually reaching 40 cents, and requires a 50 per cent increase in whatever wage rate is ruling for hours in excess of 40 per week. A majority of the state legislatures have been persuaded by druggists and grocers to prevent sales in these fields at less than invoice cost plus a (rising) percentage. Both the federal government and state governments have organized compulsory cartels in numerous milk markets.

IV. *RESTRICTION OF OUTPUT*

Restrictions of output may or may not be accompanied by direct price-fixing but of course prices will rise if the restrictions are effective. The outstanding example of governmental restriction of out-

---

* The Supreme Court has held that the Norris-LaGuardia antiinjunction act exempts unions from the antitrust laws: "So long as a union acts in its own self-interest and does not combine with non-labor groups, the licit and the illicit . . . are not to be distinguished by any judgment regarding the wisdom or unwisdom, the rightness or wrongness, the selfishness or unselfishness of the end of which the particular union activities are the means." *U. S. v. Hutcheson*, 312 U. S. 232 (1941).

put is presented by the federal agricultural program, which first used penalty taxes and benefit payments and later shifted to crop loans and "soil-conserving" payments in order to restrict production and sales. Some use of quotas (e.g., on sugar and milk) have been used to the same end. State restriction of output of the petroleum industry has also been practiced in the name of conservation, but changes in production quotas seem to correspond more closely with changes in petroleum prices than with changes in the known supply of petroleum.

v. *MISCELLANEOUS POLICIES*

In addition to the foregoing types of policies there is a miscellany of governmental contributions to the monopoly movement. The labor union has achieved its great quantitative importance only with governmental assistance; in both periods (1916 to 1919, 1933 on) probably the major factor has been the encouragement of the federal government. Sporadically large firms are heavily favored by the federal government or small firms have been urged or compelled to act together — the NRA and the World Wars are examples — and the effects of these policies have long survived the conditions which gave rise to them.

In sum, the power of the state is the chief resource of monopoly. The importance of the state in the rise of monopoly is further emphasized if one considers its negative role in failing to prevent the rise of monopoly by aggressive administration of the antitrust laws, the control of security issues, the elimination of patent abuses, and the failure to provide consumer and labor market information (see next section).

V. OTHER DEPARTURES FROM COMPETITION

The foregoing discussion has emphasized the importance of deliberate organization of monopoly in fields which would otherwise be relatively competitive. Economists have also paid much attention in recent times to departures from competition which are due to a fundamental characteristic of the consumer markets — consumer ignorance.

The typical consumer buys such a large number and variety of commodities and services that it is not reasonable to criticize harshly his lack of adequate information of the prices and technological properties, especially considering the inaccessibility of reliable and comprehensible information. The effect of this ignorance is to permit firms to differentiate virtually identical commodities and to persuade consumers to pay relatively high prices for heavily advertised brands. Each such firm has a sheltered, quasi-monopolistic position even though there be many brands of the goods which are technologically equivalent.

This phenomenon of monopoly based on consumer ignorance will be explored subsequently, but a few remarks may be made here. The fundamental fact is that a firm desiring to expand sales will find advertising a better substitute for price reductions the more ignorant consumers are of the technical properties of the commodity and the less important these properties are relative to the personal tastes of consumers. Thus advertising has led to monopolistic prices for proprietary drugs and cosmetics, because the typical consumer possesses virtually no information concerning either type of goods and because emotional elements (desire for health and romance and prestige) are strong. On the other hand, advertising of sugar, walnuts, or sheeting has not persuaded consumers that branded lines of these goods are much superior to unbranded, unadvertised lines, and for many variety goods branding has had absolutely no influence on prices.

Some of the differentiated products have attained strong monopolistic positions; thus successfully branded drugs usually sell for at least five times as much as unbranded drugs of equal quality. But it can be argued that the recent literature of economics has materially exaggerated the importance of such departures from competition.

It is frequently implied that product differentiation is exclusively monopolistic in nature, but this is surely wrong. Under perfect competition there would still be many qualities of goods of certain types because of the great variety of tastes and needs of consumers. No classical economist argued that competition would render all women's hats homogeneous. It is therefore necessary to eliminate the differences in prices due to differences in costs, for these price differentials would also exist under competition. Frequently this correction will reduce greatly the discrepancies to be explained in terms of monopolistic powers.

Moreover, it is not enough (and indeed it is not necessary!) to prove that a given industry is not perfectly competitive. The crucial question is: how far do conditions in the industry depart from competition? In many and perhaps most cases the answer is that the departures are not large. For example, despite the fact that the textile industry contains perhaps twenty times the number of firms necessary for competition, each firm has certain monopolistic powers. Even at a price higher than that charged by competitors, a firm can continue to sell to certain old customers whose attachments rest on habit, personal friendship, clever salesmanship, convenience of location, knowledge of special needs, or similar factors. The elasticity of demand of the firm may therefore be − 10, and not the minus infinity postulated by the theory of perfect competition. But the effects of these monopolistic elements will not be commensurate with the numerical difference between 10 and infinity: the prices of textile goods will certainly be less than 10 per cent higher than they would be under competition.

There is no argument that these milder cases of product differentiation should be neglected by the economist, but their secondary importance should be kept in mind. There are many other causes of departures from competitive conditions which are quantitatively at least as important and have equal claim to the economist's attention. Occupational and geographical immobility of laborers and of capital, for example, probably lead to considerably larger departures from competition. It is also easy to find important examples of what may be termed producer ignorance: the reluctance of certain industries to adopt improved technologies, the inability to forecast changes in consumer demand, and the belief of retired policemen that a successful grocery store requires only $1,000 and a friendly neighborhood.

It would be misleading to conclude this sketch of typical forms of monopoly without pointing out the fact that in the past, at least, industrial monopolies have seldom been able to maintain their positions. Except in the case of government monopolies (such as the postal service), the development of new products or new techniques or the discovery of new resources has usually led to the decline of what once appeared to be even the most strongly entrenched monopolies, and the inability to secure a continuous supply of high-quality management has contributed to the decline.

RECOMMENDED READINGS

1. Marshall, A., *Industry and Trade*, Macmillan, London, 1920.
2. Watkins, M. W., *Industrial Combinations and Public Policy*, Houghton Mifflin, New York, 1927.
3. MacGregor, D. H., *Industrial Combination*, London School Reprints of Scarce Works, No. 1, 1935.
4. Burns, A. R., *The Decline of Competition*, McGraw-Hill, New York, 1936.
5. Wilcox, C., *Competition and Monopoly in American Industry*, Monograph No. 21 of the Temporary National Economic Committee, Washington, 1941.
6. Nelson, S., and Keim, W., *Price Behavior and Business Policy*, Monograph No. 1 of the Temporary National Economic Committee, Washington, 1941.
7. Robinson, E. A. G., *Monopoly*, Nisbet, London, 1941.

CHAPTER 12

DEMAND UNDER IMPERFECT COMPETITION

Under perfect competition there are three steps in the derivation of the demand curve of the firm. First, the demand curve of the individual consumer is established by indifference curve analysis; next, the demand curve of the market is secured by summing the demand curves of the individual consumers; and finally, the demand curve of the firm is a horizontal line at a price established by market demand and supply. Imperfect competition raises difficulties at each of these steps because of two circumstances: (1) the product of the individual firm may be differentiated (in consumers' eyes) from products of other firms which are technologically very similar or even identical; and (2) there may be few independent producers.

If the firm's product is differentiated, it is still true that the individual consumer's demand will be based upon his preferences but the firm may alter these preferences by selling activities. Advertising is unnecessary when a firm can sell all it wishes at the ruling price, but as soon as a product becomes distinctive the firm may find it profitable to spend large sums on advertising to increase the attachment of existing customers and to secure new customers. Product differentiation makes it difficult to secure market or partial demand curves; one can neither add the demands for Chevrolets and Plymouths nor consider them independently.

The existence of only a small number of firms in an industry — oligopoly — makes it impossible for one firm to treat the ruling price as a datum even if the product is homogeneous. Not only does the firm sell enough to affect prices perceptibly but also, because of this, it must consider how its policies influence the policies of rivals. The problem is usually further complicated by the fact that the firms do not sell identical products.

The following analysis will begin with what appears to be the simplest situation, monopoly. It will then be extended in two

218

directions: we shall study the effects on the firm's demand curve of the existence of close substitutes and of a small number of rivals. It will appear that availability of substitutes and number and behavior of independent producers together determine all possible demand situations.

I. THE DEMAND CURVE OF A MONOPOLY

If there is only one producer of a commodity, the demand curve of the industry is obviously the demand curve of the firm. We are familiar with the determinants of this demand curve (see Chapters 5 and 6): the incomes and tastes of consumers, and the availability of substitutes. A monopoly can increase the demand for its product only by increasing consumers' incomes, reducing the availability of substitutes, or increasing consumers' preference for the commodity.

The first of these avenues, increasing consumers' incomes, will seldom appeal to the monopolist. The objection is usually simple but decisive: only a portion of the increase in income will be spent upon the monopolist's product. (There are possible exceptions, for example it is said that some coal companies mined coal in depression at prices less than variable costs and recouped at the company store. This is better viewed as a wage cut. Other exceptions can be dealt with similarly.)

It is frequently feasible to use the second method of increasing demand, namely, to reduce the availability of substitutes. The simplest way of doing this is to buy out the producer of the substitute. Then one can suppress the substitute, or increase its price, or degrade its quality. This method leads a firm to have multiple products so its detailed analysis will be deferred to Chapter 16. The state frequently lends its powers to the same end: Protective tariffs, restrictions on interstate flows of goods, compulsory purchase of local products by governmental institutions, building code provisions which forbid the use of new materials, taxes on substitutes — these and many other devices are promoted by monopolists and especially by cartels (see below). To the extent that they are successful, all such methods serve to raise the demand curve of the monopolist and usually to make it less elastic.

In the case of complementary goods, of course, the opposite goal is sought: to increase the availability of the auxiliary commodity. Thus electric utilities foster appliances; automobile producers seek repair agencies; brewers lend or sell tavern equipment on generous terms. Again the effect is to raise the monopolist's demand curve.

The suppression of substitutes, however, is necessarily a never-ending process. The limitations will become clearer if we review the nature of substitutes.* We may begin by recalling the measure of the closeness of a substitute — the cross-elasticity of demand (see page 88). The cross-elasticity of demand for commodity X in terms of the price of Y is

$$\eta_{xp_y} = \frac{\text{relative change in quantity of X purchased}}{\text{relative change in price of Y}}.$$

This is a direct measure of the willingness of consumers to shift to X if the price of Y rises. If we compute the cross-elasticity of demand for X with respect to the prices of all other commodities, we can array them in the order of their substitutability for X.

Now suppose that on carrying out such computations for (e.g.) electric power, we secure the following results:

Substitute	Cross-Elasticity
Gas	4
Coal	3
All others	less than .1

Our test reveals that gas and coal are very good substitutes for electricity — so good that electric-power rates must vary closely with gas and coal prices or sales of power (or conversely, of gas and coal) will almost vanish.

This situation cannot be accepted as one of monopoly, even though there is only one electric company in the locality. The company simply cannot establish or alter its prices without first making some estimate of the reactions of the producers of good substitutes. This attention to the reactions of rivals is the distinguishing characteristic of oligopoly, and we shall consider this case later.

We face a superficial dilemma. If there are good substitutes, oligopoly appears; yet the theory of demand assures us that there are always substitutes. But the solution is evident — substitutes

* The case of complementary products is parallel, and need not be discussed explicitly.

need not be good. A company store in an isolated mining town, for example, may be confronted by the following cross-elasticities:

Substitute	Cross-Elasticity
Mail-order stores	.1
Purchase at distant city	.08
All others	less than .05

These coefficients are all small (although their total effect may be substantial) — there is no element of oligopoly and this may properly be termed a *monopoly*. We shall in fact define a monopoly as *a firm producing a product whose cross-elasticity of demand with respect to every other product is small*.

This digression should make it clear why a monopolist does not uniformly or indefinitely pursue the policy of reducing the availability of substitutes. Eventually every commodity in the economy is a substitute, and, what is more important, the net effect of reducing the availability of any one substitute would ultimately be very small, although it might well be expensive to do this.

1. *ADVERTISING*

There is yet one alternative: to increase the consumers' preference for the monopolized commodity. One can reduce the desirability, if not the availability, of numerous substitutes. Consumers' preference for a commodity may be increased by changing the commodity, either physically or psychologically. It is worth emphasizing in this connection that a successfully advertised product can be just as different from an unadvertised product (in consumers' eyes) as a Roman chariot from the modern automobile. It may be tempting to distinguish between "real" changes (as in durability) and "artificial" changes induced by advertising, but the distinction is difficult to draw and in any case it is not necessary for present purposes. The consumer does not make such a distinction, and the monopolist considers better quality, a decorative exterior, and advertising to be (nonexclusive) alternatives among which he will choose on the basis of profitability. The immediately succeeding discussion will refer only to advertising, but other devices for changing consumer preferences could be handled in very similar terms.

Since under monopoly there are no close substitutes, there is no fear that a successful advertising program will lead to competitive or retaliatory advertising: the effect of the diversion of consumer incomes to the advertised product will be spread thinly and more or less evenly over a wide range of other commodities.

It is apparent that advertising may be profitable if there is imperfect competition among producers and if consumers do not possess complete knowledge of prices and the technical properties of all consumers' goods. It might be argued that advertising could occur in a perfectly competitive industry if customers were ignorant. This is impossible to decide in general, because perfect competition among sellers can be inconsistent with ignorance on the part of consumers. If there were a single ruling price, no competitive producer would advertise because the benefits of this expenditure (resulting from the diversion of consumer expenditures from other products) would be spread over all producers, and the producer who initiated the advertising program would lose money. If consumers were so ignorant as to pay different prices for the same goods, however, low-price firms would obviously gain by advertising. In a situation of substantial but not perfect competition, advertising would undoubtedly take place.

Little is known of the effects of advertising on demand curves. It is possible to cite cases where sensational increases in sales have resulted from small advertising programs, and as easy to collect the testimony of referees of bankruptcy courts on the opposite course of events.* This uncertainty stems in part from the consumer's perversity in refusing to react uniformly to given stimuli, in part to the usual difficulties of experiment in social sciences.† Since the uncertainty of the effects of advertising extends to businessmen, it has

* See N. H. Borden, *The Economic Effects of Advertising*, Irwin, Chicago, 1942, Part II.
† One extraordinarily successful example of experiment may be mentioned:

[Gerard B. Lambert] drove to a photographic agency, where he purchased a portrait of a girl model. She was pretty and her expression was pensive. Lambert took the picture home and propped it up on a table where he could gaze at it. . . . The girl's name, he decided, was Ernestine, and she was the belle of a small town in Wisconsin. She had good looks, culture, family position, social graces, athletic ability, and seemingly every quality she needed, but . . .
Lambert left the sentence unfinished and drew three provocative asterisks after it. Starting a new paragraph, he disclosed that with all of her advantages, Ernestine could not hold a beau, and implied by elaborate indirection that the reason was: HALITOSIS. The insidious thing about her affliction, he wrote, was that her most intimate friends shrank from mentioning it.
. . . it was agreed that test ads should be run in two Middle Western cities. In one, Listerine was presented as the advertising firm wanted — with a picture of the bottle and some text telling how fine one's mouth felt after gargling with the contents. In the other, Ernestine and her unfortunate ailment made their debut. The ads both had a reply coupon offering a free sample of Listerine.
Lambert's ad outdrew the agency's by two to one. The locales of the ads were transposed and again Ernestine won two to one. The great halitosis campaign was on.

(From J. Alexander, "Gerard B. Lambert," *New Yorker*, July 16, 1938.)

even been argued that the business community has been oversold by the advertising agencies: it is necessary only to persuade one producer to engage in unprofitable advertising in order to force his rivals to expand their advertising programs. As a corollary, the effects of advertising on the elasticity of demand are even less known.

II. *PRICE DISCRIMINATION*

We have tacitly assumed that a given quantity of a commodity will be sold at a single, definite price (once incomes, preferences, and prices of substitutes are fixed). Under monopoly this is not necessarily true, for the monopolist may be able to discriminate among various buyers and charge higher prices of those who are more anxious to buy the commodity. Price discrimination is possible and profitable only if three conditions are fulfilled:

1. There is a monopoly or collusion among sellers, for independent competitors will always profit by concentrating sales in the high-price market.
2. The total demand can be subdivided into markets with different elasticities of demand.
3. The costs of keeping separate the various markets is not large relative to the differences in demand elasticities.

Before examining the effects of price discrimination on the demand curves, it is desirable to introduce a fundamental demand concept in the theory of imperfect competition: marginal revenue. Since a demand curve represents the prices at which various amounts of a commodity may be sold, it is a curve of average revenue. Marginal revenue bears the same relationship to price (average revenue) that marginal cost bears to average cost (see Chapter 4), and it is summarized in the basic formula,

$$\text{marginal revenue} = \text{price } (1 + 1/\eta),$$

where η is the elasticity of demand. If the demand curve has a negative slope, the sale of another unit forces down the price on all of the units hitherto sold (in the absence of discrimination), and marginal revenue — the addition to total revenue — is equal to the price of the additional unit *minus* the decrease in receipts from the units previously sold. Only under perfect competition is the elasticity of demand for the output of a firm infinite and therefore

marginal revenue equal to price. The relationship between demand
and marginal revenue curves is illustrated in Figure 64.

Price discrimination may be practiced within either of two
general market structures. First, the various markets into which the

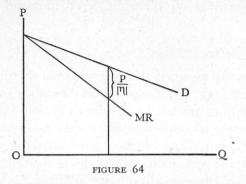

FIGURE 64

monopolist divides the total demand may be independent, i.e., the
quantity sold in any market is independent of the prices charged in
other parts. Second, there may be seepage between markets, so the
higher the price charged in one market relative to prices in other
markets, the more buyers will shift to the lower price market.

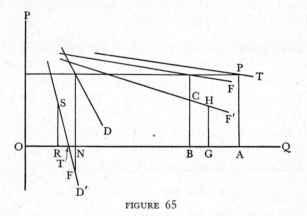

FIGURE 65

The rationale of price discrimination between independent
markets is illustrated by means of Figure 65, which represents a
division of the total demand into domestic and foreign markets. In
the figure T is the total demand, D is the (inelastic) domestic
demand, and F is the (elastic) foreign demand; D' and F' are the
corresponding marginal revenue curves. Suppose the quantity A

had been sold at the uniform price AP, then marginal revenue in the foreign market was BC and in the domestic market $- FN$. If on introducing discrimination the quantity RN ($= BG$) is transferred to the foreign market from the domestic market,

total receipts in F will rise by $BCHG$,
total receipts in D will rise by $TNF - RST$.

The discrimination will be profitable even if total receipts in the domestic market should decline somewhat. Whenever the same price is charged in two separable markets, marginal revenue will be larger in the market with the more elastic demand; this follows from the formula, marginal revenue = price $(1 + 1/\eta)$. Therefore total receipts can always be increased by transferring units of the commodity from the market with the relatively inelastic demand to the market with the relatively elastic demand until marginal revenues are equalized in the two markets.*

A classical example of price discrimination between independent markets is the pricing of medical services on the basis of the patient's income; nothing has a lower resale value than an appendectomy. Again it is feasible to sell electricity at a lower rate to industrial than to residential customers since at any practicable differential it does not pay to open up a factory in one's home. Contractual limitations may also be placed on resale: the Aluminum Company at one time sold aluminum wire (which competed with copper wire) at a lower price than ingots on the condition that it should not be melted down.

More commonly there is some seepage between the markets. Thus the domestic price cannot exceed the foreign price by more than reimportation costs, and a similar limit operates on inter-regional price discrimination. In such cases there is often a definite limit to the difference in price which can be charged in the two markets, but seepage usually takes place at all prices. Sales of first editions are smaller than they would be were there no prospective cheaper editions; attendance at "first run" theaters is smaller because of the promise of later appearances; and the incentive to buy at wholesale becomes continuously stronger the larger the

---

* Observe that it is not said that the transfer of the commodity continues until the elasticities in the two markets are equal. If the prices differ, the elasticity must be smaller in the higher price market if the marginal revenues are equal.

retail margin. The effect of seepage on the demand curves will be illustrated in Chapter 14.

II. DEMAND UNDER OLIGOPOLY

We have already defined oligopoly as the situation in which a firm bases its market policy in part on the expected behavior of (a few) close rivals.* It is convenient to discuss this problem for the case of duopoly (i.e., when there is only one close rival), but the analysis can readily be extended to larger numbers. In the course of the analysis the boundary where the number of rivals becomes so large as to lose the character of oligopoly will be developed. We begin with the simpler case where the two firms produce products which consumers believe to be homogeneous, and there are no close substitutes.†

i. *HOMOGENEOUS PRODUCTS*

It is well to begin by observing that there are several satisfactory theories of duopoly, and that there is room for many more.‡ There are many possible situations in which two rivals may find themselves, and this accounts for a portion of the numerous theories. But a second factor also deserves attention: once we leave perfect competition we enter the terrain of personal relationships. Under perfect competition the effects of the idiosyncrasies of an entrepreneur are not likely to be worth discussing; under imperfect competition they can make a vast difference in the final result.

There are certain circumstances in which a duopolist can be certain of his rival's policy. It will suffice to analyze his demand curve in three of these cases.

First, the rival may be operating subject to known restrictions on price or output. For example, the rival may be a foreign producer confronted by an import quota or by a customs duty. Or for tech-

* If there are many close rivals, the effect of (e.g.) a price cut on the sales of any one will be small, so the behavior of rivals may properly be ignored; see p. 91.

† This last condition is necessary to prevent the duopoly from becoming an oligopoly: if there is a close substitute, each duopolist must also make an estimate of the probable reactions of the producer of the substitute.

‡ Some of the traditional theories are summarized by E. Chamberlin, *The Theory of Monopolistic Competition*, 3rd ed., Harvard University, Cambridge, 1938, Ch. 3, and by George J. Stigler, "Notes on the Theory of Duopoly," *Journal of Political Economy*, XLVIII (1940), 521–41.

nical reasons he may be forced to produce at a constant rate of output. Such cases are fairly important and they offer no difficulties in analysis — the appropriate technique is suggested by the next case.

Second, there is the well-known situation of the price-leader — the case of the dominant firm. Such a firm supplies a substantial part of total sales (probably one-fourth at a minimum). It has numerous small, independent rivals, but the situation can be viewed as one of duopoly because all of these firms behave competitively (i.e., they operate at the output where marginal cost equals price). The dominant firm behaves passively — it fixes the price and allows the minor firms to sell all they wish at this price. What is the demand curve of the dominant firm? The answer is given with

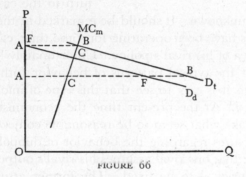

FIGURE 66

reference to Figure 66. We know, at the outset, the total market-demand curve and the marginal-cost curves of the minor firms. In the figure D_t represents the market-demand curve and MC_m the horizontal sum of the marginal-cost curves of the minor firms. At any price, OA, consumers will purchase AB of the commodity. At this price, the minor firms will sell AC. Clearly the remainder, CB, is the quantity that can be sold by the dominant firm. If we set AF equal to CB, and connect the points F, we secure D_d the demand curve of the dominant firm.

Finally, there may be collusion between the two firms. This is a simple alternative and, it will be shown later, usually a mutually profitable one. With collusion the duopolists will agree on a common price policy and make some agreement as to how sales are to be shared. There is no economic principle which governs the division of the market; more will be said on this matter later (page 275). But once the division is made, the duopolists' demand curves are completely defined. Thus if A receives two-thirds, and B one-third, of the total sales, their demand curves are such that at

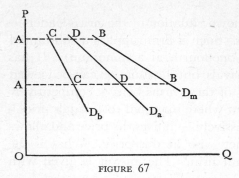

any price A's sales are twice those of B. The derivation is shown in Figure 67; AC is one-third of AB and AD is two-thirds of AB.

FIGURE 67

So much for situations in which a duopolist knows from the data of the problem what his rival's reaction to a price change will be; let us turn to the case where these reactions are unknown. It should be remarked at the outset that if two duopolists have been operating for some time, each will have a fairly good idea of his rival's policy. Unfortunately little study has been made of the typical patterns of behavior (other than collusion), although it is easy to see that this type of information is not easily collected. At the present time the economist can do little more than make what seem to be reasonable conjectures.

Two conjectures regarding the behavior of duopolists have long been popular: that one rival assumes his rival's output — or, alternatively, his price — to be fixed. The former assumption (fixed output of rival) is associated with the name of Cournot; the latter (fixed price) with Bertrand. In the Bertrand case the derivation of the demand curve of one duopolist is very simple (see Table 17): at any price less than that charged by B, A can supply the whole market, and vice versa. According to this theory, A would undercut B's price and temporarily secure the whole market, only to lose it

TABLE 17

Price of A	Quantity Sold by A	Price of B	Quantity Sold by B	Total Sold or Purchased	Effective Price
$50	100	$50	100	200	$50
49	210	50	0	210	49
49	0	48	220	220	48
47	230	48	0	230	47

when B cut his price in turn. This process would continue until the price reached the competitive level, that is, until it reached marginal cost. But long before this point was reached the most stupid duopolist would have at least a faint suspicion that perhaps his rival's price could not be assumed to remain at a higher level when he had undercut it. The assumptions of Bertrand and Cournot are unreasonable.*

There are many assumptions which are reasonable. Perhaps the simplest is that a rival will always be forced to match a price cut in order to sell any quantity at all. But then, since the product is homogeneous, customers will be paired at random with the two producers and the market demand will be divided equally between them. (The precise derivation of a duopolist's demand curve would follow the process illustrated by Figure 67.)

It is not necessary to multiply assumptions of this type. Clearly there are an endless number of reasonable assumptions, and they lead to a wide variety of demand curves for any duopolist. Among the factors which surely are relevant one may list:

1. The speed with which one rival reacts to changes in the other's policy.
2. The relative sizes of the two firms.
3. The mobility of purchasers, including the extent to which long-term contracts are used.
4. The possibility of keeping price concessions secret.
5. The costs and gains in driving the rival out of business.

Let us turn now to the case of differentiated products, where the two firms produce different products which are good substitutes for one another.

ii. DIFFERENTIATED PRODUCTS

Because of the personal element in imperfect competition, it is not possible to erect a precise criterion of when two products are good enough substitutes for one another to force each producer to watch his rival's policy and his effects on that policy. A well-informed, aggressive entrepreneur may concern himself with a rival product when the cross-elasticity is (say) .1; an ignorant and lethargic entrepreneur may disregard a rival product with a cross-

* The Cournot theory differs in details but not in principle; see problem 5 to this chapter.

elasticity of 1. A cross-elasticity of 10 certainly implies duopoly and one of .01 certainly does not, but in the absence of empirical studies it is not possible to put narrow limits on the criterion.

Many and perhaps most cases of what are commonly called *monopoly* are, in our terminology, instances of duopoly with differentiated products. It is difficult, indeed, to find a monopolized product for which there is no good substitute. Chevrolets, Fords, and Plymouths are obviously good substitutes for one another. Commonly the substitution is not so simple or complete. Gas is usually a local "monopoly," yet it must compete with coal, oil, and electricity in heating and cooking and with electricity and ice in refrigeration. Aluminum was long produced only by the Aluminum Company of America, but it competed with copper in wiring, wood in furniture, and iron and steel in a hundred uses such as automobile pistons and kitchen utensils.

The derivation of the demand curve of one producer contains one new element in the case of differentiated products. With identical products, the prices of both products must be equal if both firms are to share in the sales.* But with differentiated products this is no longer true and if the products are very different it becomes impossible to compare prices.†

The net effects of a price cut by one of the duopolists (A) now depends upon three factors:

1. The elasticity of the "total market" demand for products of the two duopolists.‡
2. The rate at which consumers shift from the rival's product to A's product, the price of the rival's product remaining fixed. This is measured by the cross-elasticity of demand.
3. The probable price policy of the rival.

When the products are homogeneous, the second factor does not require specification — the cross-elasticity of demand is always

---

* Unless, of course, there is collusion and the low-price firm accepts only a certain quantity of sales and turns all unsatisfied customers over to the high-price firm.

† Thus it is meaningless to ask whether the price of oil is higher or lower than that of coal; the answer depends upon our arbitrary selection of the units in which we measure oil and coal. For a specific use, however, such a price comparison is possible; thus if equal energy can be secured from a ton of coal or 190 gallons of oil, oil is cheap when 190 gallons sell for less than a ton of coal.

‡ This demand curve may temporarily be assigned the common-sense meaning of (e.g.) the demand for all brands of typewriters; the notion is discussed later.

(plus) infinity. In general we shall assume here that the first two factors are known to the entrepreneur. There remains the same unknown we confronted in the theory of duopoly with homogeneous products: how will a rival react to a change in price? It is not necessary to repeat the previous discussion of the large number of assumptions a duopolist may reasonably make, but with differentiated products there are several simple cases which deserve explicit attention.

First, one commodity (A) may be produced by a single firm and the other product (B), which is a good substitute for A, by a competitive industry (the analogue of the dominant firm, although here A need not be dominant and in fact may be much less important). In this case (more or less illustrated by ethyl gasoline, when it still had an uncontrolled patent monopoly, and regular grades of gasoline) the behavior of the competitive market will be known: it will of course follow the general pattern analyzed in Chapter 9. Second, the rival may be so much larger that no retaliation need be feared: telegraph companies can take the postal rates as fixed. In such cases the probable price change of the rival is known and the demand curve of the duopolist is not difficult to derive.

In any case the possibility of price competition is materially increased when the products are differentiated. It is inconceivable that the Freeport Sulphur Company think it could long sell chemically standardized sulphur at a price lower than that charged by the Texas Gulf Sulphur Company; it is much more reasonable for an electric company to attract purchasers of gas at lower rates. Retaliation may still be expected in general, but the pressure to retaliate is not so severe for the price cut reduces but does not destroy the rival's market as in the case of homogeneous products.* Moreover the obstacle to retaliation is greater: very likely B has (say) five important uses, A is a good substitute in only two. If B's price is cut in response to a cut in the price of A, B retains his share of the two markets only at the cost of reduced profits in the three more sheltered markets. (If price discrimination can be practiced, however, this objection to retaliation loses some of its force.) We may conclude that the prospects of price competition are much stronger if the products are differentiated, and in fact, that up to a

* And then probably only slowly. Recall that the short-run demand curve is usually less elastic than the long-run demand curve (p. 93).

certain point the smaller the cross-elasticity, the more probable it is that the duopolists will engage in price competition.*

III. *NONPRICE COMPETITION*

It is a matter only of terminology whether the producers of homogeneous products can engage in nonprice competition. If the products are identical in all respects — credit terms, promptness of delivery, pleasantness of personality of the two producers, etc. — obviously they cannot compete in these directions and still remain homogeneous, so all competition must be in price.† But this point should suggest two generalizations. The first is obvious: there are few cases of rigorously identical products. The second is more important: there is a strong tendency for duopolists to differentiate their products with the passage of time in order to reduce the rival's competitive power. We need not explore here all of the forms which this product differentiation may take; among the possibilities are the services just cited, actual modification of the physical nature of the product, and branding plus extensive advertising.

It might be objected that (e.g.) an advertising program would be just as likely to lead to retaliation as a price cut. But duopolists seem much less worried about nonprice competition. The sensitivity to prices is due in large part to two circumstances. First, prices are usually the most precisely measurable variables of market policy, and it is difficult to maintain a consistently higher price (for substantially similar commodities) except in the most uninformed consumer markets. But quality of product, for example, is less easily measured; it is not possible for the typical consumer to decide definitively between V–8 and six-cylinder motors as he can between prices of $900 and $800. Second, prices have been the publicized variable of market policy: there are a thousand denunciations of the price "chiseler" to one of excessive advertising, and some competitive policies (e.g., quality improvement) dare not be criticized publicly because of strong moral sanctions. It may be added,

---

* But it should not be inferred that the poorer the substitute, the lower the price. The smaller the cross-elasticity the smaller will be the elasticity of demand for one producer's output and hence the less the incentive to cut prices. The point in the text is only that duopolistic retaliation is less of a limitation on price policy if the products are poor substitutes.

† In markets where buyers are not well-informed, even price differences make two otherwise identical products seem different to the buyer.

finally, that the game of business would become intolerably dull if all modes of rivalry were suppressed. Recall the tale of Cineas.

IV. *NEW FIRMS*

Let us first consider briefly the case of duopoly with homogeneous products. Unless new firms can be prevented from entering the industry, one would expect the duopolists' profits (if any) to attract additional rivals. Some of the leading methods by which potential rivals may be excluded have already been summarized (pages 208 ff.) and the full list is long, but in many, and perhaps in most, cases new firms can enter.* The effect on the demand curve of the individual firm of an increase in the number of producers depends upon the oligopolistic assumptions we employ, as in the case of two firms. If all firms share equally (as is true when prices are matched), the demand curve of each firm shifts to the left whenever a new firm enters, for at any price each firm sells $1/N$ of the total quantity demanded if N is the number of firms. As N grows, however, the probability of price competition increases (see Section V).

Turning now to duopoly with differentiated products, we must first retrace our steps and ask: how is the differentiation determined for the two original products? It must be confessed at once that there is no general answer. If the products are technologically dissimilar (e.g., coal and oil), the differentiation rests on technological developments — a large and complex subject which is beyond our present framework. If the products are technologically similar, the differentiation is more directly related to economic calculations. It will be sufficient to discuss two cases of such market-oriented differentiation to indicate the type of factors at work.

First, the variety of tastes which can usually be found in any large group of consumers makes it profitable for the duopolists to specialize on different products. It is difficult to account for the peculiarities of other people's tastes; of even so simple a product as pease porridge it is said that

> Some like it hot,
> Some like it cold,
> Some like it in the pot
> Nine days old.

* Even more often the new firms can make substitutes; this is considered subsequently.

The ground is thus laid for a fierce advertising duel, complete with testimony from leading European physicians.* Second, even though consumers are in substantial agreement on what they want (gasoline is an example), often they lack the technical knowledge to recognize the relevant characteristics. In this case the differentiated products will be technologically very similar, although if consumers are very ignorant the cross-elasticity may be relatively small. But if the products are technologically similar, one would expect every successful claim of A to be imitated by B, while B in turn exploited new claims to keep the cross-elasticity (and hence the competitive power of A) low.† This situation is likely to be characterized by continuous nonprice competition because the duopolists are catering to essentially the same consumer needs.

In the light of even these brief remarks it is clear that the types of products that will be produced by new firms are not subject to any general rule. Where consumers' preferences are more or less evenly distributed over a range of possible products, new firms will make products more extreme than those hitherto available or products which fall between existing brands. In either case the final effect is to increase the cross-elasticity of demand for the original products,‡ but there is no assurance that duopoly relationships will disappear. Producer A may be forced to consider reactions of his policy on Producer B, who makes a good substitute, even though a half-dozen more distant substitutes are in the field.§ On the other hand, if consumers are concentrated (as in the gasoline case), the situation will probably differ little from that of homogeneous products.

v. *THE CRITERION OF DUOPOLY*

If the cross-elasticities of demand for commodity A with respect to all other prices are small, the producer of A need not consider the effects of his market policy on the makers of substitutes, for the

* This problem is usually treated by analogy to the theory of spatial location. See A. Smithies, "Optimum Location in Spatial Competition," *Journal of Political Economy*, XLIX (1941), 423–40, and references there cited.

† Relative to the previous footnote, the chief difference in this second case is that the consumers are bunched within a small "area" of preferences whereas in the former situation the consumers are distributed more or less uniformly alone a "line."

‡ The original products will also usually change. Differences from, or similarities to, the new product will be emphasized.

§ See the remarks on "chained" markets, p. 236.

effect on any one rival is small. At this end, therefore, duopoly merges into monopoly. Or the cross-elasticities may be of substantial size, but if there are enough good substitutes, the effects of A's policy on any one rival will again be small. At this end duopoly merges into a competitive (but not necessarily perfectly competitive) situation.

In investigating this latter case it will be useful to present a theorem from the theory of demand. Suppose that there are N good substitutes for a commodity A and that the cross-elasticity of demand for A with respect to each of the substitutes' prices is K. Then it can be shown that if all other prices remain fixed, the elasticity of demand for A is approximately

$$- NK - \eta_{ar},$$

where η_{ar} is the income elasticity of A.* That is to say, a 1 per cent reduction in p_a will lead to about an NK per cent increase in the sales of A if all other prices remain fixed.

It follows that the larger N, given K, the less the price reduction necessary to secure any desired increase in the sales of A, and hence the more profitable that price reduction. And the larger N, the less the effect of any given increase in the sales of A on the sales of rival products: if sales of A increase M per cent, sales of each rival fall by (less than) M/N per cent. Hence a larger N serves in two ways to bring about price competition: it reduces the amount by which p_a must be cut in order to achieve a given larger output, and it reduces the probability of retaliation.

The cross-elasticities focus attention on the gains of one firm at the expense of close rivals; we must notice also the elasticity of demand for the whole group of commodities produced by the oligopolists.† The general meaning of the demand curve for a group of related but heterogeneous products is simple: if, for ex-

* More precisely,

$$\eta_{apa} = - \sum_{i=1}^{n'} \eta_{api \cdot pa} - \eta_{ar},$$

where n' is the number of other commodities. The effect of poor substitutes (and of complements) is neglected in the expression in the text. See H. Schultz, *The Theory and Measurement of Demand*, University of Chicago, Chicago, 1938, p. 621n.

† The group may be defined as all firms whose cross-elasticities are greater than some constant. This constant can best be chosen in any particular problem by ranking the cross-elasticities and considering a group to end when a considerable gap appears in the array of cross-elasticities. See pp. 280 ff.

ample, all makes of electric irons are reduced 10 per cent in price, there will be a net increase in the sales of irons because consumers will shift to this class of commodities.* The greater this "over-all" elasticity of demand, the less any oligopolist need fear the retaliation of his rivals when he cuts price, for the greater is the share of "new" sales in whatever increase of output he secures.

But such formal considerations will never yield us a critical number of rivals beyond which oligopoly disappears. Among a handful of avaricious, double-crossing members of one industry, secret price cuts (which usually do not remain secret) may become more frequent and overt; in industries dominated by conservative bankers or vivid memories of recent " cutthroat competition," price competition may require many rivals.   In general, one would ex-pect the critical number for price competition to be smaller,

1. The younger the industry, for a variety of reasons.
2. The more uniform the size of the firms; a dominant firm can retaliate more quickly and effectively than a group.
3. The more heterogeneous the products (i.e., the lower the cross-elasticities).
4. The wider the variations in efficiency.†

In the foregoing discussion it was explicitly assumed that the cross-elasticities were of equal size.‡ If this is not true, the presumption that a larger number of rivals will lead to greater price com-petition is weakened although not destroyed. In this latter case of unequal cross-elasticities the firms may be "chained," so that a larger number of rivals merely implies a longer chain or shorter links. The following quotation concerning a gasoline price war illustrates this case, and it gives some incidental support to the argument that personal factors are important under imperfect competition:

A 2 cent discount sign went up in a station in Petworth one morning. A dealer across the street asked why. He was told it was necessary

---

* This concept is ambiguous on one point: the elasticity depends upon the structure of prices of the various substitute products. The effects of a general 10 per cent reduc-tion in the price of electric irons when all irons sell for $5 will not be the same as when they sell for various prices with an average of $5. Yet the ambiguity arising on this score is probably relatively small.

† Costs are treated in some detail in Chapter 14.

‡ That is, $\eta_{ap_b} = \eta_{ap_c} = \eta_{ap_d} = \cdots$.

because another dealer six blocks down the street had done it the day before.

The inquisitive operator went there and got the same story. He worked his way gradually downtown, getting almost identical answers. At last, near Griffith Stadium, he found a station operated by a woman and the story changed.

"Yes, I put that sign up a week ago. That (censored) so-and-so around the corner last week called my husband a (censored), and I'm going to show him he can't do that to me," she explained.

The tireless investigator sought out "that —— so-and-so," who also was a filling station operator. The latter readily admitted the incident and said he was drunk at the time and didn't mean it.

"Will you apologize to the lady," he was asked. He agreed and went around to Mrs. X, and did so. The price cutting sign came down. Slowly the Petworth dealer retraced his steps. Each time he told his story, a sign came down. Some were cynical, but a call to Mrs. X convinced them. Thus was one price war ended.*

III. THE DEMAND CURVE WHEN THERE ARE A LARGE NUMBER OF PRODUCERS

Although oligopoly disappears when the number of producers of the same product or closely related products becomes sufficiently large, it is not necessary that perfect competition appear. As a matter of fact, it is arguable that imperfect competition is quantitatively more important in the case of numerous producers simply because these industries are usually large. We shall follow the previous classification into homogeneous and heterogeneous products.

1. *HOMOGENEOUS PRODUCTS: THE CARTEL*

If there are many independent producers of a homogeneous product, competition will rule unless the producers act in concert. An agreement between producers as to price (and perhaps also outputs, credit terms, etc.) may be termed a *cartel*.† If the price is determined upon by the cartel, the quantity that may be sold is uniquely determined (given the amount of advertising expenditures, etc.) and the problem of allocating this output between the member

* *Washington Daily News*, August 13, 1940, p. 15.

† The word *cartel* is frequently used in the narrower sense of a combination of producers who enter into a legally enforceable contract with respect to price and perhaps other market variables, illustrated by the German *Kartelle* and our own NRA codes. Here it will be used more broadly.

firms arises. There are two general methods of making this allocation: by nonprice competition; and by quotas.

Under the method of nonprice competition, each firm is permitted to sell as much as it can without cutting prices. This is the
method used in some of the professions,* by retailers operating
under resale-price maintenance,† and by groups which secure "fair
trade practices" acts (e.g., barbers in Minnesota) or legal price
minima (milk in New York State). The effects of the nonprice
competition on profits and prices will be examined in Chapter 14,
so this method of allocating outputs may be passed over.

The second method of allocation is by quota. There is no general
principle by which quotas are or could be determined; the share of a
firm depends upon its importance to the cartel, the skill with which
its representatives bargain, their ability to hold liquor, and similar
factors. The nature of the determination is illuminated by the
characterization in the German literature, *Quotenkampf*. The most
common statistical bases for quotas are relative sales of the firms in
some base period and their relative productive "capacities."

The net effect of the assignment of quotas is of course to split the
market demand curve up into as many parts as there are firms in the
cartel.‡ If the firms are given fixed proportions of sales, the elasticity of demand for the product of any one firm will at any price be
equal to that for the output of the entire cartel. Various administrative devices such as penalties on sales in excess of quotas or
pooling of profits may be em-
ployed to restrict firms to
their allocated shares.

The well-known tendency
of such cartels to collapse if
they are based on nonenforce-
able agreements (as is usually
the case in the United States)
is due to the profitability of
violations. The demand and
marginal-revenue curves of a
firm in a cartel are *DBC* and

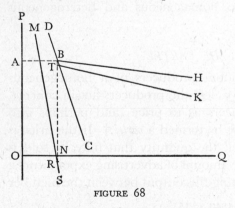

FIGURE 68

---

* Here the Code of Ethics is frequently the basis of the price agreement.

† Here an enforceable contract is the basis of the price agreement.

‡ If there are firms outside the cartel, the demand curve of the cartel is derived by a
procedure identical with that presented for the case of the dominant firm (p. 227).

MRS respectively in Figure 68; the price set by the cartel is *NB*. If any one firm secretly grants slight price concessions, its sales of the homogeneous product will of course increase greatly; its demand and marginal revenue curves become *DBH* and *MRTK* respectively. The temptation to grant price concessions is thus very strong, especially if the firm is not making large profits at output *ON*. Such secret concessions need not be granted very extensively before the more obedient members of the cartel will experience a material decline of their demand curves.

II. DIFFERENTIATED PRODUCTS: MONOPOLISTIC COMPETITION

When many firms produce a homogeneous product some form of collusion must underlie imperfect competition in the selling market. The very fact of effective differentiation, on the other hand, implies a downward sloping demand curve for the individual firm and hence imperfect competition. We shall concentrate on the case where each entrepreneur is free of cartel restrictions.

If there are numerous poor substitutes for a commodity, we have monopoly; if there are numerous good substitutes, we have monopolistic competition.* There is thus the problem of determining when the substitutes become good enough to shift a firm from the category of monopoly to that of monopolistic competition, without pushing it into substantially perfect competition.

In the discussion of the somewhat similar problem of the criterion of duopoly it was concluded that no general answer could be given but that if all the facts were known in a specific case, a definite decision could be made. Not even this latter assurance can be given in the present case: cross-elasticities can vary from infinity to a small value, and any division of this range into monopoly, monopolistic competition, and near perfect competition, must be arbitrary.

Yet there is a vast quantitative difference between the demand curve for telephone service — a product with no good substitutes — and that of any one of a hundred brands of cotton dresses; in the latter case the demand curve is certain to be highly elastic and the deviation from a competitive situation only minor. If consumers generally treated as similar (but not necessarily as identical) goods

---

* If there are a few good substitutes, we have oligopoly. Professor Chamberlin, in his pioneer *Theory of Monopolistic Competition*, includes oligopoly in monopolistic competition. Here it is deemed preferable to use the phrase to denote a more specific market structure.

which are technologically similar, it would be possible to make considerable progress in isolating these cases of monopolistic competition by counting the number of producers of what (e.g.) the Census defines as a product. But unfortunately consumers do not always display such knowledge, witness the enormous disparities between the prices of chemically similar drugs and cosmetics.* Technological similarity of many products is necessary for monopolistic competition, but so also is consumer information.

Nevertheless when there are numerous producers of technologically similar commodities there is a presumption that the demand curve for any one brand will be fairly elastic. One ground for the presumption is that consumers are not so ignorant in all their purchases as the more glaring examples might suggest. They have succeeded fairly well in resisting the suggestion that a particular color or trade name is indispensable to good gasoline, or that advertising improves the flavor of sugar. And a second factor is unfortunately more important: the competition of sellers. There are not so many important features of the usual group of commodities that each producer can long emphasize a distinctive appeal. If certain claims are successful in attracting customers, rivals will soon imitate these claims. (This suggests that within the group of products duopolistic relationships will often, and perhaps usually, appear.) There is a presumption, therefore, that when a considerable number of firms produce similar products the demand curve for any one brand will be elastic, and this presumption is stronger, the more informed the consumers and the more numerous the producers.

Observation tells us, however, that the monopolistic features introduced by differentiation are buttressed by collusion in many important cases. If the demand of the individual firm is elastic collusion is indispensable for monopoly gains, and even if the product differentiation is effective collusion will reduce competitive pressures. Since the demand problems are in essentials similar to those already discussed in the case of homogeneous products, the previous analysis need not be repeated.

* For examples, see reference 6 to Ch. 11.

RECOMMENDED READINGS

1. Triffin, R., *Monopolistic Competition and General Equilibrium Theory*, Harvard University, Cambridge, 1940, esp. Ch. 3.
2. Chamberlin, E., *The Theory of Monopolistic Competition*, 3rd ed., Harvard University, Cambridge, 1938, esp. Ch. 4, 5.
3. Pigou, A. C., *The Economics of Welfare*, 4th ed., Macmillan, London, 1932, Ch. 17.
4. Stigler, G. J., "Notes on the Theory of Duopoly," *Journal of Political Economy*, XLVIII (1940), 521–41.

PROBLEMS

1. Examine the relationship, marginal revenue $= p(1 + 1/\eta)$, in the following cases:

   a. $\eta = - \infty$.

   b. $\eta = - 10$.

   c. $\eta = - 1$ (Query: at what output will a monopolist operate if $\eta = - 1$ at all points?).

   d. $\eta = - 1/2$ (Same query).

   Draw demand and marginal-revenue curves for all of these cases.

2. Draw the following "kinky" demand curve and the discontinuous marginal-revenue curve appropriate to it:

   a. At prices above \$10, $p = \$12 - q/5$.

   b. Between \$10 and \$8, $p = \$20 - q$.

   c. At prices below \$8, $p = \$9.5 - q/8$.

3. (Review of cross-elasticities; see also p. 88.) Determine on the basis of the following data in which category of imperfect competition A falls.

   a. A and B.

Quantity of A	100	101
Price of B	\$40	\$41

   b. A and C.

Quantity of A	100	101
Price of C	\$45	\$47

   c. A and D.

Quantity of A	100	110
Price of D	\$9	\$10

4. Under discrimination the demand curve of a monopolist is made up of two parts:

$$p = 160 - 8\,q, \text{ and } p = 80 - q/2.$$

Plot these demand curves and the appropriate marginal-revenue curves. Show both graphically and numerically that if 50 units are sold, it is most profitable to sell 7.6 units in the former market and 42.4 units in the latter market. Determine prices in the two markets; compare with nondiscriminating price for this total output.

5. The total demand curve for a product is $p = 100 - q$. A monopolist A, who has no costs of production, will operate at 50 units of output, i.e., where marginal revenue equals marginal cost, which in this case is zero. Now another firm B, which also has no costs of production, enters the field and both firms follow Cournot's assumption. Ascertain the final equilibrium price and outputs.

Hint: When B enters he will take A's output of 50 as fixed and seek an output which maximizes his profit subject to this assumption. This output for B is 25; prove. Then, due to the fall in price to \$25, A will seek a new output, taking B's output of 25 as fixed. After these changes occur a few times the final position can easily be guessed.

6. Construct the demand curve for a dominant firm, given the following data:

$p = 1000 - q$ is the total market-demand curve

$MC = 2q - 20$ is the sum of the marginal-cost curves of the minor firms.

7. Let the market-demand curve for a commodity be $p = 100 - q$. Derive the demand curves of A and B, who share the market in the ratio of 4 to 1. Compare the elasticities of these demand curves at a price of \$50.

8. Draw, on one graph, the demand curves for a firm belonging to a cartel which assigns each firm a quota of $1/1,000$ and (after 500 new firms enter the industry) $1/1,500$ of the total sales at any price. The cartel's demand curve is $p = 35 - q/100$.

CHAPTER 13

COSTS UNDER IMPERFECT COMPETITION

It is possible to analyze the cost curves of a firm in a manner parallel to the preceding discussion of demand curves. Some comments will be made along this line in the present chapter, but attention will first be directed to certain general problems in the treatment of costs under imperfect competition.

I. COST THEORY UNDER IMPERFECT COMPETITION

The fundamental definition of cost is still appropriate under imperfect competition: the cost of a productive service is the amount that must be paid by the firm to secure and hold the service — the alternative earnings of the productive service. If there is competition in the other industries in which the service is used, the cost is equal to the value of the marginal product in these uses since the competitive firm buys services in such quantities that their prices equal their marginal physical products times the price of the product (page 176).

If there is imperfect competition in the competing uses, the alternative earnings of the productive services are determined by a different principle, as the numerical example in Table 18 suggests. If the price of the productive service is $290, the firm will hire only 11 units, for the twelfth unit adds only $250 to total

TABLE 18

Quantity of the Productive Service	Total Physical Product	Marginal Physical Product	Demand Price	Total Receipts	Marginal Value Product	Value of the Marginal Product
10	200	—	$20.00	$4,000	—	
11	220	20	19.80	4,356	$356	$396
12	235	15	19.60	4,606	250	294

243

receipts and hence would not pay for itself. Yet the value of the marginal product of 12 units is 15 times $19.60, or $294, which is more than the price of the productive service. The demand price appropriate to imperfect competition is easily deduced, however. The most that an entrepreneur will pay per unit for a given quantity of a productive service is the amount a unit of that service adds to his total receipts. We define this amount as the *marginal value product* of the productive service, or in slightly more general terms:

$$\text{Marginal value product} = \frac{\text{change in total receipts}}{\text{change in quantity of the service}}.$$

Recall the definitions:

$$\text{Marginal physical product} = \frac{\text{change in total product}}{\text{change in quantity of the service}}$$

$$\text{Marginal revenue} = \frac{\text{change in total receipts}}{\text{change in total product}}.$$

On substitution into the definition for marginal value product, we secure the basic relationship:

$$\text{Marginal value product} = \text{Marginal physical product} \times \text{marginal revenue.}$$

Under competition marginal revenue equals price and the equation reduces to the formula for the demand for a productive service developed in Chapter 9; in other cases marginal value product and value of the marginal product are not equal. In either case it is correct to say that the cost of a productive service to any firm is its marginal value product in other firms.

I. *TECHNICAL DERIVATION OF THE COST CURVES*

The detailed derivation of the cost curves under imperfect competition will be carried through here only for one simple case. That is the case in which a firm can exert an appreciable effect on the price of only one of the productive services it buys. It is further assumed that there is no personalized rivalry in the buying market corresponding to duopoly; this is a situation which will be discussed later (Section III).

The derivation of the cost curves will be made only for the short run.* Let the firm utilize only two productive services, a "fixed"

---

* For the derivation of the long-run curves, see problem 2 of this chapter.

service the total cost of which is $30, and a variable service the price of which rises as additional quantities are purchased. Let the supply schedule of this variable service be given by the equation $p = q/5 + 3$, where q is the quantity of the service purchased and p is its supply price. Then, using the production schedule of Table 11 (page 126), the costs are derived in Table 19.

TABLE 19

THE SHORT-RUN COSTS OF A MONOPOLY

Units of Variable Service	Total Product	Price of Variable Service	Total Variable Cost	Marginal Cost	Average Cost
0	0	$3.00	—	—	
1	5	3.20	$3.20	$0.64	$6.64
2	13	3.40	6.80	.45	2.83
3	23	3.60	10.80	.40	1.77
4	38	3.80	15.20	.29	1.19
5	50	4.00	20.00	.40	1.00
6	60	4.20	25.20	.52	.92
7	68	4.40	30.80	.70	.89
8	75	4.60	36.80	.86	.89
9	81	4.80	43.20	1.07	.90
10	86	5.00	50.00	1.36	.93
11	90	5.20	57.20	1.80	.97
12	93	5.40	64.80	2.53	1.02
13	95	5.60	72.80	4.00	1.08
14	96	5.80	81.20	8.40	1.16

The obviousness of the arithmetic in this table should not obscure a fundamental difference between the marginal costs in this case and under competition. Under competition, according to a well-known formula (page 127), marginal cost = (price of the variable service)/(marginal physical product of that service). If this formula is applied to our present example, at an output of 81 marginal cost would be $4.80/6 = $0.80, whereas actually it is $1.07. The discrepancy is due to the fact that when a ninth unit of the variable service is purchased, the price of the previous 8 units must rise $0.20 to achieve parity (unless price discrimination is practiced). If this increase in total cost ($8 \times \$0.20 = \$1.60$) is allocated to the appropriate increment of output (which is 6 units), marginal cost is increased by $\$1.60/6 = \$0.27$.

It is still possible to derive a general formula relating marginal cost to the price of the variable service. Let us define the following symbols:

> v — initial quantity of the variable service
> p — initial price of the variable service
> Δv — change in quantity of the variable service
> Δp — corresponding change in price of the variable service
> Δq — corresponding change in output

Then when the quantity of the variable service rises by Δv, total variable cost rises by ($p\,\Delta v + v\,\Delta p$), where the second term reflects the increased price paid for the initial quantity of the variable service. It follows, that

$$\text{marginal cost} = \frac{p\,\Delta v + v\,\Delta p}{\Delta q} = p\,\frac{\Delta v}{\Delta q} + v\,\frac{\Delta p}{\Delta q}$$

Multiply and divide the last term by Δv, and recall that $\dfrac{\Delta q}{\Delta v}$ = marginal product of the variable service and $\dfrac{p\,\Delta v}{v\,\Delta p}$ = elasticity of the supply curve of the variable service (see page 52). On making these substitutions, we secure the basic formula,

$$\text{marginal cost} = \frac{p}{MPP}\,(1 + 1/e),$$

where MPP is the marginal physical product of the variable service and e is the elasticity of supply of the service.*

II. THE EQUALITY OF COST AND PRICE

We may consider now an important problem concerning monopoly profits. Let the demand curve (D) and long-run average-cost curve (LAC) of a monopoly be those portrayed in Figure 69. The firm will operate at some output OA which maximizes its total profits ($OA \times BC$). Since the profits are due to the monopoly, they should be attributed to the patents, raw materials, franchise, location, or other factors on which the monopoly is based. If the

---

* Under competition e is infinity for the firm so the equation reduces to the formula given for that case (page 127).

firm is sold, its price will include the discounted value of the monopoly profits and the buyer of the monopoly will receive only a competitive rate of return on his investment. The long-run average-cost curve will shift up to tangency with the demand curve; the

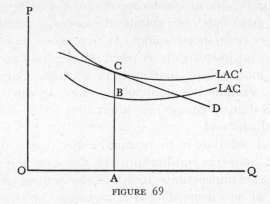

FIGURE 69

new curve is *LAC'* in Figure 69.* Even if the firm is not sold, the entrepreneur will often revalue the assets to eliminate profits. The (partial) realization of this practice is the chief reason why a low rate of return on investment is not evidence of the absence of monopoly profits.

Strictly speaking, the same phenomenon can occur under competition. If demand and hence price rise suddenly (see e.g., page 163), existing firms will make profits until new firms can enter the industry. If it requires a year to build a new plant and begin operations, an existing firm can sell its plant at a price equal to the value of the plant plus the profits which will be earned during the year. Under competition, however, the profits are restricted to the period within which new plants can be built so only short-run average costs are affected; under imperfect competition (and particularly "monopoly") the profits may continue indefinitely.

Thus if a firm makes profits, assets should be revalued upward; if losses, they should be revalued downward. Average cost always equals price; profits are zero by definition. This is of course a view of costs which clashes sharply with common sense. If *average cost* is used in this sense, it need not be used at all, since *price* is already available. Are there any conventions by which average cost can be

---

* Marginal cost will not be affected by the lump-sum increase in the interest on the increased value of the assets (see Proposition 5, p. 50).

restored to its independent status as a basis for measuring the profitability of an enterprise? Three such conventions may be suggested.

The first solution is pragmatic: eliminate from investment all intangibles such as "good will." This is the practice in many empirical studies, and it cannot be doubted that intangibles are frequently a good index of capitalized monopoly profits. Yet the method has evident shortcomings. It may leave capitalized monopoly profits in investment, as when ore deposits are valued on the basis of monopolistic marketing of the ore. Conversely, the practice may exclude nonmonopolistic costs, as when an asset is valued at less than its competitive alternative value and the difference is called *good will*.

The second solution is to reappraise the asset-valuations for conditions of long-run equilibrium. In this case the problem of profits disappears under competition and also in those cases in which the entrance of new firms eliminates monopoly profits. These are two extremely important cases, and in both long-run average costs as here defined would still serve as a guide to future investment and prices in the industry. But in the case of a well-entrenched monopoly, for example, average cost will still equal price although monopoly profits persist.

The third approach is to consider costs to be what they would be if the industry were competitive. Some technical difficulties to which this approach is subject will be suggested subsequently (page 252); here an important objection may be noted. The assumptions of competition could not possibly be met in many cases in which imperfect competition arises. It is inconceivable, because of the economies of scale, that there could be enough power companies in a small city to insure a competitive price; if this situation were brought about by compulsion the power rate would probably have to be much higher than that which an unregulated monopoly would set. One is placed in the position of asking what costs would be in a situation if that situation were impossibly different.

As a step removed, the technique is frequently to ask what investment would be if the entrepreneur acted as if he were subject to the pressure of perfect competition, i.e., if he acted wisely and prudently.* This is of course a criterion that is difficult to apply, for

---

* And as a step considerably farther removed, the historical cost is a basic factor in most public-utility valuations.

prudence must be judged in the light of the knowledge available at the time the investment was made. And since the soundness of a judgment is a matter over which even men with sound judgment may dispute, the method does not yield unique valuations of assets.

But what are the precise purposes in seeking a definition of average cost such that profits are not always zero? There seem to be two: First, to decide whether the price and investment in an industry are in equilibrium. This purpose is completely served by the second solution (in which the long-run cost curves are used), for then the equality of average cost and price indicates in all cases that the firm is in equilibrium.* Second, if there is a "monopoly" making what one suspects are monopoly profits, one may wish to know what price and investment policy should be dictated by a regulatory commission — a problem in welfare economics. But for this purpose it can be shown that average cost is a poor criterion to use in pricing; the investment and price should be set where long-run marginal cost (which does not contain monopoly gains) will equal price.† The problem is therefore largely a by-product of the common misapprehension of the nature of a system of optimum prices.

III. *RIVALRY IN BUYING*

It would be possible to develop the subject of rivalry in buying in a manner parallel to rivalry on the demand side. Thus a firm is monopolistic in buying (i.e., a monopsony) when there is no good alternative use for the productive service it buys. The firm is duopsonistic — its terminology is not the least repulsive characteristic of monopoly — when there is one good alternative use for the productive service, and the market is cartellized when there are restrictions on the freedom of the individual firm to compete. This development is so similar to that on the demand side that the details may be left for the reader to provide. It appears more profitable to consider here certain differences in emphasis on the buying side.

Competition is likely to be approximated much more closely in the purchase of productive services than in the markets for con-

---

* The present definition of average costs includes return on investment *after* those firms which can and wish to enter the industry have done so. Hence when entry of new firms is possible, the assets will be valued on the independent basis of their alternative products outside the industry.

† See A. P. Lerner, "Statics and Dynamics in Socialist Economics," *Economic Journal*, XLVII (1937), 253–70.

sumer goods. The primary explanation is quantitative: firms which have achieved protected consumer markets in which they have some discretion in price policy usually appear as relatively unimportant buyers in the markets for productive services and goods. The makers of Coca Cola, for example, have considerable control over its retail price but they have little control over the price of sugar. Another factor pointing in the same direction is the greater knowledge of industrial buyers, which restrict the scope for product differentiation in the markets for equipment and materials. Where a productive service is supplied by a strong monopoly or its price is regulated by law, the individual buyer may have no control over the price.

A second point is that when duopolistic relationships arise on the buying side, the likelihood of rivalry (rather than open or tacit collusion) is considerably greater than when the corresponding situation exists on the demand side. The explanation has already been given (page 232): aggressive businessmen who find rivalry in price-cutting too expensive or too certain to invite retaliation will nevertheless seek other methods by which to maintain or improve their positions. There are several reasons for this preference for rivalry in buying over rivalry in selling. First, the effects of many forms of rivalry (e.g., in research, advertising, location, personnel policies) are not immediate and hence do not demand quick retaliation as is true in the case of price cuts. Second, and in part because of the futurity of the effects,* there will be disagreement even among cooperating "rivals" as to the efficiency and the wisdom of various practices which will lead to differences in policy — i.e., to a form of rivalry. Thus the leading firms in the steel industry have succeeded after a long struggle in arriving at bids on governmental contracts which are identical to five decimal places, but they have disagreed sharply on wage and labor policies. Finally, there are very substantial political and administrative difficulties in arriving at a satisfactory basis for collusion, and these difficulties multiply with the increase in the number of policies on which the rivals wish to collude. This important point will be elaborated in the next chapter (page 272).

A third point is that differences in the "services" of buyers, the

---

* But also in part because it is usually impossible to isolate the precise effects of the type of rivalry under consideration.

analogue of product differentiation, are relatively unimportant. This fact is attributable in part to the greater knowledge of the suppliers of industrial materials and equipment, but it is due perhaps even more to the fact that the prices in question are of basic importance in determining the incomes of suppliers (whereas the expenditure of a consumer on any one product is usually only a small fraction of his income). The role of buying services seems to be most important in the labor market: a firm can, within limits set by the knowledge and the strength of organization of the laborers, substitute pleasant working conditions, personal relationships, etc., for higher wage rates.

iv. *PRODUCTION VS. SELLING COSTS*

Economists generally distinguish between production and selling costs, but the basis of this distinction varies considerably. One important school has attempted to erect analytical criteria for dividing costs between these two categories; thus selling costs may be defined as those which shift the demand curve or as those which do not "really" satisfy consumer needs, and production costs are a residual. But all of the definitions so far offered are either ambiguous in application or rest on personal standards of value which are hardly acceptable bases for economic analysis.

Moreover it is not always clear why a distinction between production and selling costs should be made. On the cost side, there is no difference; advertising media, for example, are also exploited in such proportions that their marginal-value products are equal to their marginal costs. Similarly one would expect selling activities to be subject to the law of diminishing marginal returns. On the demand side, it is true that selling expenditures affect the demand curve for a product, but surely it is equally true that production costs affect the demand curve. This effect is obscured in the case of competition, for it is a customary methodological device to start with a homogeneous product and define production costs as the minimum expenditure necessary (at various outputs) to produce this product. It is not a change in principle, however, to recognize that corresponding to various products there will be both different costs and different demands. The popular distinction between costs which affect demand and those which do not is equivalent to a classification of costs between necessary and useless; obviously no entrepreneur motivated only by profits will make *any* expenditures which do not affect demand.

Yet the attempted distinction is made in response to two real needs. First, it is tedious and cumbersome to write the demand and cost functions explicitly in terms of each variable, e.g., durability, size, shape, color, attractiveness of container, and subsequent usefulness of container. Second, there is the question of economic policy — are selling expenditures desirable, and if so by whom should they be made, in what measure, and in what form? Only the former point will be considered here although the latter point has probably dominated economists' discussions.

When there is a basic type of product, defined in technological terms, which consumers demand, and the differentiated products in the market do not differ greatly (again measured in technological terms) it seems feasible to divide all costs between those which are incurred to meet the technological requirements ("production" costs) and those designed to stimulate demand for a particular brand ("selling" costs). In this important case it is very convenient to talk in terms of production and selling costs even though the basis of the distinction is hard to apply in borderline cases. If, however, there is no basic technological type of product it seems quite futile to draw a line between those costs which do and those which do not affect the demand curve: in this case it will be necessary to recognize explicitly the fact that all expenditures are oriented with respect to their effect on salability.

II. COMPARISONS OF COMPETITION AND IMPERFECT COMPETITION

Despite the difficulties involved, there is an apparently irresistible urge to compare various forms of imperfect competition with perfect competition. The fundamental objective of such comparisons is clear enough: one wishes to determine which of these forms of economic organization (e.g., a monopoly, a cartel, or the ICC) is most inefficient and to formulate appropriate policies of economic reform. The chief difficulties in these comparisons usually arise on the cost side, so the subject deserves some attention at this point. Two comparisons will be made: between a monopoly and a firm making a differentiated product, respectively, and perfect competition.

1. *MONOPOLY AND COMPETITION*

Let us assume, first, that the commodity in question is produced subject to constant costs, i.e., the amount of any productive service purchased by the industry will have no effect on the price of that service. In this case the long-run cost curves of a competitive firm and the supply curve of the competitive industry are those previously given in Figure 54 (page 163). What will the long-run costs of the monopoly be? To answer this question we must know the answers to two other questions:

a. Does each competitive firm have a technological unit of the most efficient size, or did managerial diseconomies cause its long-run average-cost curve to rise before this size of plant is reached?

b. How will the managerial costs of the monopoly compare with those of the competitive firms?

If the competitive firm has not reached the most efficient technological size, the monopolist will build his plants of this latter size and hence have lower production costs. But on the other hand, if competitive firms are estopped from reaching minimum production costs because of managerial difficulties, this would reinforce the general presumption that the managerial costs of the monopolist would be higher than those of the competitive firms.* One would expect, therefore, that the long-run average-cost curve of the monopolist would lie slightly above the horizontal supply curve of the competitive industry and that it would rise at a rate governed by managerial costs. Similar remarks hold for the short-run cost curves, making allowance for the fact that the monopolist will operate fewer plants than a competitive industry.

In many industries, however, there will be important productive services the prices of which rise as the industry increases its purchases — these are increasing-cost industries (see page 163). Here is introduced a new element which is simply explained by consideration of the supply curve for such a specialized productive service (Figure 70). Suppose the industry, whether competitive or monopolized, is purchasing OM units of this productive service at a price of MP. To a competitive firm, which purchases so little of the productive service as to consider its price constant, both the

---

* If the competition is imperfect, the monopolist could make savings by eliminating certain "competitive" costs (e.g., a portion of the advertising) but such costs do not exist under perfect competition.

average and the marginal cost of the service are MP. The monopoly, however, must recognize that its purchase of the Mth unit has raised the prices of the preceding units, so that the marginal cost of the productive service is MR. This marginal cost has no significance for the competitive industry.

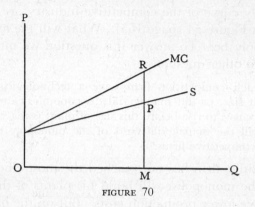

FIGURE 70

This difference between a competitive industry and a monopoly in the calculation of the marginal cost of a productive service is reflected in the cost curves in two ways. The first effect may be isolated by assuming that the supply curves of all productive services have the same elasticities. We recall the equations,

Under competition: marginal cost = p_i/MPP_i
Under monopoly: marginal cost = $p_i(1 + 1/e_i)/MPP_i$,

where p_i is the price of any productive service, MPP_i is its marginal physical product, and e_i is the elasticity of supply of that service. By comparison the marginal cost of the monopoly will be to the marginal cost of the competitive firms in the ratio of $(1 + 1/e_i)$ to 1, which of course exceeds unity in increasing-cost industries.

The second effect follows from the fact that all productive services do not have supply curves of equal elasticity: some supply curves will rise rapidly, others slowly, and still others will be horizontal.* The monopolist will use productive services A and B in such proportion that

$$p_a(1 + 1/e_a)/MPP_a = p_b(1 + 1/e_b)/MPP_b,$$

---

* The case of negatively sloping supply curves is considered below.

whereas the competitive firms will utilize them in such proportion that

$$p_a/MPP_a = p_b/MPP_b.$$

Only if all of the elasticities of supply are equal, realistically an impossible condition, will the proportions be equal in the two cases.

The rationale of this difference in proportions is simple: the rates at which prices of productive services rise are beyond the control and outside the calculations of a competitive firm; they are within the control and hence reflected in the calculations of the monopolist. The monopolist possesses, so to speak, an additional degree of freedom in his choice of productive services: he can substitute services the prices of which rise slowly (if at all) for those which rise rapidly. As a result, his average costs will be less than those of the competitive firms. (This effect may be overcome, however, by the greater managerial costs referred to in the constant-cost case.) Because of the first effect, however, his marginal-cost curve may still be higher than the supply curve of the competitive industry, and this becomes more probable (1) the more equal the elasticities of supply, (2) the smaller the elasticities of supply, and (3) the less variable the proportions in which the productive services combine.

If the competitive industry is subject to decreasing costs, the comparison turns on the cause of the decreasing costs. If the cause lies in internal economies competition is impossible and a comparison of the impossible with monopoly is uninteresting. If the cause lies in external economies, the analysis of increasing-cost industries is applicable with obvious modifications. The marginal costs of the monopolists are now less than those of the competitive firms, for the ratio $(1 + 1/e_i)$ to 1 is less than unity. Average costs will also be lower — on the understanding, here as elsewhere in this section, that monopoly profits have not been capitalized.

The comparison of costs under competition and duopoly is so similar to the comparison just discussed that it may be commented upon briefly. Only one additional element is introduced: the extent of rivalry. Rivalry introduces a systematic bias in the costs of duopolists as compared with those of a monopolist. In the unreal case where rivalry is nonexistent (i.e., comprehensive collusion) the costs of the duopolists will be approximately equal to those of the monopolist. But the costs of duopolists will rise as rivalry rises. If the rivalry is "cutthroat" the costs of the duopolists may exceed those of the competitive firms, especially when account is taken of selling costs.

These conclusions are not very definite. Greater definiteness could be secured by enumerating specific sets of conditions concerning the supplies of productive services and the comparative managerial costs. Such enumerations would be more tedious than informative; the moral is probably that comparisons should be instituted only for specific industries with which one is familiar.

II. *COMPETITION AND MONOPOLISTIC COMPETITION*

We shall consider as the prototype of monopolistic competition the firm with a demand curve with only a finite elasticity due to the effective differentiation of its product. In one respect the comparison of the competitive firm and the monopolistically competitive firm is simpler than in the preceding case: both types of firms will usually buy productive services at approximately constant supply prices. But certain new points are introduced by the comparison.

Depending upon the output of the industry and the nature of the supply of its productive services, the production costs of the competitive firm may be either higher or lower than those of the monopolistically competitive firm. If the output of the monopolistically competitive industry is larger, production costs will be higher in increasing cost industries and lower in decreasing cost industries. If the output of the competitive industry is larger, these conclusions are reversed. Unfortunately it is not possible to determine whether the output of the industry will be larger or smaller because of selling costs, to which we now turn.

The fundamental difference in costs is that a firm operating under perfect competition has little or no selling problem; under monopolistic competition the selling costs are always significant and frequently larger than production costs. As a result, the demand curve of the monopolistically competitive firm differs from that under perfect competition and this is why the outputs of the two types of industries are difficult to compare. The price of the competitive industry will certainly be lower (for given outputs) by the amount of selling costs and this tends to make its output larger, but the quantity sold will be smaller without sales promotion and this tends to make the monopolistically competitive output larger. A priori it cannot be decided which force is stronger.

The whole comparison, however, is an uncomfortable one. If consumers have complete knowledge, selling costs cannot be significant, and under this condition to compare monopolistic competition with perfect competition is to compare the impossible with the certain. If one compares costs in the absence of both consumers' knowledge and selling costs, one is comparing identical forms of imperfect competition, which again is not illuminating. Finally, if one compares two cases of imperfect competition, one with and the other without selling costs, one wonders why certain firms advertise extensively or why others do not.

A second moral may be drawn concerning such comparisons. It is too vague a project to compare competition with monopolistic competition but the vagueness can be reduced materially by specifying an economic policy. For example, it may be recommended that the state provide the information to consumers. Then, if the relevant data are available, one can compare costs of information — and the effects thereof — when provided by the state (perhaps plus whatever sales expenditures which would still be incurred by [less] monopolistically competitive firms) with provision of information by monopolistically competitive firms alone.

RECOMMENDED READINGS

1. Robinson, J., *The Economics of Imperfect Competition*, Macmillan, London, 1933, esp. Chs. 8–12, 14.
2. Chamberlin, E., *The Theory of Monopolistic Competition*, 3rd ed., Harvard University, Cambridge, 1938.
3. Boulding, K. E., *Economic Analysis*, Harpers, New York, 1941, Ch. 26.
4. Machlup, F., "Competition, Pliopoly and Profit," *Economica*, N.S. IX (1942), 1–23, 153–73.
5. Kahn, R. F., "Some Notes on Ideal Output," *Economic Journal*, XLV (1935), 1–35.

PROBLEMS

1. Derive the short-run supply curve of the firm discussed in the text (page 245) if the supply curve of the variable service is given by $p = \$6 - q/10$, where p is the supply price and q the quantity purchased.
2. Derive the long-run average and marginal-cost curves for the firm discussed in the text on the assumption of constant returns to scale of plant.

3. Derive the short-run marginal-cost curve for a duopolist (in the buying market) confronted by the production function and supply curve of productive service used in the text, assuming
   a. That his rival buys a constant quantity of the variable productive service.
   b. That his rival (of equal size) matches his price offers for the variable productive service.
4. If all the supply curves of productive services are straight lines (some of which rise and the remainder of which are horizontal), will the supply curve of a monopolist be a straight line or convex or concave to the output axis? Under what conditions is the supply curve of a monopolist a straight line?

CHAPTER 14

PRICING UNDER IMPERFECT COMPETITION

I. THE GENERAL PRINCIPLE

There is a single principle underlying the determination of price in all cases of imperfect competition. Profits are at a maximum when the firm is operating at the output where marginal revenue equals marginal cost. The principle is easily proved. Profits are rising as long as an additional unit of output increases receipts more than costs, i.e., as long as marginal revenue is greater than marginal cost. Profits decline when an additional unit of output adds more to costs than to receipts, i.e., when marginal cost is greater than marginal revenue. Hence profits are at a maximum — are neither rising nor falling — when marginal revenue equals marginal cost.

This principle is applicable to all cases in which a firm possessing the relevant information concerning cost and demand curves acts with a view to maximizing profits.* The detailed study of pricing consists essentially of the analysis of the effects of different market situations (such as duopoly and cartels) on the marginal revenue and cost curves of the individual firm. The principle is analogous to the mathematical theorem that an algebraic equation of degree n has n roots, — this theorem is of little assistance in solving an equation and similarly our principle is of little assistance in explaining any particular market price.

II. MONOPOLY PRICE

A monopoly, according to our definition, is a firm producing a commodity for which there are no close substitutes. This situation must be relatively uncommon in economic life, and the formal analysis is almost trivial for it consists only of the determination of the output at which marginal revenue equals marginal cost. All of

* Of course the principle is also true under competition, but then marginal cost = marginal revenue = price $(1 - 1/\infty)$ = price, the rule followed in Chapter 9.

the problems of interfirm and interindustry relationships are by definition absent. Nevertheless it will be useful to examine the determination of selling costs, price discrimination, bilateral monopoly, and restraints on monopoly price, for in each case the analysis is applicable to more realistic cases with suitable (but not always simple) modifications.

I. SELLING COSTS

When selling costs are distinguished, our formal pricing principle is modified slightly: the monopolist will determine both selling expenditures and output (and hence price) by equating the marginal revenue of selling expenditure to its marginal cost and equating the marginal revenue of output to its cost.* The geometrical analysis is a trifle more intricate than the usual case of monopoly for now we have three variables (selling expenditures, output, and price). We may avoid the use of solid geometry, however, by resort to indifference curves.

The fundamental data confronting a monopoly are presented in Table 20. The top figure in each cell is total receipts, the bottom figure total costs, and the figure in parentheses total profit. The cost figures are production costs (as a function of output) plus a variable amount of selling costs. The total receipts are arrived at as follows: at any output and selling expenditures (e.g., 60 and $700 respectively), there is a maximum price which consumers will pay. This price is not shown in the table but it may readily be computed by dividing total receipts by output; in the cell just referred to, price = $1570/60 = $26.17. The price falls, of course, as the quantity increases, as can easily be verified. Moreover the price increases with the amount of selling expenditures, but at a decreasing rate. The monopolist will maximize profits at an output of 35, selling expenditures of $600, and a price of $32.74. It will be observed that when selling expenditures equal $600, 35 is the largest output for which marginal revenue $\left(\dfrac{\$1146 - \$1067}{5} = \$15.80\right)$

* Selling activity is here expressed in dollars; it could equally well be expressed in number of salesmen or billboards. The marginal revenue of selling expenditures is

$$\frac{\text{increase in total receipts}}{\text{increase in selling expenditures}};$$

the marginal cost of selling expenditures is of course unity.

TABLE 20

Selling Costs	Output										
	20	25	30	35	40	45	50	55	60	65	70
$300	$476 (96) 380	$572 (147) 425	$653 (173) 480	$729 (184) 545	$800 (180) 620	$866 (161) 705	$927 (127) 800	$983 (78) 905	$1034 (14) 1020	$1080 (−65) 1145	$1121 (−159) 1280
400	632 (152) 480	729 (204) 525	811 (231) 580	888 (243) 645	960 (240) 720	1027 (222) 805	1089 (189) 900	1146 (141) 1005	1198 (78) 1120	1245 (0) 1245	1287 (−93) 1380
500	768 (188) 580	866 (241) 625	949 (269) 680	1027 (282) 745	1100 (280) 820	1168 (263) 905	1231 (231) 1000	1289 (184) 1105	1342 (122) 1220	1390 (45) 1345	1433 (−47) 1480
600	884 (204) 680	983 (258) 725	1067 (287) 780	1146 (301) 845	1220 (300) 920	1289 (284) 1005	1353 (253) 1100	1412 (207) 1205	1466 (146) 1320	1515 (70) 1445	1559 (−21) 1580
700	980 (200) 780	1080 (255) 825	1165 (285) 880	1245 (300) 945	1320 (300) 1020	1390 (285) 1105	1455 (255) 1200	1515 (210) 1305	1570 (150) 1420	1620 (75) 1545	1665 (−15) 1680
800	1066 (186) 880	1167 (242) 925	1253 (273) 980	1334 (289) 1045	1410 (290) 1120	1481 (276) 1205	1547 (247) 1300	1608 (203) 1405	1664 (144) 1520	1715 (70) 1645	1761 (−19) 1780
900	1142 (162) 980	1244 (219) 1025	1331 (251) 1080	1413 (268) 1145	1490 (270) 1220	1562 (257) 1305	1629 (229) 1400	1691 (186) 1505	1748 (128) 1620	1800 (55) 1745	1847 (−33) 1880

exceeds marginal cost $\left(\dfrac{\$845 - \$780}{5} = \$13\right)$, and that when output is 35, \$600 is the largest selling expenditure for which marginal revenue $\left(\dfrac{\$1146 - \$1027}{\$100} = 1.19\right)$ exceeds marginal cost (1).

This approach may be formalized.* Let us measure output along the horizontal axis and total selling costs along the vertical axis in Figure 71. We may then plot those combinations of output (with corresponding production costs) and selling costs (already expressed in dollars) which add up to equal total costs. If the marginal cost of

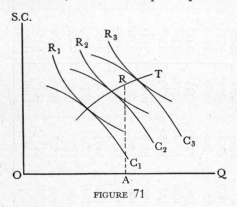

FIGURE 71

output is increasing, each additional unit of output will add more to cost, and a greater reduction in selling costs will be necessary to keep total cost constant. Hence the constant outlay curves will be concave to the origin.† They are indicated by C_1, C_2, C_3 in the figure. Similarly we may plot curves of equal total receipts from various combinations of output and selling costs. Additions to output (with constant selling costs) increase total receipts if the demand curve is elastic, so selling costs must be reduced (with a consequent fall in selling price) to maintain constant receipts. As a rule larger sales involve smaller marginal revenues so the compensating decreases in selling costs will become smaller; accordingly, the constant-receipts curves (labeled R_1, R_2, and R_3) will be convex to the origin. The monopolist seeks to get on as high a constant-receipts curve as possible with a given outlay, and this is accomplished at those points where the two sets of curves are tangent. Hence curve T represents the most profitable set of combinations of selling costs and output.

---

* For an alternative application of indifference curve analysis, see K. E. Boulding, *Economic Analysis*, Ch. 26; E. H. Chamberlin avoids the use of such curves by what is essentially the method of successive approximations, in *The Theory of Monopolistic Competition*, Ch. 7.

† If marginal cost is constant, these outlay curves will be straight lines; if marginal cost is falling, they will be convex to the origin. For a detailed analysis, see Ch. 16.

It is now possible to draw cost and demand curves for the monopolized product which will allow for the effects of selling expenditures; this is done in Figure 72. The cost curve includes production
costs plus that amount of selling costs found in Figure 71 to yield
maximum receipts. Similarly,
the demand curve represents
the quantities which will be
sold at various prices when
selling expenditures are varied
in the optimum manner. The
firm operates at the output
and price which maximize
net profits, i.e., at output *OA*,
price *AB*, and (with reference
to Figure 71) selling costs of
AR.

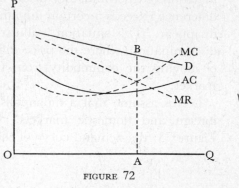

FIGURE 72

A few remarks may be added concerning the shapes of the curves
in these figures. Under perfect competition the slightest reduction
in price eliminates the necessity for any selling expenditures to
achieve a given amount of sales and, conversely, selling expenditures will have no effect on sales, so the constant-receipts curves
become vertical lines. As consumer ignorance or fancy for radio
comedians grows, the receipts curves become flatter, leading to
greater use of selling activity relative to price reductions. Decreased
efficiency of selling expenditures (due perhaps to an increase in
advertising rates) will make the constant-outlay curves steeper,
leading to less emphasis on selling expenditures relative to price
reductions. Finally, the demand curve in Figure 72 is constructed
to reflect not only price variations but also corresponding optimum
amounts of selling costs. Therefore it is not a conventional demand
curve nor is it subject to the usual restrictions, — in particular it
may have a positive slope.

II. *PRICE DISCRIMINATION*

Discriminatory pricing in independent markets is a routine
application of the basic principle of equating marginal revenue and
marginal cost. The marginal-revenue curves for the two or more
parts of the total market are added horizontally and the intersection
of total marginal revenue with marginal cost fixes total output.

The monopolist then allocates the output among the markets in such proportions that marginal revenue is everywhere equal.

When the markets are not independent the analysis is more complicated. It is instructive to analyze graphically the determination of discriminatory prices in one such case: when the price difference exceeds a certain amount sales in the high price market disappear. This situation is illustrated by the geographical price discrimination, where the price differential cannot exceed the cost of moving the commodity from the high-price to the low-price market.

Let us assume that a monopolist is discriminating between the foreign and domestic markets. The situation is portrayed in Figure 73: the demand curve of the domestic market is designated

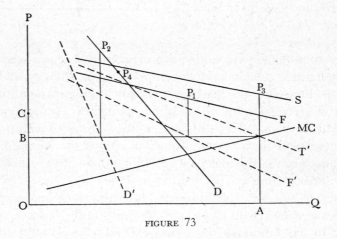

FIGURE 73

D, that of the foreign market F, primes denote corresponding marginal revenues, and MC is marginal cost. If the markets were independent the total output would be A, where total marginal revenue ($T' = D' + F'$) equals marginal cost, and P_1 and P_2 would be the respective prices set in foreign and domestic markets.

If there is seepage there will be some maximum price difference BC, and when the domestic price exceeds the foreign price by more than BC all domestic consumers (we assume) buy abroad and reimport the commodity. In order to find total output we require the marginal-revenue curve when at each output the domestic price exceeds the foreign price by exactly BC. When the domestic and foreign demand curves are straight lines this marginal-revenue curve is identical with the marginal-revenue curve (T') secured by summing D' and F',* so total output is not affected by seepage.

There remains the task of finding the prices in the two markets. One method of solving this problem is to construct a new demand curve (S): S represents the total quantity that can be sold in the foreign market at any price plus the amount that can be sold in the domestic market at a price higher by BC. One then finds, with reference to Figure 73, that the foreign price will be P_3 and the domestic price P_4 ($= P_3 + BC$).

Almost all bases of discrimination are subject to evasion, although not in so striking a form as occurs in the geographical case just analyzed. It appears well-nigh universal, moreover, that seepage increases with the difference between prices in the various sections of the market. Such seepage reduces the difference in elasticity of demand and hence reduces the profits from discrimination. A second restriction on discrimination is also important: the cost of separating the markets. All forms of discrimination involve such costs. Geographical discrimination greatly complicates the selling problem; chronological discrimination (as with popular books and motion pictures) involves delay in securing returns from the low-price market and the product may lose popularity; product differentiation involves costs of differentiation (especially selling costs). And in general the greater the differences between selling prices the greater will be the costs of discrimination. The similarity between products will have to be reduced and the necessary policing of the market to prevent seepage becomes more extensive.†

* This may be proved along the following lines: With independent markets a given increase in total output will be divided between F and D in the proportion

$$\frac{\text{slope of } F'}{\text{slope of } D'}.$$

If there is seepage, the increase in output will be divided between F and D in the proportion

$$\frac{\text{slope of } F}{\text{slope of } D},$$

These proportions are equal, for the slope of a linear marginal revenue curve is twice that of the demand curve. Hence with a given increase in total output sales in each market will increase by the same amounts, with or without seepage. The only difference introduced by seepage is that movements of output occur at different points on the two marginal-revenue curves so total revenue, while at a different level, changes in the same way with output.

† Discrimination may also occur when the demand elasticities of various markets are equal if marginal costs in these markets differ. This is most likely to occur with geographical discrimination.

III. *BILATERAL MONOPOLY*

Bilateral monopoly is the market situation in which a single seller confronts a single buyer. There must be very few cases of bilateral monopoly since there are few of monopoly; a dairy farmers' co-operative dealing with a combination of milk distributors is an approximate illustration. Nevertheless, the results hold, in a much more complicated form, for important cases such as bilateral oligopoly so the theory deserves at least brief attention.

Let *C* represent the marginal-cost curve of the selling monopoly and *D* the marginal-value product curve of the buying monopoly in Figure 74. Then *C* is the curve of average costs to the buying

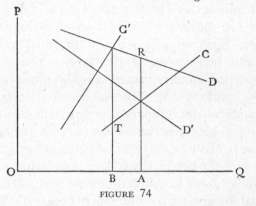

FIGURE 74

monopoly and *D* is the curve of average revenue to the selling monopoly. The selling monopoly wishes to operate where its marginal cost equals marginal revenue, i.e., at output *OA* where *D'* and *C* intersect, with a price of *AR*. The buying monopoly wishes to purchase the quantity *OB*, determined by the intersection of its marginal-cost and marginal-value product curves, and pay a price of *BT*. There is no economic principle to decide what price between *AR* and *BT* will be established; the solution is accordingly indeterminate.

It may clarify the meaning of *indeterminate* in economics as well as complement the theory to point out the facts which enter into the determination of price. Obviously there will be a definite price and a definite output; *indeterminate* means only that a knowledge of cost and demand curves is insufficient to determine these precise quantities. Special institutional circumstances will govern the price; a few illustrations may suggest their nature.

An obvious resort is compromise, perhaps in that most elementary of forms, the Aristotelian Golden (arithmetic) Mean. Condemnation proceedings are a fairly good illustration of the central element of bilateral monopoly; the owner of property is compelled to sell to the government and the government is compelled to buy a particular piece of land. The characteristics of the real-estate market do not permit of easy determination of fair value, so when New York City condemned 164 school sites,

the city experts set an aggregate value of $19,424,018
the owners' experts set an aggregate value of $30,259,808

The actual awards totaled $24,859,693, a full 7/100 of 1 per cent from the mean.* The closeness of the awards to the mean can be attributed to coincidence or the discrepancy can be attributed to the deficiencies of judicial arithmetic, depending upon one's view of the world.

The terms of compromise, however, are usually more subtle. The public's attitude toward the parties of the dispute, the "staying power" of the bargainers, and similar factors usually enter into the decision. Moreover in many cases the interest of a participant is not in maximum profits. Leaders of a new union may wish a record of wage increases to assist in unionization, and disregard the effects on employment; leaders of an established union may follow the converse policy. Leaders of a farm cooperative may wish audits of the distributor's records of division of milk between manufacturing and fluid uses. In any case, the terms of the solution are governed by political and administrative as well as by economic factors.

iv. RESTRAINTS ON MONOPOLY PRICE

It was once fashionable for textbooks on economics to list several "realistic" restrictions on the pricing policy of a monopolist. Prominent in these lists were three factors: the existence of substitutes; the threat of potential competition; and the fear of governmental regulation. The first restraint is of course inappropriate on our definition of monopoly, where there are no close substitutes. It deserves emphasis, however, that the existence of substitutes is no additional restraint on even the firm that corresponds to the popular

---

* The data are taken from Leonard M. Wallstein, *Report on Law and Procedure in Condemnation*, New York City, 1932, p. 498.

notion of a monopoly. The existence of substitutes governs the elasticity of demand, and the full effects of possible shifts of consumers to other products is already taken into account by the (long-run) demand curve used to determine monopoly price. If there are numerous good substitutes, the elasticity of demand will be great and the difference between marginal cost and price (which equals price/elasticity) will be small.

Potential competition is more difficult to appraise. It is argued that a monopoly will forego temporary high profits, which would attract new rivals, in favor of smaller but more permanent profits. The argument is illustrated in Figure 75. A monopolist motivated

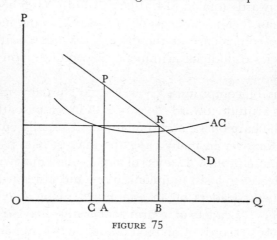

FIGURE 75

only by immediate profits would sell *OA* at price *AP;* if he recognized potential competition he would set a price of (e.g.) *BR* and sell *OB*. Then if a rival with equal costs entered the field the output of each would be *OC*, and at this output, price would be less than average cost.

We do not possess sufficient knowledge of the way monopolists think and the specific type of market situations which confront them to determine the validity of this argument. If both the monopolist and the potential rival behave with a view to maximum profits the check is a weak one: if a rival enters it will be foolish for the original firm to persist in setting the low price of *BR* since both firms can still make profits at a higher price, and the potential rival will act on this fact. In real life, however, potential rivalry probably is something of a check on monopoly price (when entry is possible), but for different reasons. A low price policy may be one means (although not generally the most effective or the most economical) of revealing the established firm's intention of combatting new rivals; and the larger a monopoly's profits, the harder it is to conceal them. These are the type of factors which give some possible scope to potential rivalry.

The threat of governmental regulation is unquestionably an effective check on the pricing policy of a monopoly. Thus it has been observed that the rate schedule for electricity in Minnesota, which does not regulate such rates, is influenced by the existence of an effective public-utilities commission in the neighboring state of Wisconsin. But the influence of potential regulation is essentially a political question; the monopolist must determine whether the political situation will dictate retaliation against a specific move. Articles of "luxury" (e.g., 60-foot cabin cruisers) will be immune from this factor whereas "necessaries" (e.g., water rates) will be very sensitive. Moreover — to revert for a few sentences to the concept of a monopoly used in Chapter 11 — it makes a good deal of difference who the monopolist is: worthy people (farmers, doctors, laborers) can do a great many things that unworthy people (e.g., rich people) cannot do. If the public officials are looking for a popular issue to help in reelection or to divert attention from other topics, the check becomes stronger. Political consequences may be avoided by such inconspicuous tactics as raising the price in several moderate steps or by failing to pass on a reduction in excise taxes.

III. DUOPOLY PRICE

Since the determination of marginal revenue and, to a lesser extent, of marginal cost depend upon the generally unknown reactions of rivals, it is not possible to formulate a general theory of duopoly price. It has already been argued, indeed, that it is not even possible to enumerate all important situations. Nevertheless, a few types of solutions will be examined, both for their own realistic importance and for their value in suggesting techniques of analysis.*

Collusion is doubtless the most important single duopoly policy. It may take many forms: the rivals may divide the territory, or (if

---

* The analyses of (1) cases in which the rival firm is operating subject to known restrictions, and (2) the dominant firm, follow directly from the previous discussion (pp. 226 ff.).

the products are not homogeneous) agree on price and resort to nonprice rivalry, or even, in extreme cases, assign quotas to the firms. Such policies will be more probable the more equal the two firms' costs, the more stable the total demand, the less elastic the total demand, and the more homogeneous the products. It is apparent that such collusion leads to a monopoly or near-monopoly price in the case of homogeneous products; and in those cases of differentiated products where nonprice rivalry is important, collusion may well lead to higher than monopoly prices because of the costs of such rivalry.

If each entrepreneur assumes (or, better, learns by experience) that the rival firm will match his price, or alternatively that the rival insists upon his conventional share of the market at any price, much the same situation arises. For, to take the former alternative, then the total sales will be equally divided if the product is homogeneous (since the customers will pair at random) and sales will be allocated by nonprice competition if the products differ. Costs may not be equal for the duopolists, however, and this raises an interesting problem. The marginal-cost curves of duopolists A and B are portrayed in Figure 76, along with their identical demand and

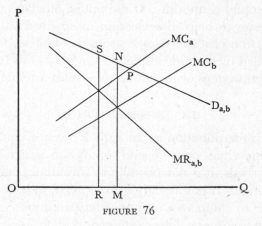

FIGURE 76

marginal-revenue curves. Duopolist A would obviously prefer an output of OR and price of RS; duopolist B would prefer the lower price, MN. Since the product is homogeneous, two prices cannot rule in the market. The lower price will be set by B and A will be compelled to follow since a higher price is impossible and a lower price even less profitable.

Suppose, however, that B is so much more efficient than A that the former wishes to set a price below *P*, i.e., below the point where A's marginal cost equals price. Duopolist A will not operate at any output at which marginal cost exceeds price. The resulting situation is illustrated in Figure 77. The demand curve for B, the more efficient duopolist, is redrawn beyond point *P* since at lower

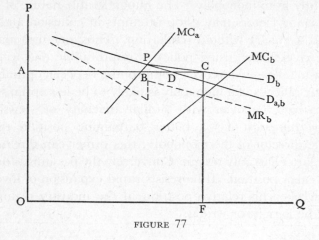

FIGURE 77

prices A will supply only the quantity indicated by his marginal-cost curve. At any price *OA*, duopolist B will supply *BD* less than half of the quantity demanded, so this quantity (= *DC*) must be added to $D_{a,b}$ to secure B's demand curve (D_b). A new marginal revenue curve for B (MR_b) is drawn and he sets a price *FC* at the output *OF* which equates his marginal cost and marginal revenue. The low-cost duopolist is of course the price leader.

The presence of more than two firms in the industry (oligopoly) does not affect the formal theory, but the content of the analysis differs in emphasis. Differences in marginal costs, for instance, will surely be greater the more numerous the firms, and this example suggests the greater obstacles to either tacit or explicit collusion. Even in the absence of cost differences, the greater the number of firms the greater the difficulty in arriving at an agreement on any one market policy (e.g., price, quality, or wage rates). Since the capacity of firms for compromise is limited — compromise is not a free good — the fewer will be the parts of market policy on which agreement is reached.

The effects of uncertainty, a factor which we generally exclude from this volume by our assumption of a stationary economy, may be commented upon briefly. Fields in which uncertainty is especially prominent are advertising, research, and investment. In each case the future returns from present expenditures are often shrouded in doubt and this makes it more difficult for rivals to agree upon the best policy to pursue. This may cause the duopoly situation to differ significantly from monopoly. The imponderable nature of some of the governing factors may estop attempts at collusion and it may even lead to rivalry without retaliation. Thus, one firm may think that the rival's advertising policy is unprofitable and feel no inclination to follow. Moreover, compromise between optimistic and pessimistic officials of a monopoly is likely to be less optimistic than that between duopolists with similar diversity of views.* The optimistic duopolist has a better bargaining position than the optimistic director of the monopoly: the former can threaten warfare, the latter can only resign. Conversely the pessimistic duopolist is in a weaker position. If he resists rapid expansion of investment he will weaken his relative position in the industry regardless of whether he is right or wrong.

IV. CARTEL PRICE

In the present section we shall consider combinations of producers who make a homogeneous product, although much of the analysis will be appropriate also to the theory of monopolistic competition. The formal analysis follows directly from the demand analysis (page 238), but it is worth while to consider the conditions favorable to cartel formation and the politics of price determination.

I. *FAVORABLE CONDITIONS*

A cartel, to recall, is here used to characterize a combination of firms which serves to limit competitive forces.† A cartel may range from a sentiment against price "chiselers" to an elaborate formal agreement in which participation may be compulsory, enforced by legal penalties for noncompliance. Whatever the form,

---

* Authority is not likely to be so closely correlated with conservatism. And it can be argued that there is usually a greater difference of opinion on (e.g.) future sales among duopolists than among officials of one company.

† Duopoly with tacit or explicit collusion could thus be treated as a form of cartel but attention will be concentrated chiefly on the problems raised by the existence of a considerable number of firms.

however, the likelihood of formation and the effectiveness of restriction of competition depend upon several factors.

The attitude of the law will of course be important in influencing both the extent of such agreements and the form which they take. The historical American policy of opposition to cartels has led to more surreptitious and, on the whole, weaker combinations than those fostered in the nineteen-thirties by Great Britain,* to say nothing of the contrast with the governmentally sanctioned German cartels. In this respect, two further points are relevant. First, statutory provisions do not constitute the effective legal setting unless they are actively supported by the political leadership and an efficient administrative force. For long periods (e.g., in the nineteen-twenties) our antitrust laws were relatively ineffectual because both of these factors were absent. Second, there are many fields in which there are a very large number of firms and for obvious administrative reasons these fields cannot be cartellized except with state assistance. Agriculture, the retail trades, and the bituminous coal industry are examples (see Chapter 11).

One may generalize that the fewer the firms, the easier to form a cartel and to administer its price policy. In any case detailed policies are difficult to agree upon and the difficulties grow much more rapidly than the number of participants.† The existence of

---

* See Ben W. Lewis, *Price and Production Control in British Industry*, University of Chicago, Chicago, 1937.

† The tribulations of a baker in a small Illinois town will suggest the nature of some of the obstacles which strew the path of collusion:

> As you know, it was the intention of your meeting at Paris to get the bakers all lined up on the price situation, and to get them more together, and for a while it looked as though we were going to get along fine. First one and then another would be contrary on raising the price, until now I believe that the bakers are in a class by themselves when it comes to being dumb and small-business men. It sure is discouraging and I don't wonder that the leaders [of the state trade association] don't give up sometime and tell the bakers to get along the best they can without any outside help. The first break came when Model, of Mattoon, raised their price in Charleston without first notifying us, and because we did not raise the same day they came back down. We were ready to raise and then did raise about three weeks later. After that we almost had to beg them to raise their price here and then they waited three weeks and knocked an awful hole in our business. We are just now beginning to recover it. Our plant and the Model plant in Mattoon got together and raised their price, and had the cooperation of another small baker there; also some assurance from Fullerton, of Tuscola, that he would not come in Mattoon; and the result was that the other small baker in Mattoon did not raise and Fullerton put a truck on Mattoon with a 2-cent cheaper price. Isn't that some cooperation. My brother and I have just about decided to be price cutters and have no regards for anybody. That is poor business, but, darn, we get so disgusted. I almost forgot to tell you that in Paris the local bakeries there are all in line and as far as I know nobody has any complaint. Our bakery there is doing good. I have been out on a couple of trips trying to get all the bakers lined up, but it seems like an impossible task. They are fine while you are talking to them, but after you leave they know what you have done or are going to do, and I'll be darned if most of them won't take advantage of what you tell them about your

large firms facilitates cartellization; these firms not only organize
the industry but also police the agreement. The geographical concentration of the industry is similarly favorable to concerted action.
Homogeneity of the products of the industry greatly simplifies the
technical problems of organization and administration of the cartel,
and in addition it gives added impetus to such organizations since
each firm feels the full force of price changes of rivals. This point
can also be interpreted to cover the case of multiple products: the
more similar the product structures of the various firms, the more
easily agreement is reached.

The role of general business conditions is at least superficially
paradoxical. It seems to be fairly well established that many cartels
are organized in periods of depressed business. The rationale is
obvious: the existence of low prices and negative profits is a more
powerful stimulus to cooperation than even higher profits would be
in prosperous times. (Moreover, in the important cases where the
state organizes or supports the cartel, the existence of depressed
conditions in the industry is usually a political requirement.) But
on the other hand, it also seems to be fairly well established that
cartels collapse more often when adverse business conditions pre-
vail. And again the rationale is simple: the cartel cannot maintain
prices and sales (certainly not both) so firms either renounce the
agreement in the hope of doing better without cartel restraints or
surreptitiously violate cartel policies.

The paradox is at least partially resolvable in terms of time. A
cartel which organizes in one depression often collapses in the next.
Its policies may have led to an expansion of investment during the
intervening prosperity, which makes the subsequent decline all the
more severe. Moreover, the differences of opinion among various

own business. I have in mind one baker in Newman who came down to the Paris meeting and was
strong for a raise. Well, he did not raise, and came in Paris and solicited business with a price
2 cents under the Paris bakers, but did not get enough orders to pay him to come down. Seass,
Clem, and I went up to see him, and were prepared to tell him that if he sold bread in Paris
cheaper than ours we were going to come to Newman and give it away. But before we got a
chance to tell him that he told us he was not coming in for the reason given above. Well, the next
day the Newman paper came out with an article stating that we were up there begging their
baker to please not come into our towns with his good bread, as if he did we were afraid that he
would put us all out of business. They gave all the names who were there. While we were there
we told him that we had raised the price in Charleston and had a nice little chat, and I'll be darned
if he didn't try to sell bread here in Charleston the next week. He did not sell any. I merely
related the above to show that in my opinion there is not a bit of chance of ever getting the small
bakers lined up, nor is there any chance of getting fellows like Fullerton, who imagine that they
are in the class with Ward's [Baking Company] lined up. (*Competition and Profits in Bread and
Flour, op. cit.*, p. 131.)

groups (e.g., high- vs. low-cost firms, integrated vs. nonintegrated firms) will be greater in depression, and this also weakens the cartel. Another part of the explanation may lie in the ambiguous term, *depression*. Cartels often collapse during recession or at the lowest level of business activity; they organize or reorganize after recovery is under way.

The paradox need not be accepted *in toto*, however. The origin of cartels has been greatly affected by factors other than the state of business activity. Two of the most flourishing periods of trade association organization — a form which may exert varying degrees of monopolistic power — were World War I and the NRA era, and in both cases governmental actions were of primary importance.

II. *QUOTAS*

In the more highly developed cartels specific outputs or proportions are allocated to each firm, and even informal agreements may rest on fairly rigid ideas of "fair" shares of the market.* There is no economic principle to guide such allocations; the situation is indeed a special case of bilateral monopoly. The more efficient firm or the firm in strategic position to wreck cartel policies will secure favorable quotas, the firm in desperate need of cartel protection will fare badly.

The most popular basis for quotas is "capacity." Popular definitions of this phrase usually run in terms of technological limits (e.g., the output of all blast furnaces) or in terms of recorded maximum output. The latter approach is patently very loose and the former is of restricted usefulness: what is the technological maximum product of a coal mine or a railroad or a motion-picture theater? Two fundamental difficulties, in fact, arise in defining capacity: the time interval, and the cost.

* The most famous of these informal market-sharing schemes is that in meat-packing. A typical example is provided by the percentage distribution of purchases of hogs in Sioux City:

Firm	1913–17	1931	1932	1933	1934	1935	1936	1937
Armour	50.3	39.8	38.2	38.7	38.6	38.1	39.2	39.3
Cudahy	49.7	39.7	39.1	38.6	38.8	38.7	38.3	38.8
Swift	No Plant	20.5	22.7	22.7	22.7	23.2	22.5	22.6

See W. H. Nicholls, *Imperfect Competition Within Agricultural Industries*, Collegiate Press, Ames, 1941, p. 4.

It is obvious enough that the capacity to produce a commodity can be increased in time — one can always build more blast furnaces or cement plants. Hence one must always specify a time interval for capacity, and even then the ambiguity is not completely removed for plant facilities can be expanded at varying rates with corresponding differences in costs of expansion. This leads directly to the second difficulty: the technological maximum output of a given plant is rarely if ever approached in real life. If the selling price is high enough relative to costs one can always secure a little more product from a temporarily fixed plant. Most discussions of capacity involve the implicit notion of a reasonable relationship between price and costs. This merely rephrases the difficulty: is the capacity of a plant reached when the elasticity of the marginal-cost curve becomes 1, or 1/10, or 1/100?

It seems impossible to formulate a theoretical criterion of capacity. One can establish a conventional criterion, e.g., the capacity is attained within the short-run normal period when the output reaches a point where the elasticity of the marginal-cost curve becomes less than 1/2. Even such a criterion, however, would be subject to many qualifications. For example, the capacity of the cotton textile industry would depend upon the technical possibilities and costs of conversion of the woolen textile industry.

From the viewpoint of cartel quotas, however, a discussion of such problems should be considered almost a digression: almost invariably the basis is historically recorded output with continuing or periodic modifications on the score of technological changes of plant. As a rule, the firm may enlarge its quota by expanding relative to the industry, although in more thoroughgoing instances (e.g., the German potash cartel, the NRA Steel Code) this is outlawed. Often the quotas are transferable; for example, under the British coal cartel it is said that some owners have closed their mines and retired on the receipts from the sale of their quotas.

A second common basis for quotas, especially in the international cartels, is geographical partitioning of the market. Thus the agreement between Röhm and Haas (Philadelphia) and Roehm and Haas (Darmstadt) provided that the former company should have exclusive rights in North America, Central and South America, Australia, New Zealand, and Japan, the latter in Europe and Asia except Japan. Similarly Du Pont divided the markets for certain products with Imperial Chemicals so the former had exclusive rights in North and Central America, excepting certain British dominions and possessions, and the latter exclusive rights in the British Empire and Egypt. An alternative basis is to divide products; in the agreement between I. G. Farben and Röhm and Haas the former promised not to produce nonsplintering glass, glass substitutes, and certain adhesives, and the latter abstained from producing photographic articles, dyestuffs, abrasives, etc. These two types of allocation can also be combined, of course, as in the agreement between I. G. Farben and Standard Oil of New Jersey where the former in general promised no competition in petroleum outside Germany in exchange for control over synthetic organic chemicals outside of the United States.*

III. *PRICE RIGIDITY*

Most of the large recent literature on rigid price is concerned with the influence of such prices on business cycles, but a brief discussion from the viewpoint of price theory will further elucidate cartel price policies.

It is not difficult to develop an analytical criterion of price rigidity: a particular price is rigid when it is not changed in such a way that the firm operates where marginal cost equals marginal revenue.† We may defer temporarily the explanation of why any firm thus fails to maximize profits in order to consider the difficulties in a concrete application of this analytical criterion. These difficulties are of at least three types. (1) Minor changes in prices to reflect minor changes in demand or cost conditions simply would not pay. Such small changes often cost as much as large ones (in terms of price lists, advertising, etc.) and frequent minor changes would irritate buyers. This does not modify our definition (which recognizes all costs and receipts) but it does entail the problem of determining when price changes would significantly increase profits. (2) It may be unprofitable to change prices even if (e.g.) demand

* The interesting mixture of cartel policies and political policies is portrayed in *Hearings*, Senate Committee on Patents, 77th Cong., 2nd sess.

† It is a corollary of this definition that there cannot be price rigidity under perfect competition, since the individual competitive firm has no control over prices. (Hence for a competitive industry output rigidity would be the corresponding measure of departure from maximum profits.) The definition assumes that entrepreneurs seek to maximize profits; the necessary modifications for the case of a multiple-purpose firm are fairly obvious.

changes substantially unless the new conditions are expected to persist for some time. Hence the element of anticipations must be taken into account. (3) Profits may be approximately maximized by varying quality, advertising expenditures, or some other variable in response to changed conditions.* As a matter of fact, one could offer parallel definitions of quality, advertising, and other flexibilities.

A quantitative measure of this price rigidity should contain at least two variables: the *amount* of the difference between current and equilibrium prices and the *speed* with which the difference is reduced. A price is rigid if it changes insufficiently or if the price change is delayed, i.e., if it fails to maximize profits at all times. It follows from our definition that a price may be perversely flexible — when it moves away from the equilibrium level — and that a constant price is flexible if the equilibrium price is approaching it, perhaps due to a secular change in demand.

No one has the information to determine for many products whether price rigidity has occurred in any period, so conventional definitions of rigidity have been devised to permit large-scale statistical investigations. Thus the number of changes per period of time, amplitude of price change, and similar criteria have been invoked. It is evident that all such tests are relatively crude: they exclude true cases of rigidity and misclassify cases of flexibility — how often, no one knows. Only in extreme cases (as when the price of steel rails did not change between May, 1901, and April, 1916, or between October, 1922, and October, 1932) can the statistical tests be considered persuasive.

The actual statistical findings of such studies need not be reproduced: in general they indicate a substantial correlation between magnitude of price changes and frequency of price changes, and stability in the pattern of flexibility since 1890, but little else.† Several circumstances combine to weaken greatly most of the findings, even if the statistical criteria of rigidity be accepted as a first approximation: First, accurate and relevant price quotations are

---

* Only approximately, however; adjustment of (e.g.) advertising is usually an imperfect substitute for adjustment of price.

† See, as examples, E. S. Mason, "Price Inflexibility," *Review of Economic Studies*, XX (1938), 53–64; *Price Behavior and Business Policy*, T.N.E.C. Monograph No. 1, 1940, Part I, Ch. 2, App. I; and *The Structure of Industry*, T.N.E.C. Monograph No. 27, 1940, Part V, Ch. 5.

extremely difficult to secure. On close inspection commodities prove to have several prices, depending upon size of order, date of contract, and similar factors, and the most important of these prices is often unknown or inaccessible. Often nominal price quotations are maintained even during the period of active price competition.* A price may be altered indirectly by changing discounts, altering credit terms, or by modifying surrounding circumstances such as promptness of delivery or subsequent service.† Among these non-price variables quality is so important as to deserve special mention: in the competitive women's clothing industry, for example, the existence of firmly established "price lines" has canalized market changes into variations in quality of product.

To return to our definition: why do firms fail to maximize profits? The answer is that they do not fail — except to the extent that they make what subsequent experience reveals to be erroneous forecasts. This is merely equivalent to saying that entrepreneurs have a reason for everything they do, and that these reasons can always be classified under the broad headings, *marginal revenue* and *marginal cost*. Thus if a cartel does not change its price when demand falls because it fears that a subsequent increase (when demand revives) would lead to an antitrust prosecution, the prospective loss in revenue or increase in cost because of such a prosecution is included in the calculations of the cartel.

How can this tautology be avoided?‡ The only escape is to specify certain factors which, for analytical or policy purposes, one wishes to measure. Thus if the central interest is a comparison of cartel with competitive prices, one may compare changes in actual prices with those which would rule under competition. Such a

---

* The reasons are numerous: prevention of inventory losses, as measured by accountants; guarantees in contracts with buyers to pass on all official price reductions; hope that the price war will soon be over; etc. See Saul Nelson, "A Consideration of the Validity of the Bureau of Labor Statistics Price Indexes," *The Structure of the American Economy*, National Resources Committee, 1939, pp. 173–84.

† For example, cold-rolled strip had an official base price of $3.05 per hundredweight in September, 1939, and $2.80 in April, 1942, a reduction of 8 per cent. But meanwhile the unofficial discount was eliminated, a size "extra" of $1.20 was added and the mill-run discount of $0.10 was eliminated, so the net price rose from $2.80 to $4.15, or by 48 per cent. See M. J. Ulmer, "Indirect Price Increases," *Monthly Labor Review*, LV (1942), 903–12.

‡ The definition of rigidity, however, does become a basis for measuring errors when applied in retrospect, for it then compares the price which would have maximized profits with the price actually charged. Such a measure would be very useful but difficult to apply.

question rarely yields a definite answer when posed as a problem in formal analysis, even waiving difficulties inherent in comparisons of different market systems. The relative changes of cartel and competitive prices, for example, will turn on quantitative characteristics of the disturbance of equilibrium.*

Although such formal considerations yield few conclusions, it is nevertheless very probable that cartel prices are more rigid than competitive prices. The administrative difficulties in changing cartel prices are substantial. No single price is likely to please all members of the cartel so a price conference may turn into a pitched battle,† which may extend also to quotas and other questions of policy. If there is even moderate reason to believe that the new conditions are temporary, the cartel may well forego some profits to avoid two controversial price changes. If a change of price requires consent of a government body, moreover, prices are certain to be rigid by almost any criterion.

V. MONOPOLISTIC COMPETITION

The important elements of the formal theory of monopolistic competition have been treated in the sections on demand under imperfect competition and the determination of selling costs. Here attention will be centered on two problems, the definition of the industry, and nonprice competition.

1. THE CONCEPT OF AN INDUSTRY

We can no longer postpone a fundamental question: what is an industry? This problem is pertinent to competition but it was not raised in Part II because the problem of multiple products was postponed. Under monopolistic competition the problem is especially acute because only one firm produces each product.

It has been argued by some economists that in this case of monopolistic competition the concept of an industry must be abandoned. The line of argument is as follows: technological similarity is not a useful guide in defining industries; the economic difference between an automobile and a tractor is greater than that between a tractor

---

* See problem 9 of this chapter for an example.

† A price which maximizes profits for efficient producers may often lead to substantial losses for "high-cost" producers; so unless provision is made for their reimbursement, they may threaten to withdraw if the price is lowered in depression.

and a horse. The criterion of substitutability between products (which is of course what is meant by economic difference), on the other hand, raises the question: where is the line to be drawn between industries? If product A is taken as our basis for measurement, the cross-elasticities of demand in terms of the closest substitutes may be

$$\eta_{ap_b} = 6; \; \eta_{ap_c} = 4; \; \eta_{ap_d} = 2; \; \eta_{ap_e} = 1.5; \; \text{etc.}$$

Does the industry include A, B, and C, or also D and E?* Any line we draw will be arbitrary — there is no clearly defined theoretical boundary to the industry.

This objection to the concept of an industry is perfectly valid but not wholly persuasive. If the industry concept were abandoned, we would be left with only a few very general theorems such as the equality of marginal cost and marginal revenue, and further progress would be estopped. Moreover we would be deserting the terrain of real economic activity, for men think and act as if there are industries. If we recognize this belief — and to fail to do so would introduce error into the analysis — the critics of the industry concept may still ask for the numerical value of the cross-elasticity which, in the businessmen's minds, fixes the boundary of the industry. But such a request would be unreasonable: the situation is comparable to that encountered in defining duopoly (page 229). It can be argued, moreover, that the difficulty in defining an industry is no greater than is usually encountered in the classification of real phenomena. As an analogy, a considerable portion of the theory of mechanics is devoted to rigid bodies, but the rigidity of a body depends upon the fineness of our measurements (and, as a matter of fact, there are no perfectly rigid bodies).

Since we employ the concept of an industry to analyze economic phenomena the concept may vary with the phenomena we are studying. This turns out to be the case. Dairy farmers in California are not in the same industry as dairy farmers in Massachusetts when

---

* It is also possible that if another commodity (B) is taken as the basis for measuring cross-elasticities, a new order of cross-elasticities may emerge, e.g., $\eta_{bp_a} = 8$, $\eta_{bp_d} = 4$, $\eta_{bp_c} = 3$, etc. It can be shown, in fact, that if "income effects" are neglected,

$$(ap_a)\eta_{ap_b} = (bp_b)\eta_{bp_a}.$$

(See H. Schultz, *Theory and Measurement of Demand, op. cit.*, p. 624.) "Chain" relationships offer a particular instance of this difficulty. But as a rule this is probably a minor difficulty.

we are analyzing milk prices; they are in the same industry when attempts are being made to secure federal antimargarine legislation. A textile mill and an aluminum plant are independent in the selling markets but they may be leading rivals for labor in a particular area. These examples suggest two possible criteria for defining an industry: demand relationships and cost relationships. In either case the problem of setting a definite boundary again appears. If we use cross-elasticities to measure demand or cost rivalry, two situations can arise.

First, there may be a definite break in the chain of substitutes. In the case of competition the break is obvious: between firms in the industry the cross-elasticities are infinite, with firms outside the industry they are finite. Under imperfect competition, other brands of coffee will have substantial cross-elasticities with respect to the price of any given brand and for most purposes other beverages are sufficiently removed to fall in other industries. Similarly one metropolitan area may be the labor market and all other areas are such poor substitutes as to be disregarded under ordinary circumstances. Our examples remind us of a previous point (page 92): for sufficiently large price changes the industry may be greatly broadened or contracted.

Second, the chain of substitutes may reveal no large break. The cross-elasticities between various kinds of cotton textiles, for example, may be no larger than those between cotton and woolen textiles and these may be no larger than those between textiles and shoes, etc. This example is surely inappropriate, and the difficulty one experiences in finding a realistic example strongly suggests that this second situation is very rare. But *if* it should occur — on the cost side also — then our industry concept is nebulous. But here an additional consideration comes to our aid.

So far only objective cross-elasticities have been considered; what of entrepreneurs' attitudes toward these cross-elasticities?* We have implicitly assumed "reasonable" behavior: the coffee importer will not fret over a fall in the price of sloe gin. In addition we may properly recognize the realistic limitations on the scope of business planning. An entrepreneur cannot watch and react to the behavior of a very large number of individual rivals; if he attempted to do so

---

* We assume throughout that the cross-elasticities are known; if not, we have a difficult, not to say insoluble, problem in dynamics.

he would soon find the cost exceeding the gain. If, then, there do exist cases in which both demand and cross-elasticities vary continuously, we should still expect businessmen to act as if there were certain important rivals, i.e., that there would be an industry.* It does not seem worth while to explain in detail what factors determine the boundary of the industry in this latter case of continuous array of cross-elasticities. It would be embarrassing to explain in detail a phenomenon which may well prove to be nonexistent.

II. *NONPRICE COMPETITION*

Nonprice competition may of course accompany price competition, and indeed there is some presumption that if rivalry is strong enough to lead to price competition the firms will also engage in competitive advertising, quality adaptation, and the like. Nevertheless attention is generally focused upon nonprice competition when price competition is for some reason restricted, on the ground that in this case all attempts of a firm to gain relative to the industry must be directed to other devices.

Are there any important differences between price and nonprice competition? The basic similarity is obvious: all modes of expanding sales are competitive for the entrepreneur's dollar, he selects those which are most efficient, and at equilibrium marginal revenue equals marginal cost in all directions. The differences between various forms of rivalry are necessarily quantitative and empirical, but even with our limited present knowledge a few generalizations may be offered.

Price competition generally yields quicker results; the short-run elasticity of output with respect to price is greater than those with respect to (e.g.) quality or selling effort. In duopolistic cases — and this relationship appears in many instances of product differentiation — this characteristic often favors nonprice competition, because of its lesser invitation to retaliation and the competitive advantage of a device which cannot be imitated immediately. The concomitant uncertainty of the effects of nonprice policies has already been noted.

* Should we expect symmetry: will all of the firms consider themselves to be members of the same industry? The paucity of good industry studies makes discussion in this field very conjectural but an affirmative answer may be ventured, unless the cross-elasticities are strongly asymmetrical. The rivalry which takes place under imperfect competition is personalized and it is difficult to imagine one entrepreneur vigorously competing with another who disregards him.

As a closely related point, the effects of nonprice competition are in considerable measure cumulative. Thus continuous advertising results in a different demand situation than an equal dollar amount of sporadic advertising. This has a double aspect: it increases the costs of entrance of new firms, but contrariwise it reduces the range of possible entrepreneurial decisions. To use the same example, a large-scale advertising program is often a long-run commitment and one which might prove, because of the nature of its appeals, to be a barrier on the adoption of new technological knowledge.

Another possible distinction lies in the stability of equilibrium. Price movements stop when marginal revenue equals marginal cost and it requires a new development (e.g., entrance of new firms, a change in technology, a shift of demand) to alter the equilibrium. Nonprice competition (particularly advertising), however, seems to be of an endless dynamic process. A firm is constantly attempting to imitate the features of successful rivals' policies and, simultaneously, to find and exploit new and temporarily unique features for its own product. An attempt will usually be made to maintain certain permanent differences in the product in order to give continuity to the firm's consumer following. But persistent differentia of product cannot often be physical; rivals can and will imitate physical differences which have consumer appeal. The firm must then turn to advertising appeals, which are in turn open to imitation. If product variation is difficult — which often amounts to saying that consumers are fairly sophisticated — a common policy is to introduce new and perhaps completely unrelated products which will be subject (at least temporarily) to lighter competitive pressures.

It would be wrong, of course, to infer that these distinctions are more than matters of emphasis. Indeed it is most difficult even to isolate nonprice competition for it shades imperceptibly into price competition: the giving of samples, for instance, can be viewed as either a price reduction or a form of advertising. There are highly competitive markets in which quality variations are as effective as price variations (and in some cases even more so) in determining sales. Indeed it is clear that if consumers are fully informed, certain forms of rivalry will be excellent substitutes for one another,* and as

* This is not universally true: advertising, for example, becomes a poor substitute for quality improvement or a price reduction.

these cases are approached distinctions between types of competition become unimportant.

RECOMMENDED READINGS

(See also references to Chapters 11–13.)
1. Harrod, R. F., "Doctrines of Imperfect Competition," *Quarterly Journal of Economics*, XLVIII (1933–34), 442–70.
2. Hicks, J. R., "The Theory of Monopoly," *Econometrica*, III (1935), 1–20.
3. Kaldor, N. "Market Imperfection and Excess Capacity," *Economica*, N. S. II (1935), 33–50.
4. Nicholls, William H., *Imperfect Competition within Agricultural Industries*, Collegiate Press, Ames, 1941.
5. Sweezy, P. M., "Demand Under Conditions of Oligopoly," *Journal of Political Economy*, XLVII (1939), 568–73.
6. Buchanan, N. S., "Advertising Expenditures: A Suggested Treatment," *Journal of Political Economy*, L (1942), 537–57.

PROBLEMS

1. A monopolist with the demand curve, $p = 50 - q$, has the costs given on page 145. Determine output, price, and profits.
2. Ascertain the subsidy per unit which would lead the monopolist described in the previous question to increase his output 25 per cent, and the lump-sum tax which would then eliminate all monopoly gains. Illustrate graphically. Analyze also the effects of a legal maximum price of \$19.
3. If the marginal-cost curve of the monopolist in problem 1 were, marginal cost $= 60 - 2q$ $(q < 31)$, where would the monopolist operate? Deduce the rule for stable equilibrium.
4. It can be shown (see R. G. D. Allen, *Mathematical Analysis for Economists, op. cit.*, p. 202) that in the Cournot duopoly problem a firm operates at half the output for which the sum of marginal revenue and price equals twice the marginal cost. Verify for the case of a straight-line demand curve and zero costs of production.
5. The demand curve in a particular market is given by $p = 200 - q$. The sum of the marginal-cost curves of the minor firms is given as marginal cost $= x/2 - 1$; that of the dominant firm is $x - 15$. Determine price, output, and profits of the dominant firm. Then investigate geometrically:
    a. The effect of a change in the elasticity of the market-demand curve.
    b. The effect of a change in the relative outputs of dominant and minor firms.
    c. The effect of a change in the elasticity of the marginal-cost curve of the minor firms.

6. Two duopolists practice price-matching. The market-demand curve is given by $p = 100 - q$. The average cost curves of A and B are: average cost of A $= 10 - q$; average cost of B $= q$. Determine outputs, price, and profits.

7. A monopolist has the average cost $= 10 - q/100$; he succeeds in dividing his market into two parts with the following demand curves:

$$\text{Alpha market:} \quad p = 50 - q/40$$
$$\text{Beta market:} \quad p = 150 - q$$

Determine prices and output; compare profits with those which would arise if there were no discrimination. [The combined demand curve is $q = 2150 - 41p$ or $p = 52.44 - q/41$ ($p < 50$). How is this derived?]

8. Assume that there are 300 firms in an industry, each with the costs given on page 145. The demand curve of the industry is

$$p = 45 - q/170.$$

   a. Verify that if the industry is competitively organized, it is in long-run equilibrium.
   b. If now all of the firms were purchased to form a monopoly, what would the short-run equilibrium price become? What would happen to (1) output per plant, and (2) profits?
   c. As plants wear out, the monopolist will not replace them since it is more profitable to operate fewer plants at minimum average cost ($15). Assume that the number of plants has no effect on costs. Where will long-run monopoly price be established, at what output for the industry, and with how many plants?
   d. Assume, now, that a cartel had been formed of the original 300 firms, and that each firm was assigned a quota of 1/300 of the sales of the cartel. Draw the cost, demand, and marginal-revenue curves of one firm, and determine output, price, and profit.
   e. If 50 additional firms enter the industry, attracted by the profits,
      (1) What would happen to prices and profits if they were not admitted to the cartel? (Isolate the demand of the cartel by the dominant firm technique.)
      (2) If they are admitted to the cartel, and now each firm has a quota of 1/350 of sales, what will happen to output, prices, and profits?
      (3) Will they be admitted?
   f. If all new firms which enter the industry are admitted to the cartel, what number of firms will eliminate all profits? Is it certain that no additional firms will then enter the industry?
   g. Suppose that the cartel collapses due to "secret" price-cutting, after reaching the point where profits have been eliminated. Each firm behaves competitively and its demand curve is horizontal. Determine (1) output of the industry, (2) price, (3) output per firm, and (4) loss per firm. Moralize.

9. Using straight-line demand and marginal-cost curves, both of which are assumed to be identical for a competitive industry and a cartel, show that

   a. If the demand curve rotates about its intersection with the price axis (i.e., maintains the same elasticity at any price), the cartel will change its price by a smaller amount than the competitive industry.

   b. If the demand curve shifts up or down a given amount (a parallel displacement), the cartel will change its price by a greater amount than the competitive industry.

10. A selling monopoly has the marginal cost curve, marginal cost $= 3 - q$; the corresponding buying monopoly has the marginal value product curve, $mvp = 60 - q/2$. Determine the range of indeterminacy.

CHAPTER 15

PRICING OF THE PRODUCTIVE SERVICES UNDER IMPERFECT COMPETITION

The general principle underlying the pricing of productive services has already been sketched in the discussion of cost curves (Chapter 12) and requires only brief restatement. The individual firm employs such a quantity of each productive service that the marginal value product of the service (= marginal physical product × marginal revenue) equals its marginal cost; this is obviously the condition for maximum profits. The rule is perfectly general: it applies whether the firm is competitive or monopolistic in buying or selling markets. The detailed applications of the rule, for example to the firm dominant in the buying market, are in all respects formally symmetrical with the corresponding cases in the selling market, and can be left to the reader to make. Moreover the addition of demand curves of firms and industries follows procedures parallel to those described for the case of competition in the labor markets (Chapter 10, Section 2).

The present chapter will accordingly be devoted exclusively to an analysis of imperfect competition in the labor markets since these are the most important and interesting markets for productive services. A brief survey of monopsony (the single buyer) will be followed by a study of wage policies of labor unions.

I. MONOPSONY IN THE LABOR MARKET

It is not possible to enter here into the popular discussion of whether employers or employees in general have the greater bargaining power in wage determinations. The question cannot be answered except in terms of specific market situations: under competition, for example, the individual employer or employee has no power to set wages, and aggregate demand and aggregate supply are equally important.* Since only a very extensive empirical

---

* The literature on this subject is very ambiguous. Thus, the assertion that one employer has a bargaining advantage relative to each of 100 employees is by itself as

study (which no one has made) would yield even preliminary conclusions on the question of relative bargaining power, the present
discussion will be restricted to an examination of the circumstances
under which an employer has significant control over the wage rates
he pays.*

In order to have control over the wages he pays, an employer
must either be the only (or dominant) employer in a given market
or collude with the other employers. But this condition is not sufficient: workers will shift to other areas or to other occupations if
wages fall below the levels in these alternative employments.
Collusion will lead to substantial control over wage rates only if
there is immobility between occupations and areas.

The extent of occupational mobility turns largely on how narrowly *occupation* is defined. If the banks of a city were to seek to
depress wages of bank janitors they would find mobility very high;
if all employers of janitors in a city were to combine a good deal
more could be achieved. There is not much evidence of employers
setting low wages for a particular occupation, nor would one expect
them to do this. If an occupation is small the gains from control of
wages are usually small; if the occupation is large the number of
employers is also usually large so collusion is difficult. Wage-con-
trol schemes commonly apply to all workers in a fairly broad group
(e.g., industry or city.)

Geographical immobility is much more important. The immobility of workers may be due to either ignorance of employment
alternatives or the costs of moving. The laborer will be immobile
if he is systematically pessimistic as to employment possibilities in
other firms.† The wretched provision of information in labor markets tends to strengthen this factor but even so it is probably of
minor importance in the United States where change per se is
sought by so many. If there is no collusion among employers,

trivial as the assertion that a fruit peddler has a bargaining advantage relative to each
of 100 housewives. Again, the statement that labor is perishable is equally true (and
untrue) of services of capital equipment. For a survey of such distinctions, see W. H.
Hutt, *The Theory of Collective Bargaining*, King, London, 1930; on the question of indeterminacy see J. R. Hicks, "Edgeworth, Marshall and the Indeterminateness of Wages,"
Economic Journal, XL (1930), 215–31.

* The quality of the labor must be specified, of course. Since typically the most
efficient worker within an occupational class is at least two or three times as productive
as the least efficient, differences in wage rates do not necessarily indicate wage control.

† Ignorance can also lead to excessive mobility, for example when exaggerated
rumors of prosperity elsewhere lead to a mass migration.

ignorance is perhaps equally likely to lead to overpayment relative to alternative employments.

The barriers to moving may be very substantial: they include transportation costs, a period of unemployment, loss of perquisites connected with seniority, and the tenacity of social ties. These obstacles to movement must vary almost infinitely among individuals. One can travel by airplane or by hitch-hiking; for the unemployed, movement will often increase the prospects of employment; the young and the old will differ greatly with respect to seniority rights; and social ties vary from inseverable to an eager posse.* Moreover, the amount of labor mobility necessary to negate employer attempts at wage control is similarly variable: even a single employer will not persist in paying low wages until all of the laborers move, and a combination of employers may break up as soon as a "shortage" of labor becomes evident.

There are two fundamental reasons for believing that geographical immobility of workers does not permit substantial and widespread employer wage control: the astonishing mobility — not to say wanderlust — of the American people,† and the ability of employers to move to areas where wage rates are low. The substantial improvement in status of the Negro — the laborer who is in general at the bottom of the income ladder, and who has suffered most from employer wage control — has been due to both an increasing northward migration (amounting to well over a million between the two world wars) and the movement of industry to the south.‡

* It may be observed that the perquisites associated with seniority can be very potent. Consider, for example, an individual who intends to work 30 more years, choosing between two positions A and B in each of which a newcomer works half-time and the fraction of time worked rises linearly until after 20 years full-time employment is achieved. If B has a nominal rate of pay $300 a year higher than that in A, a person with no seniority in A gains a present value of $3558 (at 5 per cent) by moving to B, but if he has 20 years' seniority in A he loses a present value of $3800 by moving.

† Even on the restricted definition of migration used in the 1940 Census (i.e., movement across county lines or in or out of a city with a population over 100,000), one-eighth of the heads of American families migrated between 1935 and 1940 (and over half of the remainder moved to a different house in the same county or city). See *Family Composition and Migration Status of Family Heads: 1940*, Bureau of Census, Washington, April 6, 1943.

‡ See Carter Goodrich, *Migration and Economic Opportunity*, University of Pennsylvania, Philadelphia, 1936; A. Davis, B. B. Gardner, and M. R. Gardner, *Deep South*, University of Chicago, Chicago, 1941, Ch. 20, 21.

II. THE ECONOMICS OF COLLECTIVE BARGAINING

It is not possible here to examine the whole range of objectives and policies of labor unions. Nevertheless it is advisable at least to sketch their supply and demand policies with respect to wages. Labor markets are overwhelmingly important markets in productive services and the extension of labor unions has been the most important departure from competitive price determination in recent years. Hence even a synoptical treatment of one aspect of the labor market is desirable, and it may prove instructive to examine from an analytical viewpoint questions more commonly discussed in other terms.

1. *THE DEMAND FOR LABOR*

It is commonly stated that virtually all union leaders believe that the demand for a particular kind of labor as well as the demand for labor by a particular industry are relatively inelastic. This belief, which is undoubtedly correct when restricted to short-run demand,* is attributed to two common arguments. The first is that the technical proportions in which labor and other productive services combine are relatively fixed, and during a period of variable length this is true. The second argument is that labor costs form a very small proportion of total costs; thus a 40 per cent reduction in carpenters' wages might reduce the cost of houses by only 1 per cent. This latter point of course loses its relevance if applied to large groups of laborers, and it is not invariably correct even when applied to small groups.†

In the long run, however, the elasticity of demand surely increases. The possibilities of variation of technique are almost always present and high wages encourage research for additional methods of mechanization. In the short run, moreover, an entre-

---

* The time period is of primary importance. Once a builder has contracted to build a certain type of residence, for example, his demand for labor has virtually zero elasticity up to wage rates which make repudiation of the contract cheaper than fulfillment. In even a short period, however, high wage-rate demands would be reflected in the contractor's bid (and hence lead to the construction of fewer houses) and in the specifications for houses.

† It can be shown that if the elasticity of substitution between the labor in question and other productive services (defined as the ratio of a relative change in ratio of labor to other services divided by the relative change in the ratio of their marginal products) is greater than the elasticity of demand for the product, the opposite may be true. See J. R. Hicks, *Theory of Wages*, Macmillan, London, 1932, Appendix.

preneur will find it profitable to sacrifice a share of his quasi rents rather than close down; in the long run he will move to a region or industry where unions are weak, or, in the case of an industry shift, where labor costs are small. The increase in the elasticity of demand for the products with the passage of time also increases the elasticity of (derived) demand for labor. The alternative sources of supply (imports, goods from nonunion shops) also increase the elasticity of demand for the products of unionized shops. The net effect of these forces will of course vary widely in different industries but the general conclusion is that the elasticity of demand for labor of a given type or by a given industry is substantial and in particular it is very probably greater than unity.*

Although it is not difficult to cite examples of unions which have collapsed because of their failure to recognize the high elasticity of demand for their services,† the policies of many unions reflect clear understanding of devices for economizing the use of high-priced union labor. It may be useful to survey and briefly to illustrate five general types of policy used to maintain the demand for labor of a particular type or labor in a particular industry: (1) opposition to imports; (2) combatting nonunion production; (3) opposition to introduction of technological changes; (4) preservation of jurisdiction; and (5) interindustry warfare.

Opposition to imports of foreign commodities has been characteristic of modern American labor unions, but the opposition has usually been voiced by specific unions in connection with specific proposals rather than by general federations. This is readily explicable: the interests of laborers producing a commodity are furthered (temporarily) by a higher domestic price; other laborers as subsequent processors or as consumers desire low prices. The extent of the opposition to free importation is illustrated by the Senate hearings on the Smoot-Hawley tariff: 21 unions or groups of unions

---

* There are few formal attempts to measure elasticity, although material such as that cited in the next footnote is relevant. Pigou estimates that even in depression the short-run elasticity of demand for labor is numerically greater than 1.5 (see *The Theory of Unemployment*, Macmillan, London, 1933, Part II), and Douglas estimates the long-run elasticity to be numerically greater than 3 (see *The Theory of Wages*, Macmillan, New York, 1934, Part II). Assuming that a useful meaning can be attached to the concept of the elasticity of demand for all labor, which is doubtful, the elasticity will usually be larger for particular classes of laborers.

† See G. L. Palmer, *Union Tactics and Economic Change*, University of Pennsylvania, Philadelphia, 1931, and S. H. Slichter, *Union Policies and Industrial Management*, Brookings, Washington, 1941, Ch. VII, XII.

took definite positions on particular schedules, and only in the case of two commodities did they fail to ask for higher tariff rates.* Similar restrictions have been applied to smaller areas, as in the support of legislation to require state institutions to use local products.

Only unions in localized industries (such as the building trades) have been relatively free of the problems raised by nonunion plants' competition. The most satisfactory solution from the union's viewpoint is of course to unionize the entire industry, and much of the recent activity of labor unions has been so directed.† Another device, important in textiles, has been the removal or reduction of north-south wage differentials by minimum-wage legislation. Still another device is to enlist the cooperation of laborers at later production stages, whereby the latter refuse to work with materials made in nonunion plants.‡

The attitude of unions toward technological change have been governed chiefly by their power.§ Strong unions have succeeded in some measure in outright prohibition of techniques which would decrease the demand for labor. As examples, the painters have successfully opposed the use of paint sprayers in many cities,¶ and

* Both exceptions pertained to raw materials used by the union: the cigarmakers did not wish the rate on wrappers (which are imported) raised, and the marble polishers did not wish the rate on travertine stone (which is processed domestically) raised. But both unions favored increased duties on all other commodities with which they were concerned.

† In the nineteen-twenties the United Mine Workers, for example, succeeded in securing wage rates in the unionized area (Illinois, Indiana, Ohio, and Pennsylvania) more than 50 per cent higher than those ruling in the nonunionized area (Kentucky and West Virginia). The latter area made such inroads on the national market that (after a strike which the union lost) the union operators secured large wage reductions. "The NRA brought the union a new organizing opportunity, which it was quick to seize. . . . in 1936 the [union] officers reported that 95 per cent of the industry was organized. With union scales established and enforced in virtually all mines, West Virginia and Kentucky have no longer been able to encroach upon the markets of Illinois, Indiana, Ohio, and Pennsylvania. In fact, recovery of production between 1932 and 1937 was considerably greater in the old union territory than in recently organized West Virginia and Kentucky — 52 per cent as against 37 per cent." (S. H. Slichter, *Union Policies and Industrial Management*, pp. 362–63.)

‡ For examples, see R. E. Montgomery, *Industrial Relations in the Chicago Building Trades*, University of Chicago, Chicago, 1927, Ch. X. For similar practices by teamsters, see R. A. Lester, *The Economics of Labor*, Macmillan, New York, 1941, pp. 145–55, and C. L. Christensen, "Chicago Service Trades" in *How Collective Bargaining Works*, Twentieth Century, New York, 1942, pp. 817ff.

§ It is more appropriate to speak of *technological change* than *advance*. An increase in wage rates may bring about the adoption of a long-known alternative technique which was uneconomic at lower wage rates.

¶ Indeed they have secured laws (as in Florida) against their use.

the carpenters have prevented certain types of work from being done in mills. But as a rule such frontal attacks have led to the growth of the nonunion sector of the industry, so weaker forms of opposition have been used. New techniques are delayed by requiring higher wage rates where they are used, or prohibiting their adoption if labor will be displaced, or insisting that skilled labor rates be paid even if the work becomes semiskilled,* or requiring dismissal pay, or placing limitations on the output of new devices, and similar devices.

Most, although not all, jurisdictional problems arise out of technological changes but the subject is important enough to deserve separate mention.† The classical example of aggressive jurisdictional policy is provided by the carpenters' union, which at various times has claimed all work on wood, or substitutes of wood, or work in which carpenters' tools are employed. On the second of these grounds, for example, it secured control of metal trim "only because it could fight [for twenty years] the entire building trades labor movement."‡ Such aggressive action led to a shrinkage of building construction which may well have offset the relative jurisdictional gains of the carpenters since the costs to employers of rigorous jurisdictional policies have been high.§

The source of elastic demand for labor which is generally most difficult for a union to control is intercommodity competition. It is usually impossible for a union to exert direct influence on buyers of the industry's product, or, alternatively, to raise the prices of substitute commodities, but the political weapon is often available. For example, the United Mine Workers have long been concerned over the expansion of other energy sources; the union estimated

---

* Or virtually disappears, as with the requirement that Diesel driven trains have firemen.

† Jurisdictional disputes between rival unions are the important exception to this statement.

‡ See William Haber, *Industrial Relations in the Building Industry*, Harvard University, Cambridge, 1930, p. 159, Ch. VI; also E. E. Cummins, "Jurisdictional Disputes of the Carpenters' Union," *Quarterly Journal of Economics*, XL (1926), 463–94.

§ A majority of all strikes in the building trades have been due to jurisdictional disputes. The enforcement of sharp jurisdictional lines also increases direct labor costs; as an extreme example: ". . . in order to move a pump to a different location in a foundation hole, it was necessary to get a pair of steam fitters to disconnect the steam pipes, a pair of plumbers to remove the suction apparatus and replace it, a structural iron worker to erect a rig to lift the pump, and an engineer to operate the valves on the pump — eight men for the operation. One man assisted by a laborer could have accomplished the job." (Haber, *loc. cit.*, p. 234).

that of the 42 per cent decline in coal product between 1926 and 1937, more than half (23 per cent) was due to the displacement by substitute fuels. The program outlined to combat this competition includes the following points:*

1. Extensive research in, and exploitation of known techniques for, the utilization of coal by-products.
2. Educational and legislative campaigns to secure a larger allocation of the costs of the petroleum industry to fuel oil, with a consequent higher price for fuel oil and lower price for gasoline.
3. A federal tax of 1 cent per gallon on fuel oil — about 15 per cent at the time.
4. Organization of the oil workers: "They must be actively organized with a view of raising wage rates of all petroleum workers outside of refineries."
5. Divorcement of pipe lines from oil producers.
6. Increased tariff rates on imported fuel oils, for which the union has been striving since 1921. Reciprocal trade agreements are opposed because the duty on Venezuelan oil was halved in one such agreement and Canadian import duties on American coal were not reduced in another.
7. Strengthen conservation practices in petroleum.
8. Social security funds should be raised by income rather than payroll taxes because labor costs are a much higher proportion of coal than of petroleum costs.
9. The Engineering Department of the union appeared before various commissions "in an effort to reduce uneconomic and unreasonable displacement of coal" but were apparently not very successful because "Government agencies . . . are primarily concerned with immediate dollar and cents savings on their operating expenses."

Such interindustry warfare has not been very extensive in the past because the more direct forms of substitution (such as nonunion production) had not yet been controlled by most American unions. It will undoubtedly become much more prominent in the future.

II. *SUPPLY AND WAGE OBJECTIVES*

The factors which govern the supply curve of labor in a unionized field are much more difficult to isolate. If a union succeeds in securing a wage rate higher than that offered in other occupations of corresponding requirements and characteristics, obviously laborers will flow in if so permitted, until *annual* earnings have been

* See "Report of International Officers," *Proceedings of the Thirty-Sixth Constitutional Convention of the United Mine Workers*, Columbus, 1940.

reduced to the competitive level. The supply policy of the union is therefore intimately connected with its wage policy, and both are in turn governed by the objectives of the wage policy. No systematic treatment is possible in the present state of our knowledge but a few patterns of union policy may be sketched.

The type which corresponds most closely in motivation to the usual business enterprise is the officer-dominated union. Such union leaders are commonly called *racketeers* if they extort money from employers on threat of strike,* or if they take excessive amounts from union members and funds.† Where this motive alone is dominant, the wage policy will generally be as moderate as is compatible with the maintenance of control over the union organization,‡ since a large membership provides larger union funds and yields larger entrepreneurial incomes from which to secure contributions. Those union leaders who pursue the more respectable ends of power and prestige can usually attain these ends best by meeting membership demands (except perhaps as to dues) and either rise in the union hierarchy or extend the union's jurisdiction into new industries; the various possible wage policies are discussed below.

If a given membership of a union wishes to maximize its wage earnings, an extremely high wage level is appropriate. The wage level sought should be at the maximum compatible with maintenance of full employment (assuming that the long-run elasticity of demand is greater than unity). This in turn implies a wage rate such that employment declines at the same rate that the union members retire or die. In the case of an industry with a stable demand for labor this end would be attained if the last employer were (temporarily) driven out of the industry when the last union member retired.

---

* Long a common practice in the building trades; see R. E. Montgomery, *Industrial Relations in the Chicago Building Trades*, University of Chicago, Chicago, 1927, Ch. XI.

† For example, the business agent of Local 244 of the Moving Picture Machine Operators (Essex, N. J.) received $100 to $600 from "junior" members for jobs plus a kickback of $5 to $25 a week, $150 per week salary as business agent plus a sum in excess of $100 a week as a worker although the services were rendered by "junior" members without pay, $45 per month for a car, a present of $5,000 each year, and $500 to $2,500 for convention expenses (which were also paid for by the International Alliance). See *Collins et al. v. International Alliance*, 119 N. J. Eq. 230 (1935).

‡ And this in turn depends upon the traditions, education, and skill of the union members, the movements of wage rates in related fields, and the unemployment situation.

A more realistic pattern is maximization of wage income of a given number of employees — the union accepting sufficient new members to maintain constant its numbers. The appropriate wage demands are more moderate than in the preceding case: in an industry with a stable demand for labor, for example, the wage rate will be constant at a level which permits competitive rates of return to appropriate amounts of other resources in the industry.*

It may be of interest at this point to examine the wage policy of a union which seeks to maximize the total wage bill of an industry.

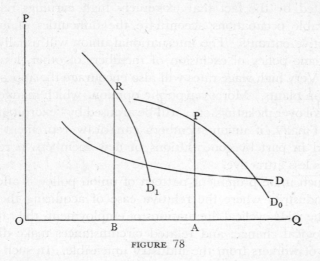

FIGURE 78

Taking as representative the case in which the long-run elasticity of demand is greater than unity and the short-run elasticity less than unity, the policy is feasible only if the union does not recognize the long-run elasticity.† This situation is illustrated in Figure 78, where D is the long-run demand curve for the labor and D_o the current

---

* An approximate illustration is afforded by Local 384 of the Moving Picture Operators (Hudson County, N. J.), which classified members as seniors and juniors. The latter could not vote on union policies, attend union meetings, or be informed of what occurred at such meetings. Their dues were $454 a year; the seniors paid $80. The initiation fee for senior members was $3,000 and a favorable vote was also difficult to secure. Senior members had first employment rights. See *Cameron et al. v. International Alliance*, 118 N. J. Eq. 11 (1933). For another example, this time the Hollywood craft unions, see Murray Ross, *Stars and Strikes*, Columbia University, New York, 1941, pp. 202ff.

† If this elasticity is recognized, the union could attain the objective only by lowering the wage rate, probably even below the competitive rate. Such a type of action is not practicable for unions.

short-run demand curve.* The union will set a wage of AP (where P is the point of unitary elasticity on D_o). In an industry with a stable long-run demand curve for labor, the short-run demand curve will fall after a certain time to D_1 as firms leave the industry, so the union is forced to raise the wage rate to BR, and so on. Thus maximizing the short-run wage bill leads to a policy similar to that a union which excludes new entrants will practice in an industry with a stable demand for labor.

In practice the foregoing types of union policy are usually moderated by the fact that extremely high earnings relative to comparable occupations accentuate the difficulties of excluding prospective entrants. The international union will usually oppose an extreme policy of exclusion of members of other, less-favored locals. Very high wage rates will also encourage the appearance of nonunion plants. Moreover public opinion, which manifests itself in control over picketing, etc., will be aroused by "exorbitant" wage rates. Finally, if union members can draw retirement benefits financed in part by contributions of new members, a restrictive policy is less attractive.

A much more prominent pattern of union policy is afforded in those industries where the relative ease of acquiring the needed skills, the wide cyclical fluctuations of employment, the rapidity of technological change, and related circumstances make direct exclusion of workers from the industry unfeasible. In such cases — and these are largely the specifications of the mass-production industries — exclusion can take place only by two devices. The first is seniority rules, the general effects of which are fairly obvious. The second device is the wage level itself: high wage rates will increase unemployment among union members and hence discourage new entrants. (As a necessary result, also, employers will insist on higher levels of performance by workmen, which again serves to exclude many from the industry.)

The wage policy which such a union will follow is difficult to formulate in precise terms. The governing circumstances are probably the relative desirabilities of high wages and full employment for union members and the movement of wage rates in similar industries. The most common rule on wage changes is to follow

---

* There does not seem to be any necessary relationship between D and D_o except the lesser elasticity of the latter curve.

employer "profits" (i.e., executive salaries plus return on investment plus pure profits).* In periods of prosperity wage requests will rise at a rate calculated to share materially (but not eliminate) unusual gains; in periods of depression they stop rising or actual reductions are accepted. The adverse effect of this policy on investment decisions of entrepreneurs is evident: the returns on new investments are almost always uncertain and although the union wage policy does not reduce the chances of loss, it does reduce the possible gains.

III. THE WAGE BARGAIN

It might be expected that a union would prefer to bargain with individual employers, each of whom would be able to offer less resistance than a combination of employers, and before the union is well established this is often true. But once the union is generally recognized, it promotes organization of employers. Thus in the once highly competitive building, bituminous coal, garment, and motor-trucking industries the unions have actively supported employer associations, quite aside from the potent motive of self-protection for employer combinations. In part the reasons for this attitude are organizational, as the case of motor trucking indicates:

> When the union first came into the picture the employers had no associations of any sort. In an industry with so many employers it would be exceedingly difficult for a union with a limited staff to conduct separate negotiations with each employer. It would also be well-nigh impossible for the union to conclude contracts which were identical in terms and expired at the same date, with a large number of employers. If this situation did not obtain, employers would charge union discrimination due to differing provisions of contracts. If contracts expired at different times, locals would probably be in a continual state of disturbance, and part of the membership would always be on strike or faced with the possible necessity of having to go out on strike. The system of negotiating contracts simultaneously with all employers in a given area, and having these contracts run for identical periods, minimizes the possibility of strikes, since locals will more carefully consider the consequences of strikes when they involve all rather than a small part of the membership.
>
> Difficulty of negotiating contracts with large numbers of individual employers led most locals to encourage the formation of employer associ-

* For a typical statement of this policy, see S. Barkin, "Wage Policies of Industrial Unions," *Harvard Business Review*, XIX (1940–41), 341–52.

ations for the purpose of bargaining with locals for the entire industry in a given city.*

In addition, industry-wide agreements minimize rivalry between local unions.†

On the other side, employers are more willing to agree to union wage demands if no other firms in the industry will have a competitive advantage due to lower labor costs. A more important factor, however, is the possibility of recouping wage increases by price increases. Such price increases are of course an inevitable consequence of increased wages even if employers are competitive in selling, although probably with a time lag if inventories have been accumulated or firms must leave the industry before competitive rates of return on investment are restored. But if a cartel is instituted the price rises may be immediate and may support monopoly profits as well as very high wages.‡ There have been numerous examples of union enforcement of price agreements among employers.§

The actual terms of the wage bargain between a union and an association of employers are of course indeterminate: this is indeed much the most important case of bilateral monopoly in our economy. The solution of such disputes is shifting to an increasing extent to the political arena. It is inevitable that when a dispute threatens to halt operation of a critical industry — and the industries which are not critical in our highly interdependent economy are few and small — the social interests demand that a settlement be reached. The principles, if such exist, on which government officials and labor boards operate, however, are not greatly illuminated by economic analysis. The sympathies of the administration, the public's attitude, the political strength of the parties —

---

* Samuel E. Hill, *Teamsters and Transportation*, American Council on Public Affairs, Washington, 1942, pp. 24–25.

† *Ibid.*, pp. 147ff.

‡ The position of the union is strengthened if price competition between employers is eliminated, since the pressure to reduce labor costs will be weakened.

§ The "Stabilization Plan" launched by the Amalgamated Clothing Workers in 1939 is an important illustration. In order to "equalize" labor costs of various firms, all products are classified into six grades and standard labor costs are set for each grade. Contractors (who do much of the work through subcontracting) are closely regulated to prevent wage reductions and the grades of products which a manufacturer or contractor may produce are designated by the union. Selling prices of garments are fixed by contractors' associations under union domination. See *How Collective Bargaining Works*, Twentieth Century Fund, New York, 1942, Ch. 8.

these and other decisive variables are beyond the domain of economic theory.

RECOMMENDED READINGS

1. Hicks, J. R., *The Theory of Wages*, Macmillan, London, 1930.
2. Slichter, S. H., *Union Policies and Industrial Management*, Brookings, Washington, 1941.
3. Bronfonbrenner, M., "The Economics of Collective Bargaining," *Quarterly Journal of Economics*, L (1938–39), 535–61.
4. Twentieth Century Fund, *How Collective Bargaining Works*, Twentieth Century, New York, 1942.
5. Dunlop, J. T., *Wage Determination under Trade Unions*, Macmillan, New York, 1944.
6. Simons, H. C., "Some Reflections on Syndicalism," *Journal of Political Economy*, LII (1944), 1–25.

PROBLEMS

1. First solve geometrically and then numerically the following pricing problems:
   a. The supply curve of the productive service is, $p = 5 + q/2$; the marginal-value product curve of the dominant firm is, $p = 50 - q$; and the sum of the marginal-value product curves of the minor firms is, $p = 20 - 2q$.
   b. The supply curve is as in part a; the marginal-value product curves of each of the two duopolists who practice price-matching in buying is, $p = 25 - q/2$.
   c. All other data are as in part b; but the less efficient duopolist has a marginal-value product curve given by
      (1) $p = 22 - q/2$.
      (2) $p = 14 - q/2$.
   d. A monopsonist has the marginal-value product curve, $p = 100 - q$. He has been buying a productive service with the supply curve, $p = q/2$. Now he finds that he can split this supply curve into the following parts: $p_1 = q_1 - 10$; and $p_2 = q_2 + 10$, and practice price discrimination. Compare the prices and quantities. Can you think of any realistic illustrations?
   e. The data are as in part d before discrimination; compare the effects of legal minimum prices of $33.33 and $50.
2. Congress passes a law prohibiting use of land in growing wheat unless rent of $12 or more an acre is paid for the land. Analyze the effects on production of wheat and other products, their prices, and incomes of landlords and laborers,
   a. If the law applies to everyone.
   b. If the law does not apply to owner-operators.
   Compare the effects of minimum-wage laws and union standard rates.

3. The data are the same as in question 2 but now the minimum rental applies to all land whatever its product.
4. An industry in two regions has paid different wage rates in the regions. Suddenly the barrier to movement of laborers is removed. What are the effects on output, prices, wage rates, and the wage bill?
5. Appraise the following quotation from *The Hot Slug*, publication of the Chicago Linotype Operators Society (taken from Slichter, *Union Policies and Industrial Management*, p. 170):

Eggs

When a linotype operator orders a dozen eggs at the grocery store, how many does he receive?

Does the grocer count out 15, 18, or 24 eggs, simply because he has good stock on hand?

Yes he does, — NOT!

He counts out exactly the number that are paid for.

But the operator considers that all right and is satisfied.

Then perhaps he goes to the print shop and hands out to the boss two days' work for the price of one.

The Intelligent Printer!

6. The following is a summary of effects of the Walsh-Healey Act (which permits establishment of minimum wages and maximum hours without overtime for laborers engaged by government contractors). Examine both the empirical implications and the internal logic.

Three groups profit from the passage of the Walsh-Healey law. They are the workers engaged in the performance of work on Government contracts; other labor engaged in similar employment, since the standards for Government work tend to become general; and employers who customarily maintain equitable standards and who formerly were adversely affected by the competition of firms observing lower working standards. The provisions of the act make for fairer competition than previously existed under the system of competitive bidding, when orders went to the lowest bidder regardless of the terms of employment of his force. Each cut in the price quotation to the Government was likely to entail a reduction in the wage rate to the workers engaged in producing the goods. . . . there is considerable evidence that the minimum wage and other requirements have not increased the price paid by the Government.

(Taken from *Handbook of Labor Statistics*, Bulletin 694 of the Bureau of Labor Statistics, 1941, II, 388.)

PART IV

MULTIPLE PRODUCTS AND CAPITAL AND INTEREST

CHAPTER 16

THE THEORY OF MULTIPLE PRODUCTS

The analysis has hitherto been based upon the assumption that the firm makes only one product. If *product* is defined broadly — for example, to mean cotton textiles or men's clothing or iron and steel — this assumption is descriptive of a very important part of our economy. But even when product is used in this broad sense there still remain firms making automobiles and refrigerators and stores selling jewelry and meals. Moreover such a broad definition of product is undesirable in economic analysis. It is part of the economist's task to explain why a firm produces diverse commodities and to examine the relationships among their prices.

Consequently we define a product as any homogeneous commodity where the test of homogeneity is that the consumers will not distinguish between any two portions of the stock.* It might appear that if producers distinguish between subclasses of the commodity (on the basis of cost), there will also be multiple products. But if consumers are indifferent between the subclasses, producers will offer only the subclass which is cheaper to produce. On this narrow definition of product, virtually all firms are multiple-product firms.

The formal theory of a single-product firm is easily generalized to include the case of multiple products. A firm produces multiple products either because the demands for the various products are related or their costs of production are smaller when jointly produced. It will be convenient to follow this dichotomy in the subsequent discussion of pricing.

I. PRICING OF MULTIPLE PRODUCTS UNDER COMPETITION

1. *UNRELATED DEMANDS*

If the demand curves for the various products of the firm are unrelated (i.e., if the cross-elasticity of demand is approximately

---

* In other words, the indifference curves between the two portions are straight lines (p. 72).

zero), the necessary condition for multiple products is that the cost of producing them jointly is less than the sum of costs of producing them separately. Such a situation obviously arises when the production of commodity A necessarily entails the production of B, e.g., no one has found a breed of sheep consisting only of wool or of mutton.

1. Variable Proportions. Typically the multiple products can be produced in variable proportions, at least in the long run. This is obviously the case in most manufacturing and service industries: a steel plant can produce sheets and rails in diverse proportions and a department store can vary the distribution of space and personnel between furniture and shoes. Variability does seem at first sight to be unfeasible in the chemical and agricultural industries. Yet the development of "cracking" processes in petroleum refining (which raised the percentage of petroleum refined into gasoline from 26 to 44 per cent in the United States between 1919 and 1932) and the varieties and changes in seeds and livestock breeds show that the assumption of variability is appropriate even in these fields. Indeed where variability is not present entrepreneurs will attempt to achieve it because of the additional opportunities for profit afforded by the ability to alter proportions. In the short run there is undoubtedly greater rigidity in proportions, but this situation will be deferred temporarily.

Given variability of proportions between multiple products, the rules of pricing under competition hold with only minor change. It is still possible to determine the marginal cost of each of the multiple products; for example, by varying the proportion of cotton to cottonseed one may secure data such as those in Table 21. The marginal cost in this case is the increase in total cost divided by the

TABLE 21

Cotton (pounds)	Cottonseed (pounds)	Total Cost	Marginal Cost of Cottonseed
1200	2200	$142.10	—
1200	2300	143.00	$0.009
1200	2400	144.00	.01
1200	2500	145.20	.012
1200	2600	146.60	.014

corresponding increase in cottonseed. The amount of cotton is held fixed so the increase in cost may (and must) be attributed solely to the changing quantity of cottonseed.

The competitive firm will of course equate marginal cost and price for each of the multiple products in the short-run normal period. In long-run equilibrium, however, it is no longer possible to say that the average cost of cotton must equal its price since the average cost of cotton does not exist. (What is the average cost of 1,200 pounds of cotton in Table 21?) Instead, we reformulate the rule and say that for the industry to be in equilibrium, so no new firms enter nor old firms leave, total cost must equal total revenue.

The former rule of distribution, that the marginal physical product of a productive service times the price of the product must equal the price of the service (page 176), must also be modified, for now a productive service contributes to several products. The extension of the rule is almost self-evident. If a productive service X aids in producing both A and B, let MPP_{xa} be its marginal product in producing A and MPP_{xb} that in producing B. The rule for maximum profits becomes

$$MPP_{xa} \cdot p_a + MPP_{xb} \cdot p_b = p_x,$$

and similarly for other productive services. This rule may be stated verbally: the sum of the marginal products of a productive service, each multiplied by the price of its product, must equal the price of the service.

2. *Fixed Proportions.* If two or more commodities are produced in rigidly fixed proportions, the marginal cost of one product no longer exists. Any increase in one product will be accompanied by a proportional increase in the other and the resulting increase in total cost cannot be divided between them. One can speak only of the marginal cost of a combined unit of (e.g.) 1 pound of mutton and 4 ounces of wool. If the proportions are fixed, however, the composition of the combined unit of output will not vary and no ambiguity is possible. The competitive firm will then operate at the outputs where the marginal cost of (A + B) equals the price of A plus the price of B, and again in long-run equilibrium total cost equals total receipts.

The prices of the joint products are determined by the condition that the quantity of each supplied must equal the quantity demanded.* The whole pricing process may be illustrated for the case of mutton and wool, on the unreal assumption that 4 pounds of mutton are always produced in conjunction with 1 pound of wool. The demand schedules for the two products are given in Table 22.

TABLE 22

Wool		Mutton	
Quantity (pounds)	Price (cents)	Quantity (pounds)	Price (cents)
160,000	100	500,000	55
180,000	60	640,000	50
200,000	40	800,000	40
300,000	20	1,000,000	35
400,000	10	1,200,000	30

If there are 1,000 identical sheep ranches, each producing 800 pounds of mutton and 200 pounds of wool, the price of mutton will be $0.40 and that of wool $0.40. Let us assume that these prices are unprofitable because the cost of producing 4 pounds of mutton and 1 pound of wool is $3.00. Firms will leave the industry and the prices of both products will rise. Since in our example the demand for mutton is elastic and that for wool is not, the latter's price will rise relatively more. If this is a constant-cost industry, when 200 firms leave the industry the price of mutton will rise to $0.50 and that of wool to $1.00 and total costs will equal total receipts.

* In terms of conditions of equilibrium,
1. For each firm
$$MC_{a+b} = p_a + p_b,$$
as stated in the text, and
$$a = kb,$$
i.e., the proportion between the products is fixed and equal to k.
2. For the industry

Quantity supplied of A = Quantity demanded of A,
Quantity supplied of B = Quantity demanded of B.

These equations are sufficient in number to determine p_a, p_b, and the output of each product by each firm. In long-run equilibrium the additional condition, total receipts = total costs, fixes the number of firms. In the previous case of variable proportions the equations of the firm are: $MC_a = p_a$, and $MC_b = p_b$.

II. *RELATED DEMANDS*

A firm may also produce two or more products simply because buyers prefer to purchase them together or to compare them at time of purchase. If the cost of handling the products together does not exceed the sum of the costs of handling them separately by more than the premium that consumers will pay for the "shopping" convenience, the two or more commodities will of course be handled together. The actual premium depends upon the market structure: if all consumers prefer joint handling, the premium will equal the cost of this service (which may of course be negative); if a considerable number of consumers do not prefer this arrangement and it is expensive, some firms will sell individual products at lower prices.*

The reverse of this situation is also possible although (for obvious reasons) less easily illustrated: consumers may have a dislike for the proximity of certain commodities and this will prevent their joint handling even though there are economies in joint production. Thus $300 evening gowns and $3.89 imitations are rarely handled by the same store; the not-too-busy rural physician could be, but is not, also the mortician.

The entire field of retailing may appear to illustrate the case of related demands. In the case of department stores the theory is appropriate. But the neighborhood retailer offers a more complicated problem. There are no production economies in handling both groceries and fresh fruits rather than specializing; on the contrary one would expect the costs of handling a full line of foodstuffs to be somewhat higher than those of handling a commensurate amount of only one type of goods. But the neighborhood market cannot support coffee stores, sugar stores, and the like, so the comparison of costs must be between very small stores each handling a single line and larger stores handling several lines of goods. The indivisibility of the merchandising unit relative to local markets usually dictates the general store, although complementarity of demands also contributes to this result.†

---

* These commodities may be either complements or substitutes. In the case of consumers' desire for variety from which to choose, there is a minor (verbal) paradox in that they have a complementary demand for substitutes.

† For a survey of the extent and causes of multiple products in manufacturing, see T.N.E.C. monograph 27, *The Structure of Industry* (Washington, 1941).

III. *THE INDUSTRY*

The theory of pricing developed in Chapter 9 is readily extended to include the case of multiple products. Unless one uses solid geometry or indifference curves (see Section 3), however, it is necessary to resort to approximations, and one problem is treated in this latter manner. The cost and demand curves for two products which are complementary in production are displayed in Figure 79; the unprimed curves indicate the initial position of equilibrium.

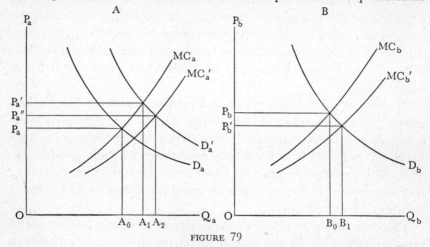

FIGURE 79

It should be observed that the marginal-cost curve for A is drawn on the assumption that B_o of B is produced, and reciprocally the marginal-cost curve for B is valid only if A_o of A is produced. Let now the demand curve for A rise from D_a to D_a'. If we break the process of reaching the new short-run equilibrium into artificial steps, we may proceed as follows. First the output of A rises to A_1 and the price to p_a'. The increased output of A decreases the marginal cost of producing a given amount of B, and decreases it more, the more rigid the proportions in which A and B are produced. This is shown in Figure 79 B by the fall in MC_b to MC_b'. As a result, the price of B falls from p_b to p_b' when output rises to B_1. The increase in the output of B reduces the marginal cost of a given amount of A, so now MC_a falls to MC_a' which corresponds to output B_1. Hence the output of A rises to A_2 and the price of A falls to p_a''. This process continues until a new equilibrium is reached.*

* The prices continue to fall, but at decreasing rates (which soon reach zero for practical purposes). The multiple products are produced in a fixed plant in the short-

It is not difficult to isolate the major variable factors determining where the new equilibrium position is reached. The greater the variability of the proportions in which A and B are produced, the less will be the fall in the price of B. (In the limiting case where costs of A and B are independent, the price of B will not fall at all, of course.) Outputs of both commodities will increase more, the more elastic the demands; and the more elastic the demand for one commodity, the more the output of that commodity will expand relative to that of the other commodity.

If the industry was in long-run equilibrium before the demand for A increased, it will now be making profits which attract new firms. Whether the industry operates subject to increasing or decreasing costs, the output of A is certain to rise and its price to fall (relative to short-run normal equilibrium) by amounts influenced by the elasticity of demand for A. The output of B is not certain to rise, however. Greater variability in the proportions may be built into new plants so advantage can be taken of the higher price of A. It is possible, if the proportions are sufficiently variable, for the output of B actually to fall (i.e., A and B may be complementary in the short run and substitutes in the long run).

It may be objected that if the price of one of the products of a firm rises, even in the short run the firm will shift facilities from other, now less profitable products. For example, a garment factory will shift from men's suits to overcoats if the demand for the latter increases. Such statements are true enough, but they do not meet the specifications for products complementary in production. Suits and overcoats must have independent marginal costs if this phenomenon is to appear.* Such products are made in one plant only if the demand curves are related, and this condition was excluded in the case just discussed.

The details of the adaptation of the analysis to the case of related demands may be left to the reader. A shift in demand for only one of a group of products with related demands is not very plausible,

run normal period and this fixity of plant dampens the reductions in both marginal-cost curves.

* Strictly speaking, it is also possible that the products be *rival* (or substitutes), so the increased production of one increases the marginal cost of a given amount of another. This condition (and also the condition of independence of marginal costs) is not inconsistent with the joint production, being cheaper than separate production, but the exceptions must be rare and need not be considered here.

however: if they are related one would generally (although not necessarily) expect an increased demand for one to be accompanied by a change in demand for others. An increased demand for gasoline is likely to lead to an increased demand for lubricating oil; an increased demand by consumers for flour is likely to go with a decreased demand for bread.

II. PRICING OF MULTIPLE PRODUCTS UNDER IMPERFECT COMPETITION

The formal theory of pricing of multiple products under imperfect competition differs in only two respects from the competitive case. First, the firm operates at the output which equates the marginal cost of each product to its marginal revenue rather than to its price. Second, the firm takes full account of the effects of one price on the sales of other products if their demands are related.

The effects of interdependence of the demand curves may be explored by means of a numerical example. The demand schedule for commodity A, on the condition that the amount of commodity B (a substitute for A marketed by the firm) is 190, is given in the first two columns of Table 23.* Unfortunately for the simplicity of the analysis, the marginal revenues of A in the third column do not represent the net addition to total revenue from the sale of an addi-

TABLE 23

Q_a	P_a	Crude MR_a	P_b ($Q_b = 190$)	Corrected MR_a
152.5	$40	—	$30.50	—
161.25	39	$21.57	30.25	$16.14
170.00	38	19.57	30.00	14.14
178.75	37	17.57	29.75	12.14
187.50	36	15.57	29.50	10.14

* One could also define the demand schedule for A on the condition that the price of B was held constant. In this case the quantity of B would vary with changes in the price of A and the computation of marginal revenue of A would be less direct. The demand functions underlying the table are:

$$Q_a = 400 - 10\,P_a + 5\,P_b,$$
$$Q_b = 600 - 20\,P_b + 5\,P_a,$$

or, expressing prices as functions of quantities,

$$P_a = 440/7 - Q_b/35 - 4\,Q_a/35,$$
$$P_b = 320/7 - Q_a/35 - 2\,Q_b/35.$$

tional unit of A. When the price of A is reduced from $38 to $37 and sales rise by 8.75 units, receipts from A rise by $17.57 per unit but the decrease in price of A will necessitate a decrease in the price of the substitute B if its sales are to be maintained at 190. By inspection of the table it will be seen that for each 8.75 additional units of A, the price of B drops $0.25 and total receipts from B drop $47.50 (= 190 × $0.25). An appropriate share of this reduction in receipts from B must be charged against the crude marginal revenue of A, so the true marginal revenue is only $12.14 (= $17.57 − $47.50/8.75).

Nor is this the end of the matter if we wish to determine prices. Since the price of B was presumably set at $30 because this was most profitable when the price of A was $38, a new price of B must be established which maximizes profits at the lower price of A. We cannot determine the appropriate prices and outputs without a knowledge of the marginal costs of the two commodities. If, for example, the marginal cost of A is $10 (and that of B, $15) the reduction in the price of A to $37 increased profits since marginal revenue ($12.14) exceeds marginal cost. (Successive approximations or algebraic analysis will show that the equilibrium prices and outputs are $36.43 and 187.5 for A and $30.36 and 175 for B.) A more powerful technique for handling such problems is presented in the next section.

Although the existence of new multiple products does not change radically the formal theory of the firm, it is probable that important substantive changes are effected. There is a presumption for greater rivalry in cases of duopoly since the difficulties of collusion must multiply rapidly as the number of products increases. The rivals must agree on an intricate and constantly changing structure of price relationships between commodities which are related in demand or production. As a result of the practical impossibility of many producers agreeing on many specific prices, one of the first steps usually taken by a cartel is to freeze existing price differentials on various products of the industry and canalize all price changes into the absolute level of the industry's price structure.

One particular case of multiple products with related demands has received much attention: loss leaders. In the case of retailing, where this phenomenon is most widely publicized, the firm sells one commodity at less than cost (usually defined in statutes as invoice cost or invoice cost plus a percentage) in order to draw in customers who will buy other products.* The chief specifications for a good leader are that it be well-known, widely and frequently purchased, unsuited for storage by consumers, and standardized so its ruling price is known and "bargain" prices are quickly recognized. The device is obviously more suited to a retailer handling a variety of items than a specialty store. We need not pass on the widespread legislation against the practice instigated by independent retail merchants but it should be observed that if leaders are prohibited, the enterprising merchant will surely turn to other methods (advertising, nine deliveries a day) to expand his sales.

Finally, it is worth noticing that multiple products modify the effects of economies of scale. If the demand curve for one product has such a height and slope that it is not possible for several firms to use the most efficient processes in producing only this commodity, several firms may introduce other products which require the same indivisible productive resources. The possibility of multiple products therefore weakens materially the tendency of economies of scale to lead to stronger forms of market control.

III. A GENERAL TECHNIQUE FOR ANALYZING MULTIPLE PRODUCTS

Although the existence of multiple products does not affect the general principles of pricing, the usual geometrical techniques are unwieldy because the cost or demand curves of the various products are not independent of one another. It is possible to circumvent this difficulty and still to retain the advantages of plane geometry by use of a type of indifference curve. The present section will explain the construction of these curves and apply the technique to illustrative problems.

1. *THE TECHNIQUE*

Two types of curves will be employed: constant-revenue and constant-outlay curves. The constant-revenue curves represent all

---

* The phrase *loss leader* has nothing but popularity to commend it. If the firm is intelligent in selecting and pricing loss leaders, it will increase its profits. Given the prices of the other products, the change in the price of the loss leader leads to increased sales (of this and other products) which add more to receipts than to costs, — a good loss leader is always a "profit leader." The fact that the cost of the leader is greater than its marginal revenue ignoring other effects is irrelevant; the true marginal revenue of the leader is the change in the total receipts of the firm if other outputs (or prices) remain constant.

combinations of sales of two commodities which yield equal total receipts. The numerical data which such curves represent are illustrated in Table 24. The combinations all yield $69.00.

TABLE 24

Combination	A	P_a	Total Receipts from A	B	P_b	Total Receipts from B	Total Receipts
1	12	$2.00	$24.00	15	$3.00	$45.00	$69.00
2	13	1.95	25.35	12	3.64	43.65	69.00
3	14	1.90	26.60	10	4.25	42.40	69.00
4	15	1.85	27.75	9	4.58	41.25	69.00

The construction of the table is simple: if $24 is secured from the sale of 12 units of A, we select a quantity of B such that its sale at the appropriate demand price will yield $45, and similarly for the other combinations. If the demand curve for B (when the price of A is $2.00) is continuous, it is always possible to find a quantity of B which yields this amount of revenue.* The quantities of A and B are plotted and then joined by a curve of constant revenue; several of these (corresponding to various levels of receipts) are denoted by R's in Figure 80.

If total revenue is to remain at a given level, the change in receipts resulting from an increase or decrease in A (denoted by ΔA) must be equal in magnitude but opposite in sign to the change in receipts resulting from the change in B (ΔB). Since the change in total receipts from A is (for small changes) ΔA times the marginal revenue of A, and similarly for B,†

---

* If the demand for B is elastic, it is always possible to increase or decrease output and increase or decrease receipts. If the demand has unitary elasticity, this is not possible but no demand curve can have unitary elasticity (or less) at all points. Why?

† This should be apparent on reflection but a proof may be given. Let p and q be price and quantity respectively, so total receipts are $R = pq$. Then a change (Δq) in output will change receipts by

$$\Delta R = (q + \Delta q)(p + \Delta p) - pq,$$
$$= p \Delta q + q \Delta p + \Delta p \Delta q,$$

and the last term may be neglected since it is the product of two small quantities. Hence

$$\Delta R = \Delta q \left(p + p \frac{q}{p} \frac{\Delta p}{\Delta q} \right),$$

and the term in parentheses is of course $p(1 + 1/\eta)$ = marginal revenue (see pp. 52, 57).

$$\Delta A \times \text{marginal revenue of A} = -\Delta B \times \text{marginal revenue of B}$$

or $$\frac{\Delta B}{\Delta A} = -\frac{\text{marginal revenue of A}}{\text{marginal revenue of B}},$$

which is equal to the slope of a constant-revenue curve. In interpreting this condition it must be remembered that the marginal revenue of A, for example, is the sum of (1) the addition to total revenue from A when its sales increase by one unit, *plus* (2) the change in total revenue from B, the output of B remaining fixed. Only if the demand curves are independent will the second component be zero; if the products are substitutes it will be negative and if complements it will be positive.*

For a competitive firm the prices are constant (and hence independent) so the second component of each marginal revenue is zero. Since prices are constant, marginal revenues are constant, and the constant revenue curves are straight lines with negative slopes. For a competitive industry, marginal revenue can be negative but the industry's marginal-revenue curve (like its marginal-cost curve) has no economic significance; it is not marginal revenue to anyone who makes decisions. The slope of the constant-revenue curves of a competitive industry equals $-P_a/P_b$ but (in contrast with the competitive firm) the prices are not constant when outputs vary. If A decreases and B increases along an industry constant-revenue curve, P_a rises and P_b falls so the curve becomes steeper — the curves are always convex to the origin.

There remains the case of the firm operating under imperfect competition. We can dismiss as impossible negative marginal-revenue curves since no firm will knowingly operate in such a region. If now A decreases and B increases along constant-revenue curves, one would generally expect the marginal revenue of A to increase and that of B to decrease, so again the constant-revenue curves are convex to the origin. But this argument is not conclusive if the demands are related; in the case of substitutes a decrease in A leads to a higher price for A which raises the demand

---

* Let $P_a = \phi(A, B)$ and $P_b = f(A, B)$ so total receipts are $R = AP_a + BP_b$. Then the marginal revenue of A is

$$\frac{\partial R}{\partial A} = \frac{\partial AP_a}{\partial A} + B\frac{\partial P_b}{\partial A}.$$

The second term in our previous numerical example (p. 313) was

$$190 \times (-1/35) = -\$5.43.$$

curve for B and this usually entails a rise in B's marginal-revenue curve. Nevertheless a convex constant-revenue curve may be taken as typical also in this case.*

The construction of constant-outlay curves follows the same procedure, and by symmetry these curves have slopes equal to

$$\frac{\Delta B}{\Delta A} = -\frac{\text{marginal cost of A}}{\text{marginal cost of B}}.$$

Since negative marginal costs are ruled out (page 202), all constant-outlay curves have negative slopes. In addition, an increase in the output of A increases the marginal cost of A and the corresponding decrease in B decreases the marginal cost of B — in both cases only as a general rule — so the constant-outlay curves may be expected to become steeper as more A is produced. In other words, the constant-outlay curves will be concave to the origin; several are indicated by C's in Figure 80. Again the conclusion is not certain

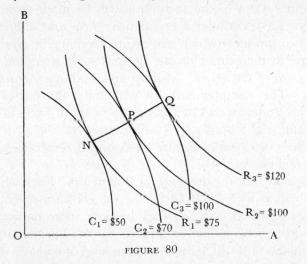

FIGURE 80

for an increase in A will raise the marginal cost curve of B if the products are competitive in production. Under competition, however, it is a condition of stable equilibrium that constant-outlay curves be concave to the origin.†

* The only requirement for a stable equilibrium is that if the constant-revenue curves be concave to the origin, they have less curvature than the constant-outlay curves.

† It may be observed that complementarity of demands is defined in terms of the effects of a change in the output (or price) of A on the price (or output) of B; complementarity of costs is defined in terms of the effects on the marginal cost of A of a change

The entrepreneur of course seeks a maximum return on a given outlay or, what is equivalent, a minimum outlay for given receipts. This condition is fulfilled when A and B are produced in such quantities that for a given outlay the combination of A and B lies on the highest possible constant-revenue curve; such points are indicated by N, P, and Q in Figure 80. At these points of tangency of the constant-revenue and outlay curves, their slopes are equal, so the condition for maximum profits is

$$\frac{\text{marginal cost of A}}{\text{marginal cost of B}} = \frac{\text{marginal revenue of A}}{\text{marginal revenue of B}},$$

which also follows from our previous discussion. The particular outlay curve chosen is that which maximizes profits; in Figure 80 this is C_2 with profits of $30 per unit of time.

II. *APPLICATIONS*

Two applications of the technique will be made to indicate its generality. First, consider a competitive firm and industry which produce two products which are complementary in production so an increase in the output of one decreases the marginal cost of a given amount of the other. Mutton and wool may again serve as examples. This complementarity will make the constant-outlay curves more concave and in the limiting case of fixed proportions they become right angles.* The situation of the firm and the industry are portrayed in Figure 81 A and B respectively, in both cases by solid curves.

Suppose now that the demand for B increases. For each firm this means a higher price for B and since the constant-revenue curves have slopes equal to $-P_a/P_b$ they become more horizontal; one is drawn as a broken line in Figure 81 A. For the industry a smaller amount of B will achieve a given level of revenue with given amounts of A so the constant-revenue curves rotate in a counter-clockwise direction; one is indicated by a broken curve in Figure 81 B. It is apparent that the output of A will decline and that of B increase (for any level of outlay). Since the industry is making

in the output of B. The demand complementarity was defined from the viewpoint of consumers; from the viewpoint of the firm it would be more convenient to define complementarity in terms of marginal revenues.

* For if the proportions are fixed (at say 4 to 1), 40 pounds of mutton will have the same cost when the output of wool varies between 0 and 10 pounds.

profits new firms will enter and their output will lower the prices of both products and hence the constant-revenue curves of both the firm and the industry.*

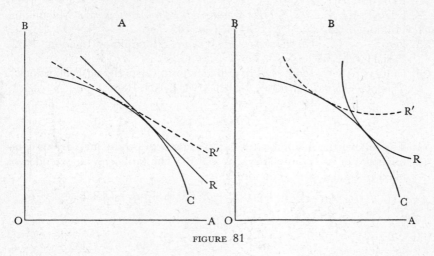

FIGURE 81

Second, the previously discussed problem of discriminating monopoly is easily handled by the same apparatus. If there are no costs in separating the two markets and the same product is sold in both, obviously the marginal cost of A will equal the marginal cost of B and the constant outlay curves will become straight lines with a slope of − 1. At the point of tangency of the constant-revenue and outlay curves they will have a slope of − 1, so the condition for maximum profits is that the marginal revenues of the two commodities be equal. Other applications of the technique are to treat as different commodities the amounts of a commodity produced in different periods,† to view money and securities as alternative modes of holding wealth,‡ and taking as the two commodities the exports of two countries.§

* The curves may also change slope as new firms enter. Thus if the demand for B is very elastic relative to that for A, the additional output of the new firms will lower the price of A all the more relative to the price of B and the constant-revenue curves of the industry will become more horizontal.

† For an elaboration, see J. R. Hicks, *Value and Capital*.

‡ See, in addition to Hicks' book, his article, "A Suggestion for the Simplification of the Theory of Money," *Economica*, N.S. II (1935), 1–19.

§ See G. Haberler, *The Theory of International Trade*, Macmillan, New York (1937), Ch. XII.

RECOMMENDED READINGS

1. Marshall, A., *Principles of Economics*, 8th ed., Macmillan, London, 1920, Bk. V, Ch. 6.
2. Edgeworth, F. Y., *Papers Relating to Political Economy*, Macmillan, London, 1925, Vol. I, Sec. II, F (pp. 143–71).
3. Pigou, A. C., *The Economics of Welfare*, Macmillan, London, 1932, Part II, Ch. 17.
4. Colberg, M., "Monopoly Prices under Joint Costs: Fixed Proportions," *Journal of Political Economy*, XLIX (1941), 103–10.

PROBLEMS

1. The following table indicates the total costs of producing various combinations of two commodities, A and B. The table can be extended or filled in by use of the equation,

$$\text{cost} = A^2/10 + 10\,A + B^2/20 + 15\,B - AB/5.$$

Quantity of A

		10	20	30	40
Quantity of B	10	$245	$355	$485	$635
	20	390	480	590	720
	30	545	615	705	815
	40	710	760	830	860

   a. What quantities of the two commodities will a competitive firm sell if the price of A is $10 and that of B $13.50?

   b. What quantities will this firm sell if, other conditions being the same, there are additional processing costs of B given by the equation, additional cost = $2\,B + B^2/20$?

   c. A monopoly has the costs given in the table, but the demand curves are $P_a = 50 - A + B/2$ and $P_b = 80 - 2\,B + A/2$. Are the products complements or substitutes in demand? Determine prices and outputs. (Total receipts = $50\,A - A^2 + 80\,B - 2\,B^2 + AB$.)

2. Solve the problems in question 1 if the products are produced in fixed proportions ($2\,A$ to $1\,B$) with total costs = $B/4 + 10\,B$.

3. Suppose there are 500 identical firms producing A and B under competitive conditions with the costs given in the table. Derive market-demand curves such that the prices ($10 for A and $13.50 for B) are equilibrium prices in the short-run normal period. Is this also a long-run normal equilibrium?

4. Construct a numerical example which obeys the usual restrictions on demand and cost schedules and which illustrates the profitability of a loss leader.

CHAPTER 17

CAPITAL AND INTEREST

It is necessary now to consider the pricing of productive *factors*, in contrast with *services*. The fundamental new element in the analysis is the interest rate, which provides the link between periodic payments for a productive service and the capital value of the resource which yields the flow of services. It will be useful to approach the problem through three approximations: first, the stationary economy; second, the progressive economy in the absence of uncertainty; and finally, the progressive economy in which uncertainty is present. (Obviously the stationary economy with uncertainty is self-contradictory.) Throughout the chapter competition will be assumed since the modifications occasioned by monopoly do not differ in principle from those encountered in price theory.

I. THE STATIONARY ECONOMY

In the stationary economy the quantity of capital is constant, so net savings and net investment must be zero. How is the interest rate and hence the value of durable resources determined under these conditions? Before answering this question a few preliminary matters must be discussed.

The content of the capital category under these conditions is relatively simple. Capital consists of those consumers' goods and productive resources, other than labor, the services of which extend over a significant period of time (to be defined later). The exclusion of labor (in a nonslave economy) is due simply to the fact that laborers are not permitted to make enforceable contracts for the sale of their services: no employer would give a college graduate (say) $50,000 on commencement day in exchange for a promise of 30 years labor without additional pay simply because he could not force the graduate to work for him.

It will be observed that "land" is treated in exactly the same fashion as other capital goods. It yields income over a substantial period of time, and hence meets the requirements of the definition of capital. Moreover one may invest directly in land by clearing, irrigation, fertilization, etc., or indirectly by improvement of transport. One may invest also in labor, and indeed a very large amount is so invested in our society. A material share of educational expenditures may be interpreted as investment in human beings, and every employer incurs costs in hiring and "breaking in" a new hand. The investment in labor (at least by families) is generally excluded from economic discussion because so much of it is non-economic in motive and the returns generally do not accrue to the original investor.

A portion of the capital will take the form of money even under stationary conditions. Payments and disbursements are inevitably periodic and they cannot be perfectly synchronized. Dividends, for example, may be paid four times a year, but a waiter is more impatient with his check. As a result the individual or firm will find it desirable to carry cash balances; the alternative would be to invest and disinvest very small sums very frequently (e.g. sell a bond to go out to dinner) and the costs at some point exceed the gain (interest). In addition, if the economy is not rigidly stationary, there will be minor contingencies against which money will be held. It is evident that the higher the interest rate, the greater the loss of interest in holding a cash balance, so this demand curve for money capital may be taken to have a negative slope with respect to the interest rate.

It is useful at this point to investigate the arithmetic relationships between interest rates and capital values.* A given capital good will yield a series of incomes through time; these are separated from the contributions of other productive services by the usual marginal-productivity analysis. If the interest rate is known, it is not difficult to determine how much of these incomes to put aside so that sufficient funds will be accumulated to replace the capital good when it reaches the end of its economic life.

---

* The chief mathematical requirement is the formula for the sum of a simple geometrical series, and this is readily derived:

$$S = a + ar + ar^2 + ar^3 + \ldots + ar^{n-1},$$
$$rS = ar + ar^2 + ar^3 + \ldots + ar^{n-1} + ar^n,$$
$$S(1 - r) = a - ar^n,$$
$$S = a\frac{1 - r^n}{1 - r}.$$

Thus let a capital good yield r_j' dollars in year j, and let the yields continue for n years and the interest rate be i per cent per year. If the capital good costs and is worth V dollars, one need not set V/n dollars aside each year since these depreciation allowances can be invested to yield i per cent.* It is known that if a dollar a year is placed in a sinking fund, after n years the following amount will be accumulated:†

$$\frac{(1 + i)^n - 1}{i},$$

so the annual depreciation allowance which at i per cent will amount to V dollars after n years is

$$\frac{Vi}{(1 + i)^n - 1} = d.$$

If this amount (d dollars) is subtracted from the value of the services (r_j') in each year, the remainder is the net income of the capital good. This may be denoted by $r_j = (r_j' - d)$.

The series of net incomes in future years have a definite capital value which is defined as the discounted sum of these incomes, i.e.,

$$V = \frac{r_1}{1 + i} + \frac{r_2}{(1 + i)^2} + \frac{r_3}{(1 + i)^3} + \cdots,$$

and the series of incomes will be indefinitely long since the capital good is replaced each time it wears out. Instead of dealing with this uneven flow of incomes, it is convenient to find a uniform series of incomes of equal capital value. For example, if a series of three incomes is $100, $90, and $80 and the interest rate is 5 per cent, the equivalent uniform income can be found from the equation,

$$\frac{r}{1.05} + \frac{r}{1.05^2} + \frac{r}{1.05^3} = \frac{\$100}{1.05} + \frac{\$90}{1.05^2} + \frac{\$80}{1.05^3},$$

or $r = \$90.33$. The same procedure is applicable to an unending series of incomes. Very distant incomes have only negligible present values: $1,000 receivable in 100 years has a present value (at 5 per cent) of only $7.60.

---

* Only straight-line depreciation is considered; variable depreciation allowances complicate the algebra but do not alter the principle under discussion.

† This formula can readily be derived by applying the rule for summing when the first dollar will accumulate to $(1 + i)^{n-1}$, the second year's dollar to $(1 + i)^{n-2}$, etc.

As the quantity of any type of capital goods is increased the value of its future services falls, and hence the capital value of a unit of the capital goods falls. This is demonstrable on the usual marginal-productivity grounds: (1) for any entrepreneur the marginal physical productivity of the services of the capital good will fall as their quantity increases, and (2) if many entrepreneurs increase their quantities of the capital good, outputs will expand and the price of the product will fall. An entrepreneur who seeks to maximize profits will not pay more for a capital good than the discounted value of the net incomes it will yield, and competition of other entrepreneurs forces him to pay this much, so the demand curve for any capital good has a negative slope.

Like all other commodities, productive services are produced by the productive services of labor and of previously existing resources. If these resources are expended only for a short period of time, interest on their investment can be ignored and the cost of a resource is the sum of the values of the services used in constructing it. But if the construction of the resource requires a significant period of time, interest will be charged on the various inputs of productive services.* The total cost of construction of the capital good (C) will be the sum of the expenditures on productive services accumulated with interest to the date of completion. If productive services worth c_i dollars are invested in year i, and investment continues for a period of k years, the total cost of the resource will be

$$C = c_1(1 + i)^{k-1} + c_2(1 + i)^{k-2} + \cdots + c_k,$$

and if the c's are equal,

$$C = c\frac{(1 + i)^k - 1}{i}.$$

Competition will dictate that the interest rate received on investments in constructing new capital goods equals the rate used to discount their future net incomes; if this is not true, it is more

---

* "A significant period of time," a phrase used also in defining capital, may now be specified. The period of time is not significant if in the opinion of the economic subject the sum of the undiscounted values of the services is approximately equal to the sum of the discounted values. Thus a significant period will be shorter the higher the interest rate. It is customary in statistical work to describe a commodity as perishable if its life is less than 6 months. If the interest rate is 6 per cent and compounding is ignored, this is equivalent to defining a capital good as one whose discounted income differs by more than $1\frac{1}{2}$ per cent from its undiscounted income. But any such boundary is arbitrary: 6 months is too short for consumers and too long for brokerage houses.

profitable to buy than to build capital goods, or vice versa. Competition also insures that, given the interest rate, at equilibrium the value of a capital good will equal its cost. If value exceeds cost, the supply of the capital good will increase and this will lead to a fall in the annual net income and also to an increase in the cost of the capital good if the industry producing it operates subject to increasing costs.

For any given interest rate there will be a certain number and quantity of investments which will be possible, i.e., yield this interest rate. The total investment can be determined by summing the demands for individual capital goods by individual entrepreneurs, taking account of interrelations of demands and costs of the type previously discussed (page 182). The same procedure can be followed for a range of interest rates to secure a demand curve for capital.

In a stationary economy the supply of capital is fixed so the interest rate is determined by the intersection of a vertical supply curve with a falling demand curve. This rate will be the equilibrium rate, and we may say with minor inaccuracy that it will be the only rate which exists. (The conditions leading to a variety of rates are discussed in Sections 2 and 3.)

It may be added that this interest rate will be unimportant in a stationary economy. The lender can either buy a capital good and lease it to an entrepreneur or lend the entrepreneur the money to purchase the capital good and receive interest. The two forms of contract are equivalent and the chief reason for the dominance of the latter in our society — the presence of uncertainty — would play no part in such an economy.

II. THE PROGRESSIVE ECONOMY WITH COMPLETE KNOWLEDGE

If a progressive economy is defined as one in which total income rises through time, progress requires either additional quantities of productive resources or improved techniques. Almost every increase in productive resources — including the laboring force — directly or indirectly requires additional investment, and hence the supply of new savings plays a fundamental role in the progressive economy. Savings may in turn be defined as the annual flow of productive services devoted to increasing the future flow of income.

It is popular to explain the supply of savings in terms of individuals' impatience to consume goods; people are held to prefer a dollar now to a dollar a year hence even when the receipt of the future dollar is certain, so interest is a necessary reward to bring forth savings. Whatever the validity of the assertion that people are impatient, the preference for a present dollar is indisputable: a dollar now is equivalent to $(1 + i)$ dollars a year hence because interest can be secured on it for the year. The existence of a positive interest rate makes it sensible to prefer the present dollar so it is not possible to use this preference as evidence of the necessity for interest to persuade people to save.

This circumstance makes it difficult to determine the influence of the interest rate on savings. In order to avoid circular reasoning one must approach the problem in an uncomfortably hypothetical manner: would people generally prefer a uniform, rising, or falling stream of receipts aggregating a given number of dollars in a given number of years provided there were no interest? Such a question can hardly be answered very persuasively but one can at least register a doubt that the common answer — a falling income stream — is obviously correct. For every spendthrift there may be a miser. No doubt some people will lack foresight or sales resistance but others (with larger incomes) will be less importunate and still others (whose incomes have forced statisticians to make extensive use of logarithmic scales) will not even be able to spend their entire incomes and still remain socially respectable. (The purchase of life insurance, in particular, is a most inefficient way of displaying a preference for relatively large current consumption.)

In our society, the conditions of which are not wholly relevant to the present discussion because uncertainty is so important, the interest rate seems to exert little direct influence on the quantity of savings. (The indirect effects by way of alteration of incomes of rentiers, effects on costs of insurance and housing, and similar factors may be of considerable importance, however.) The desire for security and for prestige and power associated with ownership of enterprise seem to be much stronger determinants of the quantity of savings and a large part must also be attributed to the social approval of savings.*

* On this last factor, see Max Weber, *The Protestant Ethic and the Rise of Capitalism*, transl. by Talcott Parsons, Scribner, New York, 1930.

Once an interest rate is established in a free market, everyone will place the same premium on exchanges between present and future dollars. Those who prefer present dollars to future dollars at this rate of exchange will borrow and hence increase their supply of present dollars and decrease their supply of future dollars, and this movement will increase their marginal rate of substitution of present for future dollars until this rate equals the market rate (see page 71). In similar fashion those who prefer future to present dollars at the market rate of exchange will lend and bring their preference rate into equality with the market rate. Among consumers this latter group is usually larger — there are net savings available for productive loans — and indeed if this is not true the economy is likely to be retrogressive.

If the state of technology were constant while the quantity of capital grew, one would normally expect the interest rate to decline due to diminishing returns.* One may prophesy with great assurance, however, that techniques will continue to improve; indeed one growing outlet for new savings is the financing of research itself. A particular invention may increase or decrease the marginal productivity of capital (i.e., it may be "labor-saving" or "capital-saving") and only in simple cases can its net effect on the demand for capital be measured with any precision. Economists are nevertheless generally agreed that inventions on balance increase the marginal productivity of capital. It is difficult to determine whether this conclusion that most inventions are labor-saving is based upon an independent view of technological processes or whether it is an inference from the observations that capital has long accumulated at a rapid rate and that the interest rate has shown no persistent tendency to fall.

In determining the interest rate at any time the time dimensions of the various quantities should be kept clearly in mind. Savings are the annual addition to the stock of capital so it is improper to draw a demand curve for capital against the supply curve of savings. One may draw a demand curve for capital against the supply curve of capital but then one must remember that the supply of capital changes very little in a year. Net savings are normally of the order of magnitude of a tenth of national income, total accumulated

* If other resources — population in particular — grew more rapidly than capital, the interest rate would rise but the opposite situation seems more probable at present.

capital is perhaps of the order of ten times national income. Alternatively one may draw a demand curve for annual new investment against the supply curve of savings, but then the demand curve is very elastic since annual investment, which is only a small relative addition to capital, will lower the marginal productivity of capital very little.

A structure of interest rates rather than a single rate will rule in a progressive economy even in the absence of uncertainty.* If the interest on any particular maturity of bond, for example, is expected to change in the future, this expectation influences the rates on loans of other maturities.

An example will serve to develop the relationship between rates for loans of different periods. Suppose the interest rate on one-year loans is 4 per cent and a year hence it is expected to be 5 per cent. Can the interest rate on two-year loans be 4 per cent? Assuredly not, for the lender will receive approximately 8 per cent on two years on the "long" loan and 9 per cent on two "short" loans. To equalize the attractiveness of long and short loans the two-year interest rate will have to be approximately 4.5 per cent. If the two-year rate were above 4.5 per cent borrowers would take only one-year loans and then renew them so the supply of two-year loans would fall, their price rise, and hence their interest yield fall relative to one-year loans. The long-run rate must be approximately the average of the expected short-run rates.†

This relationship between long- and short-run interest rates is complicated by one additional factor: the cost of investment. The

---

* Such a structure will also appear in a stationary economy in which there is saving and dissaving by various individuals for different periods. But the structure will be stable and it will be governed primarily by the investment costs referred to later.

† These figures neglect compounding of interest. More accurately, the interest (paid at maturity) of a two-year loan will be

$$(1 + .04)^2 - 1 = .0816;$$

that on two one-year loans will be

$$(1 + .04)(1 + .05) - 1 = .092.$$

If the interest on the long-run loan is paid annually, as is of course almost universally true, the return will be

$$.04(1 + .05) + .04 = .082,$$

since the first year's interest can be reinvested. The precise long-run rate compatible with these short-run rates is i per cent, where

$$i(1 + .05) + i = (1 + .04)(1 + .05) - 1,$$

or $i = .0449.$

lender must investigate the loan and usually the borrower must pay certain fees. Under these conditions it will not pay lenders or borrowers to shift from long- to short-run money markets (or vice versa) exactly up to the point where the average relationship holds since small gains in interest will not offset the costs of shifting. If, for instance, the long-run interest rate in our previous example was 4.6 per cent lenders would not shift from the short- to long-term loans if the cost of shifting exceeded 0.1 per cent per annum on the funds. In general one would expect the total costs of investment to vary less than in proportion to the amount or maturity of a loan. The costs of investment, like all barriers to movement, make the final equilibrium position dependent upon the previous market position.

III. THE ECONOMY WITH UNCERTAINTY

The analysis of this volume has usually been based upon the assumption that economic subjects have complete knowledge.* No systematic survey of the effect of uncertainty will be attempted here but a few implications for the theory of capital and interest may be touched upon briefly.

A distinction is customarily drawn between risk and uncertainty in terms of the ability of economic subjects to establish empirical uniformities as to the regularity of occurrence of events. Risks are sufficiently homogeneous, independent, and numerous to permit insurance: examples are death, fire, and theft. Uncertainties are heterogeneous and often interdependent and infrequent: shifts of demand are unique, business cycles affect almost all businesses at one time, and wars, let us hope, are infrequent. It is not possible to insure against such events and therefore new problems are raised.

A problem immediately raised in capital theory is that investments are made in various fields with very different degrees of confidence that promised returns will actually be received. There is no doubt that an industry in which 20 per cent of the firms fail annually must offer relatively high nominal rates to secure capital in competition with industries where failure is rare. It is, however,

* In addition to minor lapses (future prices, p. 95, market price, p. 148, and duopoly, p. 228) there has been the major departure of monopolistic competition, where ignorance is fundamental. In the usual treatment of this last subject, however, ignorance is not related to time.

a mildly disputed point whether "risky" investments yield on the average a higher or lower net return than safe investments. A higher net return is expected by some because of investors' aversion to uncertainty, and an equal or lower net rate by others who argue that the chance of a large gain — when such exists — is widely welcomed (and infallibly cite the popularity of lotteries). The debate cannot easily be settled by experience. Current yields are not in question, so they offer little guidance. Suppose that in a large number of investments the realized rate over a long period of time proves to be higher on senior bonds than on common stocks.* This may mean that investors have no aversion to uncertainty but it may also mean that they underestimate future earnings of the common stock. Empirical studies are also complicated by the very important role in the determination of security prices played by traditional and legal limitations upon the investments of financial institutions, which reflect differences in uncertainty only tardily and imperfectly.

There is also a more fundamental difficulty: how can one measure uncertainty? The vicissitudes to which an investment is subject are infinitely diverse and it is difficult to see how they can be reduced to any simple measure. Some securities are difficult to sell quickly without a loss but have good yields; some are vulnerable to inflation. Similarly some investors view certainty in terms of steadiness of income and others in terms of steadiness of capital value, so what is a safe bond to A may be a "risky" one to B. A consensus will emerge — that is, there will be equilibrium prices — but this is far from providing any measure of uncertainty unless it is tautologically defined as proportional to promised yields.

Previously it was stated that even with complete knowledge people would find it convenient to hold stocks of money and of goods to equalize the flows of expenditures and receipts and of production and consumption respectively. These cash balances and inventories would be stable except for seasonal and other systematic variations and their magnitudes would be small relative to the flows of money and goods. But when uncertainty is present all such stocks increase enormously because now there are many contingencies

---

* The reverse is usually true; see E. L. Smith, *Common Stocks as Long Term Investments*, Macmillan, New York, 1925; and for a summary of later investigations, C. C. Bosland, *The Common Stock Theory of Investment*, Ronald, New York, 1937.

against which to guard. The firm will hold cash for contingencies such as favorable buying opportunities or importunate creditors and coal stocks against possibilities of strikes or transport congestion or price rises. Some idea of the resulting capital requirements is suggested by the fact that inventories and cash balances in the United States are normally of the same order of magnitude as national income.

Large stocks of goods are expensive to hold and numerous devices have been evolved to economize their use. The pooling of uncertainties reduces their magnitude even though strict insurance principles cannot be applied. The necessary stocks of consumer goods are smaller, for example, if they are held by wholesalers than by retailers and by retailers than by consumers. Organized commodity exchanges increase the availability and hence the efficiency of stocks. The provision of information reduces uncertainty directly, and large sums are spent on crop reports, trade journals, market research, and the like. But almost as a matter of definition no very satisfactory solution has been found for the uncertainties arising out of general fluctuations in business.

The presence of uncertainty has many other repercussions upon investment. Changes and fluctuations in demand are combatted by building plants which are efficient over wide ranges of output (page 168), by producing diverse products the demands for which are not closely related, and by building plants suitable for conversion to other purposes. These and other methods of combatting uncertainty are all expensive, however: plants designed with an eye to fluctuations in output or to conversion will be less efficient, and production and marketing of widely different products are expensive. Similarly the prospect of further changes in technology prevents the adoption of new techniques unless their net yields are large, i.e., high obsolescence charges are made against their future earnings. Uncertainty is the foe of durability and specialization. But it may not be amiss to add that in the light of history the elimination of uncertainty by the prohibition of change would be even more costly.

The interest rate, in summary, performs two fundamental tasks in an enterprise economy. The amount of new savings is determined in part by the relative attractiveness of current consumption and increased future income, and the interest rate is the measure of this increase in future income. Given the quantity of new savings, the interest rate determines the allocation of new investment among various industries and firms: only those entrepreneurs who show evidence of their ability to earn the current rate of return will secure the use of savings and hence expand investment.*

IV. A NOTE ON THE ECONOMICS OF EXHAUSTING RESOURCES

An *exhausting* resource is one which wears out in the course of normal use and cannot be replaced identically; a coal mine is an obvious example.† An *exhaustible* resource can be defined in various ways: as a resource which can be worn out; one which can be maintained but if worn out cannot be replaced, or cannot be replaced profitably; etc. The purpose in establishing this second category of resources is apparently that agricultural land should be distinguished from (e.g.) locomotives, on the ground that if land is "wasted" the loss is irreparable whereas additional locomotives can always be built.‡ Since agricultural land can be produced or rebuilt such attempts at analytical distinctions seem mistaken, and here only exhausting resources will be considered.

The owner of an exhausting resource seeks to maximize its present value and not its current income. It has been argued that the mine owner with seven sons in college will mine coal rapidly even though he knows that a more deliberate rate of extraction will lead to a larger present value for the mine. If the relevant markets are competitive this simply will not be true: the possibility of borrowing makes it unnecessary for the rate of exhaustion of the mine to parallel the owner's personal rate of consumption. Take an extreme example: a mine would have maximum present value if it were exploited at a uniform rate for 100 years but the owner is forced to leave the industry after one year. It would be foolish of him to attempt to mine perhaps a tenth of the coal in that year; he will be

---

* The common phrase, "beg, borrow or steal," lists in wrong order the sources of funds for the entrepreneur. No matter how one views an enterprise system, begging comes second.

† It would be more precise, if somewhat pedantic, to state that the total supply of the exhausting resource in the economy diminishes with use since a given coal mine could be maintained by filling the veins with coal from other mines. This practice, however, has only two obvious purposes: fraud ("salting" a mine); and the complicating of definitions.

‡ It is an interesting problem to define "wasteful" sensibly without making the word synonymous with "unprofitable."

better off if he extracts only 1 per cent of the coal and then sells the mine; what he "loses" by the slower rate of extraction will be more than offset by the increased sales price.*

The rate of utilization of an exhaustible resource will be lower in the present, (1) the higher the future prices of the product are expected to be, (2) the more rapidly marginal costs rise with output and the higher their level in near periods and the more slowly they rise with output and the lower their level in distant periods, (3) the lower the future prices of productive resources are expected to be, and (4) the lower the interest rate. The last of these factors is a datum for a competitive industry, and the first three are determined by trends in consumption, the availability of substitutes, technological developments in extraction and use, discoveries of new resources, and similar factors. Neither the list of variables nor the method of analysis is different for exhausting and nonexhausting resources, however, and the former category would not be noticed here were it not for the popular charge that under competition exhausting resources are utilized too rapidly. Since this contradicts a well-known generalization (page 105), it deserves some attention.

Two lines of argument are used to support the charge that the competitive rate of utilization of exhausting resources is too rapid. The first is that "too high" an interest rate is used in discounting future incomes or that the market is "too optimistic" in its prophecy of technological progress or "too conservative" on the score of future population growth, or otherwise mistaken. Such criticisms are not capable of analysis unless they are defined more precisely and the empirical evidence upon which they rest is presented. One may observe, however, that unless such criticisms are merely expressions of personal taste they rest upon greater knowledge than the market possesses. It is indeed easily possible that in ignorance of future developments the market may be estimating future prices too low, for example, and hence exploit exhausting resources too rapidly. Ignorance generally leads to error and the characteristic of irreplaceability is irrelevant. There is no good reason to believe

---

* One should not infer, however, that the present value of a mine depends upon the owner's plans, for it depends only upon the offers of others. A more precise statement is as follows. The mine has a present value of (e.g.) $100,000 in its optimum use, and hence a value of $104,000 in one year if the interest rate is 4 per cent. If the mine is exploited rapidly for one year, the discounted future net income at that time plus the income from the year's operation will be less than $104,000.

that ignorance will systematically lead to overly rapid utilization of resources; too slow a rate of utilization would seem to be equally or more probable.

The second line of argument turns on the presence of external economies (page 142). The most popular application of this argument is to petroleum: even if an entrepreneur desired to pump oil slowly so profitable future markets could be explored, he dare not exercise restraint or others would drain the common oil pool. This criticism of competitive organization is quite valid in principle but the competitive rate of production is excessive because the entrepreneur does not control the technological unit (the oil pool), not because of the future irreplaceability. There are situations in which exhausting resources are not involved (for example, the erection of an abbattoir near a good residential district) where the same difficulty arises. It seems fair to conclude that there is no general analytical distinction between exhausting and other resources.*

RECOMMENDED READINGS

1. Knight, F. H., *Risk, Uncertainty and Profit*, London School Reprints of Scarce Works, No. 16 (1933), Ch. 4, 11.
2. Knight, F. H., "Capital, Time, and the Interest Rate," *Economica*, N.S. I (1934), 257–86.
3. Fisher, I., *The Nature of Capital and Income*, Macmillan, New York, 1906.
4. Lutz, F. A., "The Structure of Interest Rates," *Quarterly Journal of Economics*, LV (1940), 36–63.
5. Gray, L. C., "Rent under the Assumption of Exhaustibility," *Quarterly Journal of Economics*, XXVIII (1913–14), 466–89.

See Knight, Boulding 8?, or JPE w last s years

PROBLEMS

1. The determination of the interest rate under simplified conditions. (This example is due to Prof. F. H. Knight.) Crusoe builds a tool in 25 days and it increases the productivity of his labor by 5 per cent and lasts 5 years (and each year for simplicity has 300 days).
   a. What is the interest rate if the tool requires no repairs or maintenance and depreciation allowances do not yield interest?
   b. What is the interest rate if the tool requires 5 days of repairs a year, and cannot be used during this time?
   c. What is the interest rate under the conditions of part b if depreciation allowances can also be invested to yield the current interest rate?

* Except the academic point, which will not be examined here, that the existence of exhausting resources is inconsistent with the assumption of a stationary economy.

2. Show that the same capital value is secured for a capital good by (a) discounting its net receipts plus depreciation for the life of the asset, and (b) discounting its net receipts.

3. The rate of exploitation of a coal mine. The annual cost of mining coal is given by the equation, cost $= q^2/1600 + 50\,q + 100$, where q is the number of tons mined. The price of coal is \$1 per ton, and the interest rate is 5 per cent.

   a. Find the rate at which coal will be mined if the supply is unlimited.

   b. Find the rate at which coal will be mined if the total amount of coal in the mine is 4,000 tons.

   c. Make the comparison when the price of coal is \$2 per ton, and when the interest rate is 10 per cent.

INDEX

Abstraction, 8 ff., 23 f.
Adaptability, 122, 169, 331.
Advertising, 221, 260 ff.
Allen, R. G. D., 54 n., 57, 84, 85, 285.
Anticipated prices, 95 ff., 149 ff., 167 f., 171.

Bach, G. L., 205 n.
Balance of processes, 114 n., 202 ff.
Barter, 79 f.
Bertrand, J., 228 f.
Bilateral monopoly, 266 f.
Böhm-Bawerk, E., 41.
Bonus payments, 87 n.
Borden, N. H., 222 n.
Bosland, C. C., 330 n.
Boulding, K. E., 257, 262 n.
Bowley, A. L., 84.
Bronfenbrenner, M., 301.
Buchanan, N. S., 285.
Burns, A. R., 217.

Cannan, E., 154.
Capacity, 275 f.
Capital
  definition, 321, 324 n.
  demand for, 324 ff.
  supply of, 326 f.
  values, 323 f.
Cartel
  favorable conditions, 272 ff.
  multiple products, 313.
  nature, 237 ff.
  quotas, 275 f.
Cassel, G., 40.
Cassels, J. M., 144.
Chain relationships, 236 f.
Chain-store taxation, 211.
Chamberlin, E., 113, 226 n., 239 n., 241, 257, 262 n.
Chandler, L. V., 209 n.
Chapman, S. J., 178 n., 191.
Christensen, C. L., 293 n.
Cineas, 200 f.
Clark, C., 18.
Clark, J. M., 66, 95 n., 136, 144.
Clark, W. C., and Kingston, J. L., 121 n.

Coefficient of production, 111 f., 181.
Cohen, M. R., and Nagel, E., 8 n., 20.
Colberg, M., 320.
Comparisons with competition
  cartel, 280, 287.
  monopolistic competition, 256 f.
  monopoly, 253 ff.
Complementary commodities, 67, 72, 88 f., 219 f.
Constant cost industry, 162 f.
Constant outlay curves, 262, 317 f.
Constant revenue curves, 262, 315 f.
Continuity, 42.
Costs
  and division of labor, 107 ff.
  and prices, 103 f., chap. 9, 246 ff.
  differences between firms, 270 f.
  nature, 102 ff.
  rivalry in buying, 249 ff.
  selling, 251 f., 260 ff.
  under imperfect competition, 243 ff.
Cournot, A., 228 f.
Cross-elasticity of demand, 88 f., 220 f., 280 ff.
Cummins, E. E., 294 n.

Davenport, H. J., 115.
Davis, A., Gardner, B. B., and Gardner, M. R., 290 n.
Decreasing cost industry, 165.
Demand curves
  and selling costs, 260 ff.
  cartels, 237 ff.
  derivation, 72 ff.
  kinky, 241.
  market, 90 f.
  monopolistic competition, 239.
  monopoly, 219 ff.
  oligopoly, 226 ff.
  partial, 91 f.
  relation to expenditure curve, 78 f.
Demand for productive services, chap. 9, 243 f., chap. 15.
  determinants, 181 f.
  firm, 175 ff.
  industry, 182 ff.
Diminishing returns, *see* Variable proportions

337